The Autistic Experience

JOE JAMES AND MARIE-LAURE DEL VECCHIO

The Autistic Experience

Silenced Voices Finally Heard

JOE JAMES AND MARIE-LAURE DEL VECCHIO

First published by Sheldon Press in 2023
An imprint of John Murray Press
A division of Hodder & Stoughton Ltd,
An Hachette UK company

1

A CIP catalogue record for this title is available from the British Library

Trade Paperback ISBN 9781399806855
eBook ISBN 9781399806879

Typeset by KnowledgeWorks Global Ltd.

Printed and bound in Great Britain by Clays Ltd, Elcograf S.p.A.

John Murray Press policy is to use papers that are natural, renewable and recyclable products and made from wood grown in sustainable forests. The logging and manufacturing processes are expected to conform to the environmental regulations of the country of origin.

John Murray Press
Carmelite House
50 Victoria Embankment
London EC4Y 0DZ

www.sheldonpress.co.uk

This book is dedicated to all the invisible heroes who spend their lives helping pave the way for the next generation of Neurodivergent individuals, autism advocates who are actually Autistic who share their lives and experiences with the world in the hope of creating better knowledge and understanding from those who stereotype us and put us all in a box labelled 'broken'. They are the unsung heroes who we should all be learning from, and hopefully one day, the world will accept us as equals and not treat us like we don't belong.

We would also like to dedicate this book to those Neurodivergent people that didn't make it to adulthood. Your voices will never be heard, your lives never fully lived. The system let you down. We hope we have done enough to give your loss meaning by creating this book and trying to change the future for all Neurodivergent people to come.

Contents

Acknowledgements ix

Foreword xi

Introduction xiii

1 Bullying 1
2 Perceptions of autism 23
3 Diagnosis 57
4 Meltdowns 89
5 Emotional regulation 101
6 Masking 117
7 Mental health 131
8 Interactions with medical professionals 153
9 Special interests 177
10 Friendships 193
11 Couples 213
12 Parenting 241
13 Advice 263

Conclusion 287

Glossary 289

Acknowledgements

From Marie-Laure

Greg, you are my rock. I will always cherish how excited you were when I told you that this book was happening. Somehow, you even managed to be more excited than I was (I didn't think that would be possible!). You are the most wonderful and supportive person in this world and behind each of my accomplishments (especially this one), there are countless hours of your wonderfulness!

Mom, your contribution to this book has been huge. You have spent hours helping us out and so many voices wouldn't have made it into the book if it weren't for your incredible dedication.

I would like to sincerely thank all my patients. I have learned so much from each and every one of you!

A massive thanks to all the participants of this book. Your generosity, authenticity and braveness have made this book what it is. I have been so moved, inspired and impressed by all your life stories and am so thankful to you for trusting us on this project.

From Joe

I want to thank my amazing wife Sylvia for always keeping me on track and helping me with my demand avoidance and anxiety when it came to writing this book. It is not easy to write about my life as it has been very traumatic at times, but with support I have managed to overcome my fears.

Thank you to my family and friends for always supporting me (is this an Oscars speech?), especially my children Simon and Sophie and my best friends/brothers, Richard, Alex, Jake Graham and Carl. You accept me for being me and that matters more to me tan anything else in the world.

Thank you to all the Neurodivergent voices who have contributed and even the ones who didn't make it into the book. It is an honour to be sharing your experiences, both good and bad, with the world and I think you are incredibly brave for doing so. Hopefully we can really help many people by opening up about being Autistic.

Thank you so much to my friend Luke Beardon for supporting and championing me and helping get this book published, you are a legend dude.

Last but not least, thank you to my co-author Marie-Laure for working tirelessly putting this book together – I know how difficult I can be and you have been amazingly patient.

Foreword

As someone with an academic title in the autism field I maintain that the best way to learn about autism is to engage as often as possible, as much as possible, and as in depth as possible with the autistic community. Since first becoming fascinated with all things autistic I have read so many autism-related books – and my favourites have always been autobiographical in nature. This book, then, ticked more boxes for me than I could ever have dreamed of. With such authenticity, so many autistic voices, covering such a range of invaluable concepts, the book entranced me from beginning to end.

The richness within this tome is undeniable. Equally undeniable is the fact that many of the voices in the book have such tragic stories to tell – the suffering at the hands of others is something that is deeply troubling and worthy of note – as Nia-Eloise wrote: 'The only thing that I suffer from is people's ignorance and prejudices and the spread of misinformation. And clothes labels'.

Perhaps it's unfair of me to choose that particular quotation out of the plethora of supreme narrative littered throughout the book, but I think it sums things up very aptly. One other quotation that leads to a brilliant section is as follows: 'Autism to me is like cake!' You'll have to read the rest of the book to find out what this means – trust me, it's worth it.

I cannot thank Joe and Marie-Laure enough for allowing me to be one of the first people to read this – it is quite possibly one of the most important books giving voice to autistic people that has ever been compiled. The phrase 'must-read' is surely overused – and, equally as surely, is 100% applicable in this case. Whoever you are, whatever your relationship to autism, reading this book will give you something that you will not find elsewhere.

Dr Luke Beardon
Senior Lecturer in Autism, Sheffield Hallam University

Introduction

We are often told that autism is a communication disorder. We beg to differ, because if people just listened more to us, they would soon find out that more often than not, we have plenty to say, even when we don't speak. There is no communication disorder; most Autistic[1] people communicate fine with each other. However, many misunderstandings arise when neurotypicals and Autistic people communicate with each other. Our goal in writing this book is to begin to bridge the gap. In response to being continually ignored, we have collected Autistic experiences, that is experiences written by us, about us, for anyone willing to hear our voices. So, if you really want to learn about autism, learn it from those who live it every day, and please, forget every stereotype you have ever been shown. The word Neurodivergent will be used quite often in this book. Neurodivergent means to have a different brain type than the typically evolved brain. You may have heard of the word neurodiversity, which is often used when describing Neurodivergent people, but neurodiversity actually means everyone, including neurotypicals. So, we are Neurodivergent, everyone is Neurodiverse.

Let us begin, and we warn you now, it won't be an easy read, but believe us, it was far harder to write this than anyone will find it to read it. In this book, you'll read stories from more than 80 Autistic people from many different countries, aged between 16 and 74, of various genders. Our participants display different forms of communication. Some people are or have been mute or selectively mute, while others have always felt comfortable expressing themselves orally. Some prefer to express themselves in spoken form, others in written form. We have offered different ways of collecting our participants' stories in order to show stories of people who have had different life experiences. While we – the authors – don't necessarily agree with each and every one of their statements, they show a wide diversity of experience. We wanted to show the variety of humans that are often silenced behind the narrowness of stereotypes. We hope Autistic people will be able to

---

1   We are using a capital letter for the words 'Autistic' and 'Neurodivergent', which is an identity, as opposed to the word 'autism', which is registered as a disorder.

relate to our participants' experiences and medical professionals can learn from them. We hope this book gives everyone the permission to be who they are, authentically.

There are many myths and mistruths about Autistic people perpetuated by medical professionals, the media and clickbait science. In this book, we, the Autistic community, speak for ourselves, give our side of the story and show what we as Autistic people have experienced living in a world that blanket labels us all as a disorder, a condition, a disease and a disability. We firmly believe we are supposed to exist, we are necessary for our species to make change, and the way our brains differ from the typical has been crucial for the advancement of humanity. We hope that from reading this book, you will begin to see the people behind such hurtful labels and realize the damage that has been done to a minority of people who simply were born different.

1

Bullying

Joe James' experience

The more I think about the word 'bullying', the less meaning it starts to have. It is a word that is thrown around a lot these days, especially on social media when people argue and disagree. There is still so much bullying going on and, even though we are living in a world that is supposed to be more accepting and understanding, it seems we are more divided than ever. In my childhood, the bullying was up close and personal. Not that it's worse than today's bullying, but back then I definitely wished I could have blocked and deleted the people that tortured me every single day.

My first memory of being picked on is from nursery school. I must have been about three or four and I'd asked a child if I could play with a truck they were playing with. They said they were finished and happily let me use it. The teacher stormed over to me and snatched the toy from my grasp. I was so scared and didn't know what I'd done wrong (a common theme in my life). She accused me of taking it from the other child and made me apologize to them. Even the child said I didn't take it, but she said they were just being nice and lying to protect me. I have never really trusted people – this was perhaps the start of it all.

My birth mother was incredibly loving. That was, until she didn't get her own way, or anyone said anything she didn't like. Then it was like a war zone and I was the target. Somehow everything was my fault. Even when my dad had a meltdown and lashed out at us, it was apparently my fault for making him so angry. I was an Autistic/ ADHD (attention deficit hyperactivity disorder) child who had serious

1

anxiety issues and was scared and angry all the time, but to hell with my feelings, I was the one who needed discipline and that meant beatings and psychological bullying. My mother would pit my siblings and I up against each other, constantly comparing us and making out as though she loved each of us the most while poisoning us against each other with lies. She would throw things at my head and hit me with kitchen utensils and anything else she could get her hands on at the time. I was mocked and made to feel like the freak of the family. I never wanted to leave my room, only to go outside, and I ran away constantly, taking my favourite cuddly toys with me in my pillowcase like a little hobo.

School life was a continuation of the torture I endured at home. I was always singled out as the odd kid, the weirdo, the nerd. Once, when I was nine years old, I was cycling to the next village to secretly buy some sweets. I was denied anything with sugar or chemicals because it was thought at the time that sweets would make my hyperactivity worse, so even on my birthday I wasn't allowed chocolate cake. On the way back it was pouring with rain and when I crossed the road, I was hit by a car. I had a broken leg, but luckily that was all. When I got the cast put on, the nurse told me that everyone would sign it and I would get loads of attention. That sounded so great, as mostly I was ostracized and had no friends at all. When I got back to school the kids all laughed at me and called me stupid because a few days before the teachers had done an assembly on road safety and used me as an example of what not to do. They had no idea what had happened, they just decided to make me look like an idiot so they could prove a point. They had zero care for the reper-cussions for me and how much the kids would use it as another reason to pick on me. I was so hoping for a big welcome and to be awash with sympathy and compassion, but the opposite happened. Six weeks later, when my cast came off, the nurse was kind enough not to mention that it was as bare as the day she had applied it.

Even though things were tough, I did have my older brother, Simon. He looked after me when my dad ignored me and he taught me many life lessons I would have struggled to learn on my own. He was the only one I could count on as my older sisters had been driven away by my birth mother and my dad was neglectful and distant most of the time. Simon took me on camping trips, holidays, to the cinema and off-roading in the Land Rover he built from scratch. He was 11 years older than me and I thought he was the coolest person alive. He showed me music and movies that I still treasure today, especially Bon Jovi and Queen. So much of who I am is because of his guidance and I know he would be proud of me if he was around today. Unfortunately, when I was 16, just before my exams, he was killed in a motorcycle accident and I never even got to say goodbye.

Before Simon's death, my school life consisted of me avoiding or defending myself against bullies. I had the occasional friend, but they never lasted long as others would make sure they were also bullied until our friendship ended. Some of those friends even turned on me and that hurt the most. I was really good at school despite hating many of the teachers. I was academically gifted and was destined to go to Cambridge like my heroes Charles Darwin and Sir David Attenborough. I wanted to study Zoology and certainly had the drive and enthusiasm to get there. Every day seemed like a battle, having to cope with my volatile home life, then dodge and weave my way through secondary school. It was so tiring but, somehow, I managed it.

After Simon's death, things changed dramatically. I stopped avoiding the confrontations and actively began looking for them. Soon the kids who thought I was an easy target found out that they had just been lucky enough to have got away with it for so long. My brother had taught me how to bo x and how to fight dirty, so that's what I did. I took my pain and hatred out on every single child and adult who got in my way. I was on a path of destruction and no one, even the deputy head teacher, was off limits. I began getting detentions, then suspensions, my work suffered as I had stopped caring, and I even got in trouble with the police for breaking a fellow pupil's eye socket. I was violent, and I loved it.

Meltdowns had been common for me, but after Simon died, they became who I was, an integral part of my identity. I was feared, looked up to, talked about. I was finally no longer a victim of bullying; I was now a victim of my trauma. I fought constantly with my dad and my birth mother was terrified I would hit her back, so she stopped attacking me. Eventually she kicked me out when I was just 17 and my exams had ended in failure. A few days before that I had decided to kill myself.

I was walking out of my school, alone and angry as usual. I hated my home and believed no one loved me and no one would care if I was

3

gone. As I crossed over a bridge I was overcome with a sense of calm and thought, 'I'm ready to end this'. I'd had suicidal thoughts a lot in my life but had never really taken them seriously. I was about to jump, but the thought of my dogs not knowing where I was, and an image of them sitting beside my grave like Greyfriars Bobby, made me think twice and I kept on walking. I want you to understand that I came extremely close to ending my life simply because of how I was treated by others. I have not gone into details as research has shown this can be dangerous. But this was a serious attempt and is not to be taken lightly or dismissed as the fleeting thoughts of an angsty teenager.

I think the worst thing to come from my brother's death was the final realization that even that tragic moment couldn't make my dad step up and be the man he needed to be. All he did was shut himself away even more and fight with me when I tried to spend time with him. All I really needed was a hug, all I got was a cold shoulder.

I was a victim, then I was a fighter, but even when I was sticking up for myself and having to deal with so much pain, I was labelled the troublemaker, the thug, the bad kid. Luckily, I met my best friend and wife when I was 18 and she helped heal the wounds that I sustained in my childhood. Without her I would still be lost, with her I have become a great dad, a great photographer, a neurodivergence specialist, a motivational speaker, an author and the happiest person I have ever been.

Participants' experiences

We wanted to begin this epic journey of understanding Autistic people from the mouths of Autistic people with a subject that I believe affects the overwhelming majority of Autistic individuals and has the most negative impact on who we become later on in life. So much of our struggling within social situations and day-to-day life is down to bullying and how we were treated by others when we were young. It can fundamentally shape who we are, and I for one have been mentally scarred and carry a lot of emotional anger and baggage because of the experiences above. Even the diagnostic criteria focus so much on our childhood and how we got on with others, it almost defines us as Autistic people, but it absolutely shouldn't. I'm hoping that by reading this book, people will take notice of our struggles and how we are treated so badly. Many of us choose to end it rather than face another day of persecution and judgement.

We asked our participants, who come from all over the world and have different heritages, upbringings, ages, abilities, disabilities and personalities: were you bullied as a child? The response was yes for more than 90 per cent of them and the ones that weren't had to mask to fit in and weren't allowed to be their true selves, which in a way is another form of bullying in itself. The saddest thing for me to discover while reading through these experiences is that no matter the decade, even today, things have barely improved in terms of how we are treated. This is unacceptable and needs to change immediately.

Please keep in mind, as you read on, that these are real people, not made-up characters in a fantasy novel. These are real experiences, and for many the bullying doesn't stop in childhood. From physical to mental bullying, ostracization and cruel jokes at their expense, we do not deserve this treatment simply because we are different.

We will start with Dan, who describes his experience in just a few words. These few words mirror what so many of us asked ourselves repeatedly: 'Why me?' He says:

> " At school I would get bullied every day. I used to ask sometimes why they were picking on me and the answer always came back 'because you're there.' "

Gillian was bullied through ostracization, in an 'Oh my god, you play with her?' way. She was really quiet, but a ball of rage. If you picked on her, she'd take it and just go into herself. But if you picked on her siblings, she'd absolutely lose it. She adds: 'I'm such a pushover, until somebody picks on my relatives or friends.'

Eva remembers having struggled once with two girls while trying to make friends:

> " They said that I was staring at them but I wasn't. I would be looking at people, trying to understand things, and then I would be misunderstood. I just struggled; it was not fun. And that has affected my whole life really. "

Sarah says secondary school was kind of ok for the first few weeks:

> ❝ I seemed to be making friends, or so I thought. I wasn't overtly bullied, but I wasn't accepted into groups and cliques. I was mostly left alone, although there would be some snide remarks, jibing, taking the piss out of me when I just 'didn't get it'. I remember teachers being a bit like that too. I didn't understand it though and I constantly felt on edge. I always had a friend, but again, they were bossy, strong-headed, and it was almost like I was tagging along with them. I was probably three years behind everyone else emotionally/socially, reflecting back. I was naïve, didn't understand jokes, just didn't really get any of it. Being left out is a far too common thing for Autistic people. It is that sense of loneliness and isolation that may result in us not being sociable later in life. So don't immediately blame autism for our social struggles, the fault may lie in the hands of others, not our neurotype. ❞

Richard speaks about his experience:

> ❝ I was bullied because I did not hang out with the local kids and didn't give a crap about peer pressure. And to be honest, I still can't fully understand why I was bullied by the local kids that lived in my street. But they would chase me all the time. And to be honest. I loved outwitting them. I liked to answer back with wit and never let myself get mentally bullied. Unfortunately, I was physically bullied a lot. The outcome being that I learned to be a fast runner. I was a complete chatterbox. I was cheeky because I liked to argue, especially with teachers. This obviously (to me now) pissed people off. I had a lot of trouble making friends. Because of trust mainly. ❞

Charles reminisces about his time at school:

> ❝ I moved primary schools due to severe bullying from staff members and teachers. The school I am referring to here is the second one I attended. I don't really remember interacting with

friends outside of school. I don't remember if I had any best friends, just a few people that I do remember. There are a few incidents I remember, such as having a girl tell me I wouldn't be able to cut her finger off with the pair of scissors we were using in a crafting session and then subsequently getting in trouble when she let me try. Or the time when I was shoved backwards in the coat room by a bully I was standing up to and having one of the coat racks go into the back of my head. **"**

Beckie remembers being the weird child, wearing glasses and needing braces, and being an easy target for bullies. Also, she didn't really communicate well as a young child. The volcano inside her would erupt, she'd explode, be aggressive, violent, and the bullies would then regret picking on her. As she got older, she had a reputation as the crazy girl you didn't mess with.

So often we are seen as the ones in the wrong, when in fact we are simply defending ourselves. This is just another way that we are bullied and forced to accept our role as the victim that should not be heard.

Ben, Emily and many others also experienced this. Ben recalls:

" I always felt a little out of step with the world. I loved learning. Sometimes I think I could have gone to school for ever. Relating to other children was a huge struggle and I dealt with a lot of bullying. I learned martial arts to defend myself. This was effective, but frequent fighting added to the perception of me as a problem child. Teachers often perceived me as having an attitude and other children saw me as weird, annoying and arrogant.

Bullying was near constant. I always tended to stand and fight. Teachers were useless to the point that my mother threatened to call the police and sue. Moving schools made it worse because that meant losing what friends I had, and also that I had to fight every bully at the new school. **"**

Emily speaks about her experience:

" I had no idea I was Autistic when I was a child. I was the weird kid, the outsider. I was the one with my nose always in a book. Adults and children alike found my inquisitive nature and deep sense of justice intensely annoying. I guess the good thing about it was that I could complete most of my academic work without it even looking like I'd been paying attention.

I was horribly bullied, verbally and physically abused pretty much every day. Beaten to a pulp on more than one occasion. It began at primary school and followed me until GCSE level. When I reached out for help, teachers would tell me that I should stand up for myself and not be such a wuss. I did stick up for myself, somewhat explosively, on a few occasions. Then it would often be me who got in trouble and the other kids branded me a 'psycho'. It left me with deep wounds and a sense that I was weird, annoying, geeky and completely unlikable. "

Sadie also had a terrible time at school:

" When I moved to secondary school I was bullied constantly during those five years. Every time I reached out to someone it got worse so I just put up with it. It was the same as home life so I could easily put up with it. The only reason it stopped, despite having new bullies each academic year, was that I stood up physically to one of the bullies in my year. I had finally had enough. I would try to go to school early and be the last to leave to avoid a particular set of bullies waiting for me at the entrance/exit on my route. "

The thing about bullying is it affects us so deeply, but we don't always express or show that. We often internalize our pain and it manifests in harmful ways towards ourselves, as Christina and many others experienced. Christina recalls how bullying was a big problem for her even into high school:

> I could never understand why I was targeted constantly for ridicule. I was so quiet and never spoke to anyone, but for some reason other kids still felt the need to say horrific things to me. It reinforced the idea that there was something very wrong with me. During my sixth to eighth grade years, I would spend every recess sitting up against the building watching the kids play on the playground. All of them knew how to engage and seemed to enjoy being there. I remember only once did a playground monitor ever approach me to ask me why I didn't go play with the others. I didn't have words to answer and was embarrassed, but also relieved someone noticed me.
>
> Around the age of ten was when the self-harm began. I started with lighting matches and burning my skin, then eventually moved to cutting. It was intoxicating to me to see my physical pain. While I would cut myself, I would imagine someone noticing my injury and that person getting me the help I desperately needed. In real life, however, I always kept my injuries hidden. Out of all the years of my cutting and self-harm, only twice did someone notice it.
>
> Around my preteens, I started struggling with suicide ideation. I remember making a promise to myself that I would kill myself when I finished making a tablecloth for my mother. I would fantasize how I would do it. I became obsessed but had it in my mind to wait until I completed my project so as not to disappoint my mother.

Christine was teased but was rather violent in defending herself, giving one boy who took her beanie an arm lock and knocking down a boy who stole her milk. After that, no one messed with her any more.

Hayley remembers her experience:

> Public school also meant I was an easy target for bullies. I used to have food thrown at me, I was punched, kicked, someone kicked the bathroom door in while I was in there. I had kids make fun of me, call me names, make fun of my stims, throw rocks at me.

I was too nervous to ever stand up to bullies. I took it every day, it was relentless torture. It ruined me as an adult. I don't have any self-confidence, I have very low self-esteem. I started self-harming. I tried taking my own life on multiple occasions. All this ended up with me being sectioned in hospital for months. I don't think I would have ended up in hospital if it wasn't from the constant bullying. 🎤🎤

Nicky recalls her time at an all-girls school:

🎤🎤 I was bullied at the girls' school. It's left me with an inherent distrust of women. It was mainly verbal, which I couldn't cope with. A little pushing and shoving but nothing really physical, which I was always disappointed with as I was sure I could hold my own in a fight much better than I could with the verbal bullying. I didn't tell anyone about it. I tried to steer clear of the bullies and mainly ignored them, but all these years later I can still remember their names and faces. 🎤🎤

C.A. was harassed by a group of bullies:

🎤🎤 There were a few specific bullies that targeted me, but on the whole, it was just the generic 'you're annoying', 'you're loud', 'go away, we don't like you' type of behaviour I received. For the most part I wasn't worth their time. But there were also those who went out of their way to try to help, who didn't shut me down when I reached out and tried to guide me in what people were needing me to do/not do, to accept me. I could never reach their expectation. I'd commit to trying, doing my best, but ADHD would mean I'd forget I was even doing that within a few hours and the mask would drop and natural me would come back out. I'd feel shame that I couldn't keep it up, commit to doing better next time … and the cycle would start over. I could never get it. I appreciated those who showed compassion in this manner though. 🎤🎤

When people try to help us by encouraging masking, changing who we are to fit in and fundamentally reshaping us, as C.A. experienced, it often makes us feel undervalued and that who we are is just wrong. Those people seem to be trying to help, but in fact they can cause more harm in the long run because we aren't accepted for who we are. People should be taught to be more accepting and appreciative of difference, so we don't have to warp ourselves into their idea of what is normal.

Joanne recalls her time as a child:

" It was only in my final year of primary school that I started to struggle with my peers. I didn't know why they reacted to me in a strange way when I talked about my interests. I tried to like what they did, but boy bands really weren't my thing. Big cats were my thing! Animals, nature, climbing trees, exploring the world, finding out how things worked, that was what got me excited. I never really felt comfortable with them. They started ignoring me or pretending to be nice only to suddenly do something unexpected and laugh at me with others.

I was always on the outside of the group looking in. The forgotten one. I stopped trying to interact so much. I lost all the confidence I had and became easily led, desperate to feel belonging and acceptance, desperate to be liked. It led me into uncomfortable situations and eventually to sexual assault.

I confided in a friend who passed it around and suddenly I was the talk of the school. I was confronted by gangs of his friends (in the year above me). It got round to teachers and I was taken aside. The police got involved and I was asked to make a video statement at the police station. But I couldn't. "

Some of our experiences are so traumatizing they are extremely vivid many years later. No matter how extreme these may seem to others, the fact remains they are extreme to us.

Fabrizio remembers how he felt when he was targeted:

> ❝ For no reason, one of my ex-classmates started to pick on me. He was a big fat guy. He had older brothers with him. He tried to chase me, but I was faster. Then his brother came in front of me with his scooter, while another person came after me. They took me by the arms and threw me in a bush of roses. Then the brother of this classmate started beating me. All ended when a person that was living there came out of his house, in a dressing gown, shouting at the guy to stop. He took me into his house and tried to help me. I was deeply shaken and traumatized. I left that group and I didn't speak with any of them. I still resent these people, mostly this classmate and his brother. They never apologized. This had a huge impact on my life. I was traumatized for many years after that. ❞

Geraldine recalls how one girl felt the need to verbally bully her one day in art class, as Geraldine was always good at art and the other girl became jealous of her. The art teacher saw the girl's antics, told her to stop and asked Geraldine to move away from her, which she did. The girl then took her physical bullying out onto the playing fields during break times.

Karol reminisces:

> ❝ I got bullied in secondary school by a few people, but one that was particularly interested in bothering me was a girl with the same name. She was Carolina and I'm Karolina, so it's spelled slightly differently but pronounced the same, and that apparently really bothered her. She told me to tell people to pronounce my name in a different way. I didn't really get that because, well, it was my name, I couldn't just change how I pronounce it, and also I couldn't care less that we had the same name so why did I have to be the one to change it? So she would criticize me to her friends when I was around, making sure I heard her, and I would hear her say really mean things about me. That shattered my self-esteem and made me really unhappy. ❞

Linda reached out to her parents when the beating up started and they contacted her worst bully's parents, which only resulted in the bullying getting worse. This led to Linda not mentioning it again, pretending it was over and just finding a way to survive day by day.

> Not being supported, especially at school, is a common theme for many Autistic people, as we can read below. We are seen as a burden or hindrance rather than the potentially world-changing individuals that we could be. If the education system invested in us, instead of creating obstacles that we must fight against, we might just have an entire generation of amazing people who are not traumatized by their educational experiences.

Isabella recalls:

" Nobody knew I was Autistic. Everybody knew I was not normal, weird, physically slow and clumsy. I was often depressed. I hated waking up early, I was tired all the time, I was feeling weird all the time and used to feel like I didn't get the 'how-to-be-a-human manual' while everyone else got it.

I hated school. Sometimes other children and even teachers made fun of me and I was bullied sometimes. I used to daydream during school. I hated numbers, I love science, history, literature, geography, I hated physical education because I was clumsy (because of dyspraxia but nobody wondered why).

The school system was totally inadequate and ignorant – they knew I had problems but they never cared about finding out why and they never ever tried to help me in any way.

And my parents were disappointed because I was not like other kids. "

Jennifer talks about how it wasn't just children that bullied her:

" I was bullied by both students and teachers. I had a teacher point out in the middle of class that I was picking my skin

(I have a skin picking disorder and do this when I'm trying to block out external stimuli). I had both students and teachers make fun of the type of clothing I would wear since I preferred comfort over style. I've had both students and teachers make fun of me because of my inability to be good at sports during PE class (I am dyspraxic). I've had both students and teachers make fun of me or punish me for crying because they didn't see a reason for it. I've always been the type to avoid confrontation and would rarely stand up to any of them, especially the teachers. I also never really told others much, except for maybe my best friend or sister. I survived by forcing myself not to dwell on it, to mask and just escape to my favourite fantasy worlds. **"**

There are exceptions to the rule when it comes to school, and individual teachers can shine and see our potential. Kate remembers her teachers, but also remembers the horrific treatment she experienced that went alongside their support.

Kate speaks about how not knowing she was Autistic affected her childhood:

" I am a late/adult diagnosis, so when I was a child, everyone just thought I was weird. I remember being told I was too loud and annoying frequently and told that I shouldn't still like dinosaurs or have stuffed animals as I got older. I never really had friends. I had one or two people who would be nice to me for a while, but ultimately they never really stuck around and I could never figure out why. I remember desperately trying to be everything that I thought people wanted me to be – to look like them, to talk like them, to act like them in the hopes that someone would stay my friend for longer. On the positive side, academics were very easy for me. I learned quickly and retained information well. Tests felt like an algorithm that I could solve even if I didn't know the answer by using a simple statistical analysis. This often resulted in my being the 'teacher's pet' if you will, and the vast majority of my teachers were supportive and assured me that I was meant for great things.

The actual tasks at school were generally easy. Learning was easy and translating that learning into writing or testing was easy for me. Socially, school was impossible. I never felt like I fitted in, no matter how much I changed myself. The other children were cruel, often bullying me for seeming different. I've had people hit me, call me names, even cut my hair while I was in school. This led to me feeling extremely isolated and lonely for much of my childhood.

Kids threw things at me, called me names, left me out of their games and groups. A girl in sixth grade who sat behind me cut my hair during class. A teacher in seventh grade told me that no one liked me. The Christmas before the Columbine massacre happened, my parents gifted me a trench coat that became my favourite thing to wear. After Columbine, kids would accuse me of being a school shooter and approach me and ask me what I was hiding under my trench coat. In high school, bullies started trying to pick fights and one student even called a fake tip into crime stoppers to get me arrested. I told my parents about it, but they mostly just told me to stay away from anyone who was mean – which was nearly everyone. I told teachers and administrators, but their suggestions were pretty much the same. I was taller and stronger than most girls my age from growing up on a farm, so my coping mechanism became to just be scary to make people stay away from me instead. I walked around looking angry all the time and really isolated myself so that no one would feel like they could bully me. When the girl called crime stoppers, I was in tenth grade. Even though there was zero evidence and I'd done nothing wrong, the administration held me in the office for four hours and searched all of my stuff without consent or contacting my parents. They suspended me 'just to be safe' and made me submit to a psychological evaluation before I could return to school. After that, I went into dual enrolment and got away from the public school system. "

Kelly had a few close friends, but she remembers falling out a lot with them. She felt she annoyed them. If she had an obsession, such as a new boyfriend or a new interest, she would be all-consuming about it, talking non-stop, totally fixated on it, and she now feels that maybe that was hard to take for some people.

Kevin, Lauren, Michelle and Mickey share how even though they excelled educationally, due to their differences, socially they were treated badly. While Kevin did well academically, getting As and Bs, socially it was a different story. He ended up having to move away from his freshman residence hall in the middle of the year because he had difficulty understanding boundaries and when people wanted to be left alone. It was difficult because no one ever talked to him directly and told him he was interfering with their space; they just stewed privately about it and by the time he found out about it, it was too late.

Lauren recalls:

> **❝** I was very passionate about science and reading books, especially interested in physics and geology. I went to a public school, then college and now university. I found school mostly easy – I could churn out good exam results and I was well behaved in class. Teachers never had a problem with me and I enjoyed school. I was bullied sometimes for being 'too weird' and having interests that the other girls didn't. I never understood why the girls liked makeup and boys, and people considered me a tomboy for most of my life. I struggled with my confidence and anxiety, as did my other friends who were also Autistic. My friends are part of the reason I was bullied because they also had interests and ways of communicating that were considered weird. However, they always taught me to never care what others think and to keep being weird. It knocked me slightly, but in a way it's the reason I'm so assertive today and know how to be myself. **❞**

In elementary school, Michelle was bullied a lot, both verbally and physically. She always got top grades in every subject – the schoolwork was almost insultingly easy. It never occurred to her to report the bullying because she was also verbally and physically abused at home. In high school, her grades declined because she was tired of getting straight As and not getting any benefit from them – only snide comments. So, she began skipping school.

Here are a few more experiences before we move on. These are just more examples of what we must endure simply because we don't act like other people expect us to.

S.E. reminisces:

> 66 I was bullied, treated like a freak by my classmates. On the other hand, I was always way ahead of people my age. Instead of wasting my time playing their illogical games, I spent my time reading and understanding things that didn't even interest them. I always had a great memory and understanding of things that interested me. And I didn't have this urge to 'want to grow up and fit in' and stop doing the things I liked just for the sake of that. I was capable of just enjoying myself without feeling the social pressure that other kids seem to be exposed to. 99

Sarah speaks about her difficulties:

> 66 The hard stuff was interacting with my peers and some teachers. I was relentlessly bullied, never fit in, didn't understand all the undercurrents. Some teachers liked me because I was bright and a good student. Others hated me and gave me a hard time because I was challenging and pushed back against pointless rules. 99

S. was very badly bullied in boarding school. She was the only services child there and got beaten up on several occasions and was the target of practical jokes.

Bob remembers:

> 66 I was bullied at junior school for being 'teacher's pet' and the entire class ganged up on me, including my best friend. I didn't understand what I'd done wrong, I just helped the teacher by doing jobs when he asked. I was very glad to leave junior school and my parents moved away so that I wouldn't be at secondary school with the same people. 99

We close this part of the chapter with Mark, although these experiences are but a fraction of the abhorrent treatment we Neurodivergent people go through every day. Mark says what a lot of us who survived the trauma wish we could do.

> 66 I just wish I could go back and reassure that terrified, confused small chap that it will be ok, your brain is different but that makes you special. There are all sorts of ways to cope, here's what you need to tell people and this is why. Have a hug, little man, you deserve one. 99

Jordan's story

We wish to share some words Jordan wrote:

> 66 I am writing about my day-to-day life. I have always struggled and it's hard for me to learn things. I have always thought I was someone that was just so stupid as I couldn't learn as well as everyone else. Later I found out I have dyslexia but I still didn't understand everything about it, I still thought of myself as just someone that was thick, even though my mum told me I wasn't.
>
> As I have got older, I know that I don't learn in the same way as everyone else as my brain is made differently, but I can learn things in different ways. I think everyone thinks I don't care, but often it is the opposite.
>
> My possessions and my bag are important to me. I struggle in the classroom and many social situations, often being too bright or loud, there are often too many people about. I try to appear normal every day, but often by the time I get home I am mentally and physically tired. I don't want to be different, so I try to fit in. I often get overwhelmed with emotions when I try to be normal. I have not managed to get a grip on these, I have anxiety about talking it out loud and then struggle to say the words as they get jumbled.
>
> I worry about so many things. I can have short periods of quite intense OCD (obsessive compulsive disorder), like when I used to

wash my hands constantly until they were really bad. Trying to be positive is hard but I try to be creative – I can make and do things better than writing and subjects. My family try to help and tell me positive things about my abilities, but that isn't going to help me in the real world.

My daily life is mostly planned out. I follow a daily routine as I find it easier because I don't like change. High school life is very overwhelming and I struggle these days. I try to do my best but sometimes it's just not good enough. A never-ending cycle that I can't get out of. I don't think I will be able to stay in my classes as my latest school report shows that my teachers believe I will fail my exams. My parents have taken me for extra maths, she (the tutor) believes I need more visual aids, but I just don't know.

How I act caused a real struggle in my life as some people just don't understand me. They make fun and I can't get Bethany [my sister] to fight all my battles, and it's hard for me to cope with it all on a day-to-day basis. I am trying to work this through with my family. I need to speak up, but it's hard when you struggle with a full mind to stay on track, so it's easier to keep it hidden. **"**

Jordan's mother gave us permission to share this piece of writing and she adds her own words, as he is unable to write them himself.

" This is just a small section of a reflective piece Jordan had put together. It broke my heart helping him get out the words he wanted. He masked so much. I had asked time and time again about Jordan being Autistic, but got shot down by many. I was made to feel that I was way off base. How could I say he was Autistic? Just because I had fought and he was diagnosed as dyslexic didn't mean he was Autistic as well. I was just a mum.

It wasn't until after this piece was written, and he had failed at his exams, that I had to fight harder for him. We sat down on the floor, back to back, and I asked him to shut his eyes and tell me every single thought he had about himself. Within minutes I had a page full of pain. A visit to the doctor with this piece of paper began the diagnosis journey.

He had such a big heart, he listened to others when they were struggling, maybe not giving them answers but someone that didn't judge just really listened. I had been in a car crash in December 19 and he was such a support helping me. In hindsight I said that he was so busy helping me that he had too much pressure and he was distracted during his exams. His response, 'No, Mum, it's just me and my brain.' The school system did not work for him, his Air Cadets family with routine and support helped him achieve much more than his school life, but he just so wanted to fit in. He had a girlfriend but that had ended badly. When he had suicidal thoughts, I slept on his floor for six weeks. We sat and talked each night into the early hours. Why had he reacted so? Why didn't people like him? Why was he so odd? So thick? A burden to his sister? To his dad and me? To have such weights on his shoulders at his age, the anxiety tracking through the hours, I would talk quietly and gently try to get through to him, or we would shout at each other until we were spent, hugging him until he relaxed with Pooh Bear in his arms.

Jordan was a quiet child. Bethany, his sister, talked for him in his formative years. He did struggle, with bright lights, loud noises, his ear defenders beside his bed for so many years. You knew how his day had been by the way the back door shut on his return from school. Or going to collect him at lunchtime as the toilets at school were dirty, hiding away as he hadn't understood someone and didn't know why he was the bad one. Sometimes he needed to decompress and I would just get him a snack and leave him for a while, sometimes it could take days before he would let you know what was bothering him.

The time that he got detention as some fellow students had taken his bag, with his laptop in, and chucked it across the class, and no one would listen so he kicked cabinets. He was so frustrated – why was he getting into trouble when they had taken his stuff? Then he got so very upset as he had lost his temper. I could give you so many instances where Jordan felt inadequate, or lost himself and would start hitting himself or objects, but I can't have this entry full of negatives.

We tried to help others understand him, as his diagnosis didn't define him or his abilities. He felt a failure, only some understood his quirks – 'Jordanisms'. He felt so strongly that sometimes it felt that he took on others' pain. Covid didn't help, all his routines were shot, Cadets were online, and he never felt comfortable, the assessments were tiring, he hardly spoke for six whole sessions, I sat holding his hand. He grew more anxious, he was isolated like so many, and struggled mentally to keep focus.

Jordan had so many plans and imagination, he was an amazing, loving, empathetic son. I loved hearing him laugh at things: I have no idea how they were funny, but they were to him. His love of everything *Doctor Who*, each series and individual and what was contained in them. 'Timey wimey wibbly wobbly' stuff. (If you know, you know.) Anything Marvel, the chronological order of the films, his ability to tell me the links without missing a beat when I got confused. Lego had been a constant, his ability to see past instructions, once he had checked off each piece the manual would be set aside. His love of wood and creating pieces, his ability to teach others PT, he loved his Wednesday Cadet evenings, being able to track 50-plus apps to create meaningful overall sessions. He had started college and we saw a difference – when he was interested in a subject it was like he was a sponge. He had dropped biology previously, but seeing him link muscles and bone structure into his classes was amazing.

It was only when I found Joe James and his page that Jordan and I felt that we had some answers through all the fog.

Jordan had started to grow, we were learning, the belief was that because he had masked and had such a supportive network, he had not been identified as Autistic, but the diagnosis was supposed to help him get more support as you know, people like labels.... I myself prefer them for jars.

Jordan died by suicide on 28 November 2020, four days before his 17th birthday, I hurt each and every day, how did I not see his pain that afternoon....

I try to honour him by living and breathing each day. Trying to help those that are lacking in voice. For those who have different abilities, the ones that people may not see. For those that suffer from mental health, to strive to break down stigma that surrounds us, one conversation at a time. **"**

We hope by sharing Jordan's story that it shows how serious not being treated positively and equally can affect our lives. Studies show that up to 60 per cent of Autistic people have considered suicide. This desperately needs to change and it starts with the way autism is portrayed by the medical community, charities, the media, teachers and other professionals. The responsibility lies at the feet of every person who can make a difference and they need to understand the consequences of their actions when they portray neurodivergence as a negative 'thing' that 'afflicts' people's lives. How can we ever feel good about who we are if we are constantly told there is something wrong with us?

2

Perceptions of autism

Joe James' experience

What is autism? According to most 'experts' it is a broad range of *conditions* characterized by *challenges* with *social skills*, repetitive behaviours, speech and non-verbal *communication*, or a *lifelong developmental disability* which affects how people *communicate* and interact with the *world*, or a *complicated condition* that includes *problems* with *communication* and *behaviour*. It can involve a wide range of *symptoms* and skills. ASD (autism spectrum disorder) can be a minor *problem* or a disability that needs full-time care in a special facility.

These are all negative opinions and stereotypes – my opinion differs significantly.

Being Autistic (according to me, an Autistic person and Autism specialist whose special interests are neurodivergence, the brain and evolution), I believe autism is a prioritizing of learning (usually by one's self) over communication, but we are more than capable of doing both if given support, time and guidance. It is part of evolution and is supposed to exist.

A lack of synaptic pruning in the toddler years and again in the teen years makes the Autistic person more vulnerable to their surroundings due to having the neurological pathways of a new-born baby, which also changes the way they learn as they grow older. So instead of being able to learn an average amount about multiple subjects, the person can only learn a great deal about a few subjects that have piqued their interest. If they were to try to learn in this extreme way about all subjects, they would most likely burn out and in some cases either shut down or go into a meltdown. I have a hypothesis which suggests that the reason some Autistic children never fully mentally develop into adulthood is due to the synaptic pruning process hindering the synaptic building of new pathways. So, every Autistic brain will have a capacity for a certain number of pathways, and the fewer that are pruned, the fewer that can be built. This may also be why so many of us struggle socially with our peers, because we are younger in nature. But we are also great mimics and learners, therefore we learn to adult, and can often do that at a younger age because we mimic parents, teachers and grandparents. So, we can be simultaneously immature and very mature for our age. I myself feel more like a child or teenager most of the time and just act like an adult when I must. Again this is another form of masking and takes its toll on my mental capacity.

Autistic people have been responsible for some of the greatest innovations, inventions, ideas and creativity in human history and have advanced the species beyond its nearest competitors in the animal kingdom. We are the leaders of change and out-of-the-box thinking and don't like being told what to do without questioning it. This is commonly seen as behaviour or communication 'problems', but in fact it is the problem of the other person not understanding why we don't take things at face value.

Autistic people do not need to match their neurotypical peers because we are not supposed to, any more than the average person is supposed to match us in our ability to learn or have hyper-senses which enhance or harm us depending on our environment. We are different for a reason and it creates diversity within the human species, which is vital for adaption.

Autistic people all have different experiences, intellect, upbringings, values, cultures, disabilities, strengths and weakness. We are a minority of different thinkers that need support to navigate a world enhanced by us but not suited to us. Autism is not a disorder, it is a difference.

Autism is genetic, it's hereditary and nothing causes it other than procreation. The idea that it is caused only suggests it is damaging a human, when in fact it is the environment that damages the Autistic person, not their own brain.

The problem is that there is not enough information out there that is easily accessible to the general public, and the information that is there is biased towards negative stereotypes and unfair assessments of our people, mostly for the financial gain of organizations in disguise as charities. This is harming us because so many Autistic children and adults feel there is something wrong with them, that they are broken and nothing but a burden to society. This couldn't be further from the truth and I will not rest until ALL Autistics understand how valuable they are, even if they cannot speak or have severe disabilities. We ALL have value, even if others cannot see it.

Participants' experiences

Over the years, experts have changed the definition and medical representation of autism. We thought it would be about time we heard the Autistic community's thoughts on how autism is perceived. In this chapter, we've asked our participants to tell us how they see autism. We've asked them how they feel about the different terminology. Do keep in mind that behind the choice of words lies the representation we have of autism. Through the power of words, we can change how we perceive autism, whether it's to define it as a disability or as a different neurotype.

What is autism?

Definition of autism

Rather than provide you with one huge definition, we've asked our amazing participants to share their definitions of autism. Here's what they came up with:

'A gifted person trying to fit in to this reality, that can never [fit in].'

Geraldine

'Autism is where people see the world through a different set of lenses.'

Faith

'Autism is a neurological difference that causes changes in the way a person perceives, experiences and understands social interactions, communication and sensory input.'

Kate

'When I was a little girl, I knew a girl living down the street who had a brother who was blind and Autistic. He was sitting in his room and would scream and scream and it scared the hell out of me to be honest. It physically hurt me seeing him so unhappy and not being able to communicate with the world. The picture of that rocking child locked in a room and a body is what autism was to me for the very longest time.

'By now, obviously, this perception has changed and for me, being Autistic (not having autism) is simply a different way of perceiving the world on all levels. Fewer filters from the outside world, which brings its set of challenges with it. Sensory overstimulation is no joke. But then again, autism (I believe) comes with a more organized way of thinking, a more thorough way of thinking, more logical, more depth to it. The curiosity runs deep and the independence of mind and creativity can be wonderful. Unfortunately, balancing all these things can be a challenge and the challenges can be a huge hurdle while getting through today's world's expectations. Often, it comes with anxiety and an amount of curiosity making one obsess to a level where one forgets oneself. The very raw, unfiltered feelings that bear no logic and must be slowly learned to be understood and tamed. They are in strong contrast to the logical mind. The physical shortcomings can be crippling and limiting.'

Katharina

'Capacities and X-Men abilities way beyond this reality with super-power gifts.'

Geraldine

'As I understand it, autism is classified as a developmental disorder with variable presentation. From my reading, I've learned that it affects the nervous system and is often characterized by heightened or reduced sensory sensitivities and communication difficulties. An Autistic person's brain and nervous system are differently wired than neurotypical people's, so Autistic experiences are outliers when plotted on a bell curve of the typical–atypical. Autism is considered developmental because Autistic people develop differently (perhaps due to differences in synaptic pruning, growth and firing rates of different sections of the brain) compared to neurotypicals' nervous systems. Autism is classed as a disorder (sometimes disability) because aspects of neurodivergence are seen to negatively impact on ND people's ability to function in their daily lives. I hope that in the future, neuroscience technology will give us an improved insight into ND vs NT brains and nervous systems for a clearer understanding and definition.'

M.

'A higher-than-normal sense of *everything*! Anxiety, empathy, fear, special interests, awareness, pain, drama, super-intelligence.'

Sarah

'For me, autism is very much like a computer operating system ... it may be a different system than the majority use, but it's internally consistent and works just the way it's intended to! It's a specific neurology that affects everything about how we see, experience and interact with the world.'

Sarah

'For me, autism is down to my brain being wired differently. This means that there are areas where I may struggle, e.g. communication, sensory issues, social issues, struggling with motivation. Different, not defective (as I feel we are often seen).'

S.

'My definition of autism is that it is part of the way my brain functions. It is a difference, but it is definitely not "less" or a "disorder". All Autistic people are individuals though, with their own abilities and struggles. For me, being in the right job and relationship has helped me to utilize my autism for the sometimes amazing skills it has given me. I believe all Autistic people do have something they can do really well – sadly, not all of us have the opportunity to find it or use it and that is often due to perceptions in society.'

Virginia

Marie-Laure often likes to point out how being Autistic makes sense in terms of perception of the world. It is true that many of us live in a highly stimulating society, with a lot of noise, people and agitation. If we're more sensitive, we're bound to notice it more and be more affected by it. It is also true that we live in a rather complex society, with a lot of expectations, stress and pressure. Also, human interactions are complex when we think about it: people lie, cheat, are dishonest, leave, etc. Being aware of it makes sense, it simply means noticing something quite factual. Therefore, it also makes sense that in order to survive in this stressful environment, people need to have a sense of control over their lives: the need for routine, predictability, clear roles in social interactions, intense interests, profound relationships to people we can truly trust, among many other traits, can simply be viewed as an efficient way of adapting to an otherwise somewhat chaotic environment. In that sense, being Autistic can almost be seen as a philosophy, a certain awareness of the complexity of the world we live in – which makes complete sense.

Criteria defining autism

The official diagnostic criterion for autism is generally considered to be the *DSM-5* (*Diagnostic and Statistical Manual of Mental Disorders*). But we have asked Autistic people what they think the diagnostic criteria for autism should be.

In Najib's opinion, autism is characterized by specific interests and behavioural issues, especially around social interactions. According to Neville, the criteria would be someone who struggles with social interactions, overloading or overstimulation of the senses, someone with a narrowed range of interests or special interests and someone that may rely heavily on strict routines, being somewhat inflexible.

Fabrizio shares what the criteria should be based on his personal experience:

> 66 Difficulty to focus, interest in science, animals, insects, physical and chemical phenomena, informatics and computers. Difficulty to have relationships and friends. Difficulty to have romantic relationship. Loneliness. Sensibility to light, smell and sound always or in particular conditions. For instance, I am extremely photophobic. I dislike noise and chattering when I am focusing. I don't like crowded restaurants or pubs (with a lot of people talking) although, with some effort, I can go there. 99

Bob mentioned what a hard question that is and added that she doesn't think she has a proper answer as it seems so diverse and individual. Here's her attempt at listing some criteria:

> 66 It involves seeing things differently, not picking up on non-verbal communication, being very focused on some things and missing others, struggling to show emotions in a neurotypical way and liking things to be the same. There is a huge variation in Autistic people and different people show these things to different degrees. Some Autistic people also don't like making eye contact and speak with different intonation. 99

Sunny made an interesting list of specific traits to look for:

> ❝ I think key traits to look for would be sensory issues of any kind, complex and creative thinking (rather than linear), strong visual thinking, pattern recognition, focus on details, deep knowledge in specific areas, preference for facts and truth, using clear literal language and expecting the same from others, stronger emotional empathy than cognitive empathy. These things affect the environments we are comfortable in and how we socialize with others. Autistic people will feel at home in Autistic cultural environments. ❞

Amélie says that as Autistic people, we are direct people, we have a certain hypo-/hypersensitivity, we struggle to adapt, we struggle with social communication, we have strengths and giftedness for certain things, weaknesses for others, we experience moral and psychological suffering, tiredness, and we're emotional sponges.

Eva's perception of autism is a different way of being:

> ❝ I think people who are Autistic tend to be more sensitive to their environment, sensitive to other people, sensitive to the world, which can be a disability. In many ways, it is a disability, because if you are sensitive, you have like a less thick skin, you get hurt easier and the world is louder, the world is more painful. But it can also be positive. If you are more sensitive, you can decide to help people, decide to help animals, fighting for justice, you care more. ❞

Naomi has shared her very interesting thoughts regarding her perception of autism:

> ❝ It's very complicated. I don't even know if autism is the right word. In comparison to what we call the norm, there is something a little bit out of place … I would start with three criteria: a kind of lag, an intensity and a sensitivity. 'Lag' in the sense of another wiring, another way of apprehending things in a profound way. I see it when I work with people who are not Autistic, I don't understand their logic and I think, 'how did they get there?' There might also be a kind of authenticity, a kind of integrity, something a

bit raw, a bit naive in Autistic people, something very direct, there's not so much of a filter. For me, there is no protection; I am raw. That goes with sensitivity too – I feel like I'm a kind of character who walks around the world a bit naked and gets scratched by the slightest external friction, all the time, because I have zero shell, nothing at all. Everything affects me! In relation to sensitivity, I often think of antennae: very, very long and fine filaments that reach out very far and that can feel a lot of things that others don't feel. Maybe others have lost the means to feel them or decided not to feel them … I don't know … Actually, I'm not sure what a non-Autistic person is. Sometimes, we talk about 'neurotypicals' and I don't really know what that means. That's something that I find a bit dodgy, the idea of neurotypy.

Many participants, such as Noah, have mentioned that the criteria should be more adapted to different genders, as well as to people who mask very well or manage to function within mainstream society effectively. Lauren thinks the current *DSM-5* criteria are almost there. She adds:

> However, it needs to be more inclusive of intersectionality, for example people of different races, cultures and genders. It also needs to acknowledge that masking is a thing and many people do it. This means that people can appear ok but really aren't, and they shouldn't diagnose based on how someone appears.

Sébastien hopes that in the future, the criteria that define autism will be based on our abilities instead of our disabilities, that autism will be recognized as a specificity and not a disorder, whether it is thanks to cerebral imagery or tests based on our ability to notice details or our prodigious ability to recognize patterns. Hannah also regrets that in the *DSM-5*, the language that is being used is negative – all about deficits and impairments. She adds:

> I feel there needs to be a total overhaul in the way autism is diagnosed, the way people see it, the way medical professionals treat it, define it and discuss it. Autism is not a bad thing. It's a neurotype – a difference in processing and experiencing.

As a psychotherapist, Marie-Laure also sees the importance of characterizing autism not only through possible difficulties but also through the very real abilities. If we only define autism through struggles and disabilities, it conveys the impression that autism is a problem. When we tell someone they're Autistic, it sounds disastrous to them. However, when we tell someone they're Autistic and explain it means feeling emotions and sensations more strongly, having more empathy, certain social preferences (rather than inabilities), the ability to feel very passionate ... then people are more open to recognizing themselves in that way of functioning and can see it as information, not a death sentence. Also, if we only define autism through defects, it doesn't leave any room for a happy, well-functioning Autistic person to exist. Adding a list of abilities to the characterization of autism would allow people to know that if they become more self-confident, get more motivated, look after their needs and themselves, they will still be Autistic. Autism defines a structure, it's deeply rooted. It's not a form of symptoms that can be alleviated. Our social preferences or passions or emotions can vary with time. But we will still be Autistic.

Joe James says that when doing an autism assessment test simultaneously with a friend whom he suspected was Autistic, they answered nearly all the questions in the same way. The only questions they differed on were the ones about social interaction and friendships. Since Joe's photography and social media success, he has many Autistic friends, a new mum, is in touch with most of his siblings, loves doing talks and visiting schools and colleges to speak about neurodivergence, and is socially very successful. Joe's friend is the opposite, doesn't really like socializing and has a deep mistrust of people due to the way he has been treated. According to the assessment results, Joe's friend is highly likely to be Autistic and Joe, who is more sociable but answered all the other questions the same, only 'shows traits of autism, but not enough to be Autistic'. So, apparently, Joe's autism has disappeared because he is happy and has friends. What a load of nonsense these snake oil salespeople are peddling! Autism according to Joe should be defined just as much by what we can do as by the things we struggle with. Anything else is harmful and will only lead to misdiagnosis and people not knowing who they really are and not getting the right sort of support so they can reach their Autistic potential.

Terminology

Words are important, they shape our perception of reality. Depending on the words we're using, we're describing autism as a pathology – implying the Autistic person is ill – a different neurotype, or even a superpower. We thought we'd ask our participants the words they prefer when it comes to describing autism. Ideas differ in that regard, depending on people's experience. Marie-Laure has been surprised to notice that the words the Autistic community usually prefers are the complete opposite of the words clinicians are taught during their studies, or that the media uses, or that a lot of the scientific community uses.

Joe James says that the difference between having autism and being Autistic is the difference between saying there is something wrong with this person or this person has an identity and a tribe they can relate to. His personal preference is Neurodivergent because he understands it as one single brain type that when scrutinized by medical professionals will be split into 'disorders', depending on what the professionals have been taught, what they define autism, ADHD, dyslexia and so on to be, what they are apparent experts in, and what the person struggles with the most on a day-to-day basis. But Joe James believes it would be far more beneficial to discover someone is Neurodivergent, then individually what they struggle with, and support them as a person, not a disorder.

Should autism be considered a diagnosis or a different neurotype?

The meaning behind this question is that a diagnosis refers to an illness whereas a neurotype refers to a difference. We asked our participants if they feel that autism should be considered a diagnosable illness in the medical sense of the word or a different neurotype, within the realm of neurodivergency (meaning that it would be a different way of functioning but not considered as pathological). The answers were varied. Some people really disliked labelling autism as a diagnosis, while others thought it made perfect sense.

Emily feels that the answer to that question really depends on the person:

> 66 For some people, like me, it's a neurotype. My autism impacts my life all the time, sometimes positively, sometimes negatively, but overall it's manageable. For some people, their autism (or their co-morbidities) has parts that are debilitating and need medical attention. The tendency of the medical profession to treat Autistics as a monolith is really unhelpful. 99

Lauren thinks autism should always be both a diagnosis and a neurotype:

> 66 It is a neurotype because our brains are wired differently, and that's ok, however we need a diagnosis of autism to access support and understand ourselves. In today's society, we do not have the privilege to just treat autism as a neurotype because the system does not support us and people are not aware of autism, nor accept us for being Autistic. If there's a point in time where everyone can very easily access the exact support they need and we are treated as equals with allistics, then that may change. (Autism would still be disabling for me even in this ideal society, so maybe it always will be a diagnosis, who knows?) 99

Charles feels that autism should be considered a diagnosis of a neurotype. He says:

> 66 Having such an explanation of why you are the way that you are can be very beneficial for mental health and can go a long way towards helping someone to come to terms with being who they are. Also, by having such a diagnosis, it can help pinpoint what kinds of treatments or methods, if any, might be appropriate to help with some of the more debilitating aspects of autism, if they are present. 99

Mark comments on how society deals with diversity, including neurodivergence:

> 66 I think that there is a direct parallel between Neurodivergent acceptance and the acceptance of other marginalized and repressed groups – the visibility of the LGBT+ community and the rise of the BLM movement are two immediate examples. NT society as a generalization still fails to understand that those who do not somehow conform to their understanding of difference within a population are not a new phenomenon, all the 'non-conforming' groups have always been there and it is only the current generation's reaction to the apathy of the generation before it and the conservatism of the generation before that, facilitated by the vast leap in opportunity for communication and finding niche groups within society, that has become available only in the last 20 years or so, which is allowing the marginalized to become visible and validated. We've always been here. We've just had to hide until now. So, yes, autism is a different neurotype and diagnosis is an inappropriate word, as it implies a failure of the system, a disease, a problem, a disorder, something that could be cured once identified. We don't 'suffer' from it, we are it. 99

Gillian is one of the organizers of the Neuro Pride festival in Ireland. She shares the thought process behind building that community:

> 66 None of us is *just* Autistic. Why do we keep siloing everything off? Like, 'We have a group for Autistic people, another group for ADHD people, etc.' Literally every person I know is multiple Neurodivergent. It's so important for Neurodivergent people to be finding a community. It's one of the most important things for me. There's this nonsense idea that Autistics don't have any social skills. I don't think people have ever sat in a room with a lot of Neurodivergent people where they're all talking. Just sit there and tell me we have no social skills!
> A few years ago, I went to a conference set up and run by an Autistic woman. Everybody who was involved in it was Autistic, including the photographer. I didn't have anywhere to stay and this

woman said, 'You can stay in my room', so I was going down to spend an overnight in a room with a woman I didn't know, to meet a group of people that I didn't know and spend the next few days at this conference with a group of people that I didn't know, and I remember going down there thinking, 'Oh my God, this is going to be awful!' And I went into the room and I sat down, and this person started talking to me and we just started talking about loads of different stuff, straight in, no 'Hello, how are you?', none of the neurotypical nonsense. And I remember sitting there and at one point just looking around the room and everybody was just chatting, everybody was talking. At some point, somebody said, 'It's getting a bit too late for me, I'm gonna go to my room' and nobody was annoyed by that, it was really accepting. And this man walked into the room, looked around the room and dimmed the lights and everybody's shoulders just relaxed.

It was my first experience of being in a room filled with people and being relaxed. It's really sad that I was 40 when I had that experience. It was the first time in my life that I was relaxed. I didn't worry about 'Oh my God, did I talk too much? Did I talk enough?' – because I'm a terrible oversharer. I didn't do that thing of replaying every social interaction to see where I went wrong. It was so relaxing. The next day, at the conference, you could spot the Autistic people because they were the ones who took their shoes off. So, I was like, 'Oh, we all do that!' And that was the moment where I was like, 'I want other people to experience that.' Being Autistic doesn't mean being antisocial. It's a different way of socializing. There were people joining us, wondering 'I don't know if I'm Neurodivergent enough to be joining you' – if you're asking yourself that question, you 100 per cent are! If you're wondering 'I don't know if I'm Autistic enough', it's like, 'You are, here you go!'

How do you feel about saying someone 'suffers' from autism?

Kate believes some people are suffering. She says, 'When I'm having a sensory episode and my entire body itches and I'm fighting the urge to slap myself, it is suffering.' Neville says he can understand the phrase 'suffers from autism' as it can cause massive struggles, but he doesn't like to read it in words.

Many people have shared that they do not suffer because of autism, but rather because of people's lack of understanding. Joanne, for instance, said:

❝ The world just isn't designed for people who think differently. Ironically, it is the people who think differently who can have the most impact on the world – innovation, design, investigation are all led by thinking about things from a different perspective. ❞

When asked if she suffers from autism, Linda said: 'Nope, I suffer from the lack of understanding, respect and appreciation and the lack of accommodations I need because I live in a neurotypical world that expects me to fit the neurotypical mould – which I don't.' Michelle said that rather than suffering from autism, she suffers from uneducated and ignorant people who have no idea what autism is and treat her poorly as a result. Nia-Eloise wrote:

❝ The only thing that I suffer from is people's ignorance and prejudices and the spread of misinformation. And clothes labels. ❞

Eva doesn't like the phrase 'suffers from autism':

❝ I am not suffering, it is just part of who I am. It is kind like saying 'I suffer from my brown eyes'. It is a ridiculous thing, unless I am in Nazi Germany and they are trying to exterminate my brown eyes and then I am suffering because of the Nazis and not because of my brown eyes. ❞

Noah feels that the only suffering is that people in society are so fixated about the importance of appearing normal. He personally doesn't suffer with autism, although he is aware that sometimes his autism does make things more challenging.

Paul dislikes saying 'suffers from autism' for the following reasons:

❝ It is condescending, meaningless and possibly ignorant. Each Autistic person's circumstances are different and so are their environment, support and degree of difficulty. It also earmarks autism as entirely negative without any positive attributes. "

How do you feel about high-/low-functioning labels or that of mild/severe autism, or the characterization of level 1/2/3 autism?

There are several ways of medically characterizing autism in an attempt to make the diagnosis more specific. For instance, some people make a distinction between high- or low-functioning Autistic people, others between mild or severe autism, or level 1/2/3.

Joe James says that if you use a degree of autism when describing an individual person, you are essentially tarring them with the same brush as every other Autistic individual who is seemingly similar based on parameters set by a non-Autistic medical community. It is more harmful than helpful because it is suggesting that there is a lid on their potential since they don't function as society believes they should do. Synaptic pruning takes place twice before a person reaches adulthood, and it has been proven that Autistic people can make huge strides in their ability to 'function' as they get older. So, labelling someone from a young age only hinders them. Also, by assuming you know how to help an Autistic child based on their level is completely nonsensical – you should be learning from that child how to help them, not from a textbook. The phrase 'high-functioning' is also problematic as it suggests to the average person on the street that we are completely capable of living our lives without any additional support. I know a young man who has been labelled high-functioning, yet he lives in an assisted living facility and cannot cope by himself, even though his label suggests he should be able to deal with all aspects of life without any issues whatsoever.

The other issue Joe James has with functioning labels is that if there is 'low' and 'high', what are the parameters for just functioning? Where is the medium functioning? It's all just such rubbish in his opinion and we should spend more time getting to know the individual and not treating them like a patient. The spectrum is not linear, it's not a line with one type of Autistic person at one end and another at the opposite end. It's a circle of colour and all of us belong inside it, being part of it, but at no point being compared to each other, like neurotypicals compare us to them. You can't be on a spectrum, only *in* it. What these labels are also doing (which the medical community seems to love doing) is making autism out to be a 'thing' we have, like a disease, or condition, when it is in fact a neurotype that is supposed to exist as part of the human evolution and progression of our species. We need to stop villainizing autism and embrace the idea that we are all equally Autistic, but some of us are more impacted by the lack of synaptic building than others.

Here's how our participants feel about these severity and functioning labels.

Isabella finds her needs and challenges hugely different from those of people at different levels and that it is very wrong to deny the differences between Autistic levels. She does feel that functioning labels are helpful:

> 66 Because people are different and autism doesn't pick a type of person, you can have any type of intelligence, you can be affected mildly, severely, and we should use the functioning labels, they are so useful. I don't know why some people think they are bad. It is not an insult for anyone. If you are high-functioning it doesn't mean that you are not struggling, but you are high-functioning. If you are low-functioning, it is not an insult, it is a thing, I am not functioning. I think I am disabled. It is not an insult, it is just a thing. It is how it is. 99

Kate makes the point of how severity labels can help some people access the support they need:

> 66 I think that there needs to be a separation between severe and less severe autism in a way that validates the supports necessary for the non-vocal or severely impaired population. Services need to be accessible to all at the level that they need it. I do feel that merging the prior 'Asperger's' community with all of ASD has reduced the availability of services to the severely impaired by reducing the perception of the severity of the possible impairments. 99

Christine makes an interesting point regarding how anxiety impacts the person's experience:

> 66 I am Autistic and non-verbal. Talking, either on my own or to others, is debilitating to me. I can tolerate an hour unless everyone

is talking at once, then hardly any time at all. I get increasingly unable to think and form coherent answers, I say things I know are wrong, and then I can't say anything at all. Severe or mild to me is an indicator of how much anxiety a person is experiencing. Find ways to reduce the anxiety and it may be easier for the person to function. **"**

Luka considers himself low-functioning and uses that terminology because he has multiple disabilities and disorders. However, he is against a neurotypical person identifying their child/teen/partner, etc. with one of those labels without their consent or understanding. That, he feels, is where the issue is being misled. He says these words should be used only by Autistic voices sharing how they want to describe themselves.

Jennifer thinks all these terms try to oversimplify Autistics' experiences. The terms 'severe' and 'mild' autism are more based on other people's experience of the Autistic individual rather than on the Autistic person themselves. Lorraine also feels that these labels only describe how her autism affects someone else and not how it affects her.

Noah is ambivalent regarding functional labels:

" On one hand, it is very necessary for access to support, and the spectrum does vary from those who are able to blend into society almost seamlessly to others who require support in all areas of their life. I understand that the spectrum of ability and weakness isn't linear, but I do think in some environments functional labels are necessary. **"**

Paul says that 'severe/mild autism' lends itself to stereotypes:

" It ignores individual differences and also the fact that people's functioning levels can fluctuate for various reasons and are not constant. It ignores what support is being given to allow people to express themselves. However, having a classic 'Asperger's' profile myself, I wish I had an acceptable way to easily communicate to people that being Autistic does not mean I am incapable. I am self-sufficient, educated, have worked and am still partly self-employed in retirement, can drive and can make eye contact. I have been married. If all someone knows is that I am Autistic, would they infer all that about me? 🙶

AutieMum doesn't like the terms 'severe' and 'mild' and feels they can be harmful:

🙶 None of us presents the same and so it's not accurate to call a non-speaking person 'severe' and a speaking person 'mild' when they both may struggle the same amount but with different things. This is where autism awareness and acceptance come in, as the severity labels are linked to stereotypes and the more society learns about autism and how it presents differently in different people, the less likely severity labels are to be used. 🙶

Jess's thinking most closely aligns with the social model of disability:

🙶 An individual is not disabled unless their society does not accommodate them. My brother-in-law would probably be traditionally described as 'severely' Autistic. I do not like this phrasing, he is not more Autistic than I am, he just has a different presentation of autism. He requires more support with communication, but is a lot more emotionally stable than I am. Traditional ideas of the severity of autism seem to stem almost entirely from how well an Autistic person can appear to be neurotypical. My brother-in-law cannot appear neurotypical, he does not communicate especially well and has very obvious stims. However, he experiences a lot less depression and far fewer meltdowns than I do. 🙶

Nia-Eloise says that autism is just autism, there's no level to it. She adds:

🙶 We don't say that some people are severely neurotypical or mildly neurotypical so why do we say that about autism? 🙶

How do you feel about the wording 'autism spectrum'?

Most participants do not mind the word 'spectrum' itself, as it does convey the idea that there is some diversity, but many participants have noticed how misunderstood the notion of spectrum is.

Joanne, for example, says that autism is described as a spectrum, but that is a difficult concept as most people don't understand what a spectrum is. She clarifies: 'It isn't linear. One place on the spectrum is no more "severe" than any other.'

Grace also doesn't think of it as a 'high/low' spectrum but rather a spectrum (or wheel) of many different colours, like the light spectrum or a colour wheel, where everything on the spectrum or wheel is its own unique colour or shade and is not 'more' or 'less' or 'higher' or 'lower'. Karol, too, has used the image of the colour spectrum:

> 66 The 'spectrum' still makes it sound like there's a scale of how Autistic you are, but it always makes me think of the colour spectrum and how when you mix different colours you get a new unique colour which is kind of like autism – you've got different Autistic traits and the different ones come together to make a unique experience of autism and not everyone has all the traits or maybe the traits have variations like the different shades of a colour. 99

Nia-Eloise feels that calling it a spectrum has led to the belief that anyone is Autistic if they share a potential trait of autism. She has been told many times by neurotypical people that 'we're all a little Autistic', which is frustrating.

Do you prefer to say 'I am Autistic' or 'I have autism'?

Marie-Laure still remembers how during a course on autism at university, the professor explained to a full auditorium the importance of telling the patients they 'have autism' rather than they 'are Autistic'. The professor explained that saying 'have' means that we are not reducing the person to their diagnosis but instead showing them that they are a whole person, worthy of appreciation, and that their pathology is only a part of them; there are many other parts of them that are good and lovable. To make explicit what that teacher was implying: autism is a disability, it is not lovable, but thankfully the Autistic person is also a human being and not only sick, so we can appreciate the person if we leave aside the sickness. Back then, Marie-Laure was a young student hearing about autism at a university level for the first time. Naïvely, she thought: 'Wah, that makes perfect sense! This gives such hope to all those people, knowing there's more to them than their diagnosis!' She then went on to work for a few years, diligently saying 'you have autism' and sharing that 'optimistic knowledge' with her patients. Needless to say, she now cringes very much at the thought of that.

Later on, when Marie-Laure started learning *from* the Autistic community (instead of listening to neurotypicals talking *about* the Autistic community), she was surprised to hear people were actually demanding to be described as 'being Autistic' instead of 'having autism'. What a shock! That's when Marie-Laure understood that if we do not view autism as a pathology but rather as a different neurotype (different, not less), there's no need to feel shy about using the word 'Autistic'. It is not an insult. It does not diminish the person. It simply describes how they function, in a very valid way. Just like describing someone as 'tall' or 'short', 'left-handed' or 'right-handed', it does not mean we're criticizing the person: we're simply describing them. From that understanding followed the next one: autism does not describe only a part of you, it describes you entirely. It impacts your passions, your conversations, your relationships, your triggers, your feelings, the food you eat, the clothes you wear, the places you go ... It is not just a small part of you which you could remove as an accessory, it *is* you. And that's a good thing!

A vast majority of people have shared that they prefer to say 'I am Autistic' rather than 'I have autism'. Emily prefers to say 'I am Autistic', but mentioned she would defend to the death an individual's right to choose. Najib prefers to say 'I have autism' and explains that it sounds less pejorative this way. Amélie says she definitely wouldn't like to say 'I am Autistic' because autism does not define her as a person. That being said, almost all of our participants did express their preference for saying 'I am Autistic'.

Katharina, for example, explains how understanding that she is Autistic has helped her understand herself better:

❝ During the process of getting a formal evaluation for autism, it gave me plenty of opportunity to put things into perspective. Finally (!!), so many situations, feelings and struggles but also talents made sense in hindsight. So, for me, autism is who I am, since on every single level it impacts who and how I am. I believe that I perceive the world fundamentally differently than many other people and it changes the way I feel, think, love and live and can't be separated from my being. ❞

Ben explains that in his perspective, being Autistic is a permanent condition, as opposed to 'I have a cold'.

Sarah made an interesting point, saying she chooses to say 'I am Autistic', raising the question:

❝ If I were neurotypical, would you say I had neurotypicalism? No, of course not! ❞

Joanne uses a great image to illustrate why she prefers to say 'I am Autistic':

❝ Autism to me is like cake! There are so many different cakes in the world: chocolate cake, carrot cake, Victoria sandwich, Battenberg ... the list is endless. They are all cakes. No one is more of a cake than any other. But they are all different. And that's because of the ingredients. You see, all cakes have similar ingredients, a type of flour, sugar, egg or fat, but all the other ingredients are what gives the cake its flavour, it's appearance even. Even those ingredients which cakes have in common can vary slightly. Plain flour, wholemeal flour, rice or cornflour, that is what makes the huge variety we see in cakes. Autism is the same!

We all share some similarities, that's what makes us Autistic, but even those things can look different for each individual. We also have other 'ingredients' which work alongside our Autistic traits. Some are commonly found, like developmental delays, hyper-mobility, sensory processing differences, just like there are some flavours of cake that are more common. But even when you meet two Autistic people with the same traits, they are still individual, different from each other, due to their experiences and under-standing, just like two cakes made with the same ingredients may not come out the same. One cake is not more 'cake' than another because it has more ingredients.

Here are some examples of what it would sound like if we applied the person-first model to a Victoria sandwich vs the identity-first language:

This Victoria sandwich has cake. Cake is only a part of the Victoria sandwich and shouldn't define what it is. If this Victoria sandwich didn't have cake it would still be a Victoria sandwich.

This Victoria sandwich is a cake. The whole of this Victoria sandwich is cake. If this Victoria sandwich was not a cake, then it wouldn't be a Victoria sandwich.

Lola made a very powerful statement regarding how 'Autistic' is not a pejorative label and that she's happy to be characterized by it:

> 'Too loud', 'Annoying', 'Stuck up', 'Know-it-all': just a few of the labels which have stuck to me my whole life. I'll proudly wear the Autistic one, thank you very much.

S. has an interesting theory regarding how moving from 'I have autism' to 'I am Autistic' might be part of a self-acceptance journey:

> I am now saying I am Autistic – it has taken me a while but the memes about it not being a bag you can carry around with you have helped me make the changeover. I feel that this choice is down to the individual. While others may take offence at people saying they have autism, I can't help but wonder, is this part of an acceptance stage when an individual uses the term 'have autism'? It's like they haven't quite accepted it as an integral part of their being, rather that it is a part they are still growing accustomed to.

Ups and downs of being Autistic

In your experience, what is the best thing about being Autistic?

While many participants found it difficult to select the criteria that should define autism, the majority of them were inspired when it came to sharing the best sides of being Autistic. So, without further ado, here are the 'bonuses' to being Autistic!

Joe James says that the best thing about having an Autistic brain is the ability to hyper-focus and learn things to an extreme degree. Also, the natural ability to see things from a different perspective and to think outside the box. Our abilities are so valuable, yet so many of us go under the radar of opportunity and success because of stereotypes, misinformation and a public school system that lets us down every single day.

Emily's capacity for strong emotions allows her to love without boundaries and fight for what she believes in without growing weary. Christine's favourite thing about being Autistic is her empathy for others. Corrinne loves to learn and learn intensely about something. She finds it fun and it makes her good at what she does and able to help others with what she has learned. Jennifer also feels that one of the best things about being Autistic is feeling so much joy when participating in her focused interests.

C.A. said that the best part of being Autistic is what they're capable of:

> 66 The tenacity with which I approach things, the resilience of overcoming anything in my way, the 'failure is not an option' attitude I carry with me; succeeding to spite everyone and everything that is designed to want and actively seek my failure. I may not have experienced a lot of the trials of my life were I not Autistic, but I survived them because I am. 99

Hannah feels that being Autistic gives her an ability to think outside the box and see things that others don't notice, to create worlds in her mind and connect to others differently, in a more meaningful way.

S. has also been known to think outside the box and come up with solutions that others haven't even thought about considering. She is meticulous in her work, sometimes putting more in than necessary. She also notices the subtle changes in people's non-verbal communication pretty quickly.

Beckie has made a fantastic list of such wonderful bonuses to being Autistic:

> 66 The best bit of me being Autistic is my child-like self, the way I experience the world through my heightened sensors, how fast my brain works, my need and thirst for knowledge, how I hold on to everything I've learned, experienced. My logical thinking ability, the lack of the grey haze in my life, how easy I work things out. 99

What Kate loves about being Autistic is being able to separate her emotions from logic in a way that allows her to make decisions without being biased.

Jodie, who grew up in a Jehovah's Witness cult, feels that the best part of her mind is that she has a questioning one:

> 66 I ask a lot of questions, which is not suited to the cult lifestyle, you can't brainwash someone who is aware. Getting out of the Jehovah's Witness cult was the best thing I ever did and I'm not sure I would have been able to if it weren't for the PDA (pathological demand avoidance) part of me. Sorry guys, brainwashing doesn't work on me. 99

Fabrizio states that he would not have been a curious, scientific mind had he not been Autistic.

Jess says that the best thing about being Autistic is most of it! She goes on to say:

> 66 The best thing about being Autistic is – most of it! While my experiences around autism as a child and being diagnosed were distressing and have left me with a lot of trauma, I would not be who I am without being Autistic. I am kind and compassionate because I am so in tune with my own struggles. I have an incredible memory for things I find interesting. I find such incredible joy in my special interest. I love my family and friends and my partner so

incredibly intensely because of my autism. I can feel music when I listen to it. I would not change being Autistic purely for the feeling of music, if nothing else. **"**

Lorraine feels that the best thing about being Autistic is that she is able to learn new skills very quickly. Also, she is able to be very still and observe, which means that she has a great rapport with animals, both domesticated and wild.

M.'s favourite sides to being Autistic are related to how she sees the world:

> **"** I think my favourites are my strong ability to see incredible beauty in the world of nature, which allows me to love and communicate well with pets, as well as enabling my favourite hobby of taking and editing thousands of photos that I love because of how I can capture my view of amazing nature and cute animals as I see and feel them. **"**

Sadie appreciates the ability to see a bigger picture with all the details and everything, not just one thing but the whole thing with all the little bits.

Sarah can't say that there is only one best thing about being Autistic; there are many great things about it. She will list a few:

> **"** I seem to notice more detail in things than other people, it's almost like I automatically home in on the minute details first and then focus more on the bigger picture after. A bit like if you were to have a camera on full zoom and then slowly turn it back to normal view. I don't just do this with images or scenery, it can be with people, sounds, situations or mood too. It's difficult to put it into words to explain it properly, but I will give an example for the sound one. If you listen to a song, you will notice the words, the basic tune and the beat. I will notice all those things but also the sounds in the background too, like the tiny tambourine sound, clicking, tapping, even the breathing-in sound of the artist before singing their next line. That sort of thing.
>
> I have a very creative brain and am constantly coming up with different ideas.

I find lots of little things amusing (like a child would).

If I want to learn something, I won't just learn the basics, I will investigate the subject much more deeply than the average person. For example, if I were to decide to learn about an onion, I wouldn't just learn about how it looks or tastes or how to plant and grow it. I would investigate how many layers it has, how thick those layers are, if they differ per variety, what colours they have in them, what PH level they grow best at, their names and where they would originate from, etc.... I would be the master of onion knowledge. **"**

Here's the list of Lola's preferred sides to being Autistic:

" What I love about being Autistic is ... where do I begin? There's so much I love about being Autistic. But here are a few of the great traits that I attribute to my Autism: good at focusing, attention to detail, enjoy repetitive tasks (I do a lot of these at work), excellent long-term memory, stubborn (yes, I consider this a good thing – a lot of people seem to give up on something if it doesn't go their way at first), highly empathic (contrary to popular belief, Autistic people *are* capable of empathy, it's more the body-language stuff we struggle with), always wanting to learn more about specialist subjects, musicality (once I know a song, it's pretty much there for life. I don't often get lyrics wrong!). One thing in particular that I love is that I get to be a part of an amazing community. There are so many wonderful people out there advocating and educating the world about us, and so much emotional support online. **"**

In Sarah's experience, the best aspects of being Autistic are the way she experiences the world in glorious vitality, her innocence, her joy, valuing simple things, being kind, sensitivity, as well as deep thinking and feeling.

In your experience, what is the hardest thing about being Autistic?

Although our participants were inspired when sharing their favourite things about being Autistic, they also didn't hold back when it came to describing the most difficult aspects of being Autistic.

Joe James says that the hardest thing about being Autistic is people assuming they know what it's like for him based on stereotypes or them knowing a completely different Autistic person. People make assumptions about him based on what they have read or learned autism is, but it isn't anything per se, it's just a type of person who differs from the average person.

Here's what our participants had to say.

Emma feels the hardest part about being Autistic is how misunderstood she can be:

> ❝ Worst thing is the way people fundamentally misunderstand me sometimes when I can't express myself. I go away, write it down and send it, but they look at me like I have three heads because I just couldn't say it. It's caused me problems getting medical assistance before now and it's really impacted my life. ❞

Emily feels the hardest side is having to always make adjustments to fit into a neurotypical world. She adds: 'It's draining and I get eye strain from rolling my eyes so hard.'

Danielle explains how difficult it is to have people not being aware of the fact that we're Autistic:

> ❝ The worst thing about being Autistic for me is almost that I am not obviously Autistic enough. People can't see it. Even if you tell them, they don't get it. My head can be misfiring all over the place with millions of thoughts and worries but I still maintain an appearance of being fine. Looking back over my life I recognize that I have put massive effort into trying to appear the way I should. I have developed multiple versions of myself to suit multiple people. ❞

Nia-Eloise feels that the hardest thing about being Autistic is dealing with the stereotypes and misinformation about autism. She says:

> ❝ Anytime I tell someone I'm Autistic, I get the 'compliment' of 'you don't look/act like you're Autistic' or 'I'd never have thought that about you'. It's really hurtful and irritating and it used to make me feel like I was an imposter pretending to be Autistic. ❞

Kevin says that his least favourite thing about having autism is how isolating it can sometimes be:

> 66 I feel incredibly lucky to have built the community I have, but even today I still have moments where I feel like a fish out of water in a room full of neurotypicals. I also have moments where I get overwhelmed, I don't know why, and it makes me upset. And I have moments where I do something that alienates other people, but don't know exactly what that is. 77

Neville would say the hardest thing about being Autistic is the struggle in social situations, especially events such as parties, weddings or anything where he would try to interact with people he doesn't know, and the burnout that can come with it.

Beth feels one of the most difficult aspects to being Autistic is being told 'You can't be Autistic because you make good eye contact', or 'You're a girl', or 'Well, you don't look Autistic to me'.

The hardest thing about Karol's autism is her struggle with being sociable:

> 66 I mask, hide my Autistic traits and pretend to be an extravert, so when people talk to me, they're not really talking to me, they're talking to what I think is the neurotypical image of myself, and that makes it hard to connect with people. Even when I'm around someone, it mostly feels really lonely. 77

Some hard things about being Autistic, in Grace's experience, have been never feeling like she quite fits in anywhere and being misunderstood a lot of the time. Hannah really dislikes feeling like you have to stand there and listen to others, otherwise you are being 'rude'. According to Isabella, the hardest things about being Autistic are the sadness, loneliness and incommunicability, and the health comorbidities. Beth finds it difficult to navigate the social world, making friends. The hardest thing about being Autistic for Kristel is how sensitive she is and how she always expects people to be as loyal as her, when they're not. And it hurts.

Corrinne describes how difficult it can be to have different needs than others:

> 66 The hardest thing about being Autistic is not being able to cope with the noise and stressors of everyday life. I need a lot more quiet and down time than others, and I don't feel like I can be anywhere near as productive as most people. It's hard having different needs and knowing how to embrace that and not compare myself to others. 99

S. struggles with the constant feeling of exhaustion:

> 66 The hardest thing about being Autistic is this constant overload. This constant hyper-vigilance and stress is slowly killing me, I can only take that much of it, it makes me just want to end it all a lot of times. This world can be so loud, so overwhelming, I cannot handle any more a lot of times. My brain is tired, my body at 19 too tired from pressure and constant stress like an old person would be. My high standards of loyalty, truth, honesty and my blindness to social cues and sign/body language or simply indirect speech always leave me like a blind sheep in the middle of a wolf pack, lonely, abandoned and hurt all the time. 99

In Jess's experience, the hardest thing about being Autistic is having meltdowns:

> 66 I find it very difficult to control anger and can feel absolutely fine and then be sent over the edge almost instantly by a tiny trigger. I initially pursued diagnosis after realizing how abnormal it was for me to have such explosive meltdowns; to be frank, my meltdowns are violent and loud. I will scream and shout, throw objects, throw myself against walls, pull my hair out and attempt to injure myself. I am aware of all of these actions but unable to stop myself. The entire experience is absolutely terrifying. Meltdowns happen for me about once or twice a month, more if I am stressed, less if I am not stressed. 99

M. describes the toughest part as being the fact that everything feels very intense. She adds: 'I'm hypersensitive and get overwhelmed and burnt out easily and struggle to keep earning a living, which is very scary.'

One of the parts Christina is still trying to navigate is mirror touch synesthesia. She explains:

> This element of myself can sometimes feel debilitating as I must avoid nearly all distressing situations. This means movies, news, TV, radio, social media, blood draws ... I can feel pain in my body just by seeing a scab or a scar. Witnessing something physically traumatic causes immense and overwhelming pain in my body, typically starting in my chest and radiating to my limbs. The intensity of the pain depends on the trauma someone is experiencing. In the past I've seen videos of kids sticking their heads out of a moving car and losing their breath from the wind in their face. While watching this, I also lose my breath and have to re-centre my focus on my own breathing, so I don't choke.

C.A. began by saying that the worst part of being Autistic is the way they're treated for it. Nothing they have to say is considered as heavily; no knowledge they offer is as credible; no expertise is taken seriously. They then go on to describe the feeling of displacement, which they experience as an Autistic person and can be understood as a cultural experience:

> In Australia our indigenous populations continue to feel the intergenerational trauma of white colonization by way of health and education gaps, substance abuse, higher incarceration rates, the list goes on. This *still* occurs in indigenous people who have grown up in our metropolitan cities, showing the dispossession of lands, the disconnection with their culture and the displacement of feeling 'not right' is innate within people who are expected to live in worlds not built for their natural way of life.
>
> Being Autistic colours every experience: every colour seen, every blade of grass run between our fingertips, every flavour on our tongue, every thought that runs through our minds. As such, being Autistic is absolutely a cultural experience and

being forced into a society where we inherently feel 'wrong' is a major contributor to poorer wellbeing outcomes in Autistics due to this very similar sense of displacement, something well documented in other cultures. **"**

AutieMum hates how there's a pressure to be like a genius at something, like 'Rain Man', when she feels actually just slightly above average in some things but doesn't have any special talent with numbers or art, for example.

In S.'s experience, the hardest side to being Autistic is when we're told we're being hurtful – when that definitely wasn't our intention:

> **"** The hardest thing for me involves saying something that hurts another unintentionally or saying something that is taken the wrong way because I'm not good at sugar coating. Sometimes, people explain to me where I went wrong and I still don't get it. I find this really frustrating and sometimes upsetting. It gets to the point where I start thinking 'I hate people' and just want to spend time at home with my dog. **"**

Lucy feels that the downside is the exhaustion. She says:

> **"** I don't think I've had a day where I haven't felt exhausted. I constantly have to plan how I'm going to get through the day. And it's a worry: "I might not get through the day." And I have to get through the day and be ok for my children. **"**

How do you feel about the way media and pop culture represent autism?

Media and pop culture have an important impact on the perception of autism among the general public. A lot of people will never read a book about autism but will still have an image in mind of what an Autistic person 'looks like'. We've asked our participants how they feel about the way media and pop culture represent autism, in order to see if they feel that it is an accurate description or not.

Beth chose not to watch any TV shows on autism because they didn't represent her as a female. She adds: 'I thought if I watched these, I'd get serious imposter syndrome!' Grace also feels as though she has only seen male Autistic characters and would really like to see female Autistic characters portrayed in movies and TV shows.

C.A. describes how stereotypically the Autistic characters are usually represented in movies:

> **❝** They are presented in a way that makes them 'obviously' Autistic, by ways of behaviours and social awkwardness, despite the fact that much of the Autistic experience is internal and so not observable, but when the only information you're getting as a neurotypical actor is neurotypical information based on neurotypical observations of Autistics, the result on screen is not going to be representative of the lived experiences of most Autistics. Often, they are expected to specifically push to make behaviours more noticeable so the character appears 'more' Autistic, otherwise how would audiences know? But this only adds to the ongoing stereotyping of Autistic behaviour and leads to incredibly poor directorial and production decisions. Your audience might not be able to tell the character is Autistic? *Good*: many Autistics are denied support specifically because they are not *obviously* Autistic. **❞**

AutieMum says that pop culture certainly hasn't helped society's perception of autism:

> **❝** I categorically refuse to watch any programme that purports to be about autism or contain an Autistic character (unless the actor is actually Autistic) because I don't want to see what the world thinks of me. I saw a snippet of *The Good Doctor* once and I was horrified that the character was so robotic and cold. I thought, 'Is this really how we come across to people?' I don't know if that character relates to other Autistic individuals but he was basically my fears and insecurities confirmed on my screen. Also, the actor wasn't Autistic and so I felt he couldn't portray what he doesn't understand. **❞**

Lauren describes Autistic representation in media as 'shocking'. She says:

> 66 I don't think I could actually name one piece of good representation. We're usually viewed as unfeeling geniuses and are never even played by Autistic people. When I see this media, it doesn't make me feel represented, it makes me feel like I'm publicly being made fun of. 99

Paul explains why he can't relate to the Autistic characters:

> 66 Before my late diagnosis the only 'Autistic' characters I knew were Rain Man and Espenson. I did not relate to either. I wasn't a savant or someone with high support needs. I didn't stim ostentatiously. I think all the shows miss the introversion, loneliness, masking and shutdowns, which wouldn't make good TV. I don't see myself in any media portrayal of autism and think the shows accentuate very stereotypical behaviour. If all I knew about autism was those TV shows, I would never have self-diagnosed as Autistic. If anyone asked me to recommend a film or TV show to demonstrate what autism was like for me, I couldn't. I would spend too much time explaining what I wasn't like. 99

Thomas, who is 14 years old, has said something incredibly powerful:

> 66 I feel the way social media represents autism is always showing the side of the most severe autism. This makes me not want to tell people I am Autistic. 99

What Thomas has said there is incredibly important, in our opinion. The way media conveys certain messages around autism will greatly impact whether one person will be proud or ashamed to be Autistic. It will also have a great influence on how people are likely to react when they learn their friend/relative/colleague is Autistic. We hope that in the future, representations will be accurate enough to help people relate to the characters and feel safe in telling people they're Autistic.

As you will probably have noticed in this chapter, there are many different ways of perceiving autism. Some see it as a gift, others as a pathology. In the end, what matters is mostly to respect the person's choice of words as they describe their own experience. There is so much diversity within diversity that it makes sense that each person might perceive and experience it differently. It wouldn't be helpful to dismiss someone's struggles, just like it wouldn't be helpful to pathologize a way of functioning that can be healthy.

3

Diagnosis

Joe James' experience

I was watching television with my wife, Sylvia. We were snuggled up on the sofa watching a programme about children who had 'challenging behaviours'. Much of the time, it was the parents who I found to be challenging as they completely ignored their child's obvious difficulties and chose to blame autism. It was called *Born Naughty* on Channel 4. The doctors on the programme visited the families to assess if the child was Autistic, had ADHD or whether they just had bad parents. I don't know why it couldn't be both, or neither, but that was the show.

I'll admit I knew nothing about autism or Asperger's and only a little about ADHD, even though I apparently had it. I had never been given help at school after my hyperactivity diagnosis and pondered whether it was even real, as no one in my family ever mentioned it to me. It was almost as though if I was hyper, it was my fault because I like chocolate, so it was my responsibility to control it.

So, there we were, three episodes into the series and a little boy called Thomas appeared. He was sweet, chatty *at* you not *with* you, liked Lego, had siblings but would only play with them if they joined in with his games, was constantly running around and seeking stimulation, and rarely listened to his parents. He tended to be quite violent and would have very destructive meltdowns. He was nine and had been so badly bullied he refused to go to school. My wife's eyes darted towards my face, then back to the television, then back to my face.

'What?' I asked as she stared at me, aghast.

'This boy is you!' she said.

'How?' I always listened to her, even if I didn't always agree with her.

'Just watch it again, he's just like you when you were a child.' She would know as my family always spoke about how 'difficult' I was and how much of a 'pain' I was. Sylvia didn't like hearing this stuff, but she put up with their bashing of her husband because she hates confrontation.

I obliged and pressed rewind on the remote. We watched again and this time I concentrated much more and intently analysed Thomas, not what they were saying about him. People had said stuff about me all my life, so I didn't want to hear their thoughts. I watched him, watched his movements, his eyes, his passion when talking about Lego, his face drop as he spoke about friendship. My eyes began to water, my stomach turned, I had flashbacks to my childhood and there it was, Sylvia was right. I paused the show and looked at my best friend.

'He's just like me!'

'Does this mean you have autism?' That's what the programme called it.

'Let's watch and find out if the doctors think Thomas does.' We hadn't actually got that far at that point.

Suddenly it was like I was being diagnosed myself. I heard words like 'medical condition', 'behaviour problems', 'underlying problem', and those words made me angry. I didn't feel like I matched any of these phrases, and neither did Thomas. I wasn't a problem, the way I was treated and the environments I was forced into were the problem.

We watched on tenterhooks as the parents sat at a table with the doctors and Thomas played with his Lego. The results were in and they were told Thomas was on the Autistic spectrum and was 'high-functioning'. I remember thinking this was an odd way of describing it, as then they went on to tell the parents all the help he needed. If someone was high-functioning, surely that meant they were better than average-functioning, so who was average?

So, there it was, the answer to why all my life I had felt so different from everyone else. The reason I struggled to fit in, even as an adult. The reason I fell out with work colleagues, friends and family. The reason I struggled to socialize and lost my temper and hurt myself. The reason for all my problems became very clear. But I didn't blame my autism for those problems, I blamed everyone else, for the way I was treated.

Even though I didn't have a formal diagnosis I went into full-blown research mode and found out everything I could about autism. There was a lot of information out there and most of it contradicted itself. I found out that the type of autism I had was called Asperger's, named after a doctor who called his patients 'little professors'. I quite liked that as it fitted the way I felt about being an 'Aspie'. I was highly intelligent, loved science, art, documentaries and research. It was all falling into place. I spoke to some of my siblings and even my parents. My dad said I was just Joe, my sister and younger brother said it made sense, my birth mother said she had suspected for some time. *Wait, what?* I asked why she hadn't said anything and she told me she thought I was doing fine, so why upset things? I could have screamed. Years and years I'd felt out of place, Sylvia and my nephew Jake being the only ones who understood me and apparently the answer to my lifelong question 'Why me?' was on the lips of my so-called mum all along. I don't know if she was trying to be smug, supportive or vindictive, I could never tell with her.

Sylvia thought it would be a good idea to get a formal diagnosis because I'd had some fallings out at work and she wanted to make sure I was legally protected by the disabilities act. I agreed, as I do most of the time, her feelings and worries trumping my opinions on the subject. I went to my GP (general practitioner) and chatted away, barely letting her get a word in edgeways, and she agreed very quickly with my well-put analysis of my life to this point. I was lucky to have a GP who understood autism and who didn't think it was all about rocking in a corner and lacking empathy. With me, I had a small library of proof of my self-diagnosis printed out from the internet, but it turned out I never needed it.

A few months later, I was chatting with a lady from the local mental health clinic. I couldn't understand what it had to do with mental health, but I just took it in my stride. She asked me about my childhood, she asked me about my friendships, I told her about my special subjects and saw her smile slightly as she clearly made up her mind that I was indeed an 'Aspie' (I now know better and despise the terminology). It took her just over an hour and she confirmed the diagnosis. She said, 'Welcome to the club', which I really liked, and made me feel like I wasn't alone as I had once thought. She told me about services and a support group, I told her that none of that was necessary, but I was interested in some more information. We booked a follow-up appointment which I missed due to being easily distracted and she never replied to the voicemail of apology I left her. I decided that she was too busy for me and to just get on with it myself.

That was it then, I was officially Autistic (Asperger's), my paperwork said. I messaged everyone I knew a photo of the signed paperwork, almost rubbing it in their faces how wrong they had been to judge me as they had. I felt vindicated, relieved and bitter at all those who had ignored me and made me feel bad about being different. I told everyone I knew, even my trainer at the gym. I was really proud and kept reminding them about Charles Darwin and Albert Einstein who were said to also be Autistic like me. I truly saw the positives, but not everyone I met had the same opinion.

When I informed my manager at work, he told me to keep it to myself. He told me it could negatively impact how people perceived me or stop me from getting promoted within the company. He said that people would see it as a weakness and not take me seriously as a supervisor any more. Luckily for me, I ignored him and at least for the next few years I remained positive about my new-found understanding of who I was.

My dream for the future is that being Neurodivergent will not be seen as a diagnosis but as a type of person who experiences the world differently and each individual will get support based on their specific needs and not as a blanket label. We should discover our neurotype and embrace who we are.

Participants' experiences

There is quite a controversy around whether or not we should use the word 'diagnosis' when referring to autism. In this chapter, we will not explore that controversy in depth, but you can read more on that question in Chapter 2. Here, we will explore the journey our participants have described regarding getting a diagnosis through formal assessment. We will discover our participants' motivations in getting a diagnosis, what it has changed in their lives, the reactions of their beloved ones, and share our participants' opinions regarding telling your child they're Autistic.

The process of getting a diagnosis

If you're considering getting a formal assessment and are wondering what to expect, know that there are different ways of doing the assessment depending on your age, your gender and the professional doing the evaluation. In general, you can expect there to be some questionnaires to fill out, as well as a meeting with the evaluator, in which you'll be asked questions about your past and present, your strengths and struggles, and how you deal with certain situations. It is likely that the evaluator will be asking some questions of the people who know you well, with your agreement, so that they can know a bit more about you as a child and you in the present. Depending on the country, there can be an extremely long waiting time in public services (up to ten years!). Private assessments usually give an answer much faster (a few months), but can be very costly in countries where it is not covered by insurance. These factors mean it can be difficult and perhaps discouraging to get a diagnosis for people, especially adults, often discouraging people from going through that whole process.

Lauren tells us about her assessment, which she did in 2021 in the UK:

> ❝ I filled out 23 pages of questions about my upbringing and childhood, all the way up to the present. I filled in the AQ 50 and another self-referral questionnaire. I was given an assessment date and in that one session after about half an hour, the psychiatrist stopped me and told me she could already confidently diagnose me with ASD. She congratulated me and commended me on the extent and quality of the research I had done. ❞

When Fabrizio got diagnosed in 2022 in Switzerland, he was sent several tests to do, one of which completely surprised him:

> ❝ This test asked me to point out to which emotion a photo of eyes corresponded (from a slice of a photo of a face). I was completely puzzled by this test, realizing that I am unable to read eyes emotions. The diagnosis came in the worst moment of my life, where I am far from my family and under treatment for stress/depression. When my psychologist confirmed my suspicions, I was not surprised, but the confirmation still stung. I was already realizing my condition and this brought me a deep sense of desperation. It's not the environment around me that is difficult, it's just me. There is no shortcut, there is no denying and there is no excuse any more. I am weird and I will always be struggling. ❞

Corrinne explains the fears she had when starting this process in the USA at 25 years old:

> ❝ I was anxious about the process, that I wouldn't say what I needed to, or I would mask too much and they wouldn't pick up on my autism. But they did and it went really well. The waiting process for a week to hear the results was very difficult. I was anxious. Finally, I got the diagnosis and it was more accurate than I thought, I was very happy. ❞

Nia-Eloise, from England, finally got diagnosed four years ago, when she was 15 years old:

> ❝ When it came to getting my diagnosis, all of the questionnaires were aimed at autism in males and it was clear that autism in females is barely understood, even by mental health professionals. My mother sent them all back with notes saying that they don't apply to females. I had to bring in my own research and notes about female autism for them to read. It honestly felt so bizarre that I had to teach them about autism before I could get my diagnosis. My mother was so supportive and fought so hard for me and I'm just so appreciative for all that she did to help me. She let me speak when I felt like I could but was ready to talk for me when it got overwhelming. I definitely couldn't have done it without her. ❞

Jennifer decided to seek a diagnosis at age 30, in the USA:

> ❝ I already knew I had sensory processing issues, but started to listen to other Autistic female YouTubers and found I highly related to their experience. I mentioned to my GP that I wanted to seek a diagnosis and they were understanding and referred me to a psychologist. Unfortunately, this psychologist wasn't well versed in autism and had a very outdated view. She told me that despite the fact I have multiple 'symptoms' of autism, the fact that I wasn't diagnosed as a child, that I could mostly hold a conversation and make some eye contact, that I wasn't obsessed with trains or math,

and don't seem overly affected by it, meant she was refusing to move forward with a diagnosis since there wasn't a reason to label it.

It took all I had to even finish this appointment. The moment it was over I cried. I felt like I had hit the end of the road and that maybe I was just making this all up. However, I couldn't let go of the feeling that I had finally connected with something that explained my life in a way that nothing else did. I decided to fight for it. After discovering there was only a handful of doctors in my area that would even diagnose an adult with autism and that the wait would take years, I almost gave up. 🙶

Thankfully, she did not give up and found a Canadian centre where she could get a proper assessment. She describes the process as having been incredibly smooth and was seen in months, not years. She adds:

🙶 I didn't feel like I had to prove myself to even be acknowledged. For the first time, someone listened. Not only that, but they validated my struggles and pointed out some things I do that are actually very common among Autistics. 🙶

Sarah had an absolutely horrific experience with her autism assessment in the UK, offered by the public services:

🙶 I was repeatedly told, 'Autism is almost always diagnosed in childhood and if you weren't diagnosed as a child, you almost certainly don't *have* it' (EXACT words, repeated over and over). When I was mute, they told me, 'If you refuse to speak, we won't be able to assess you.' They talked over me, silenced me, refused to ask me or my husband about any of my struggles or sensory difficulties, repeatedly tried to force my husband to leave, and made me play stupid, childish games. Then, they kicked me out after 1 hour 15 minutes, saying I showed zero signs of autism (ironic, given my mutism, inability to make eye contact, 10/10 on the AQ10, significant sensory issues, and social and communication difficulties, for starters). They told me that without having a parent there, they wouldn't consider *anything* from my childhood. They were rude, bullying and lied repeatedly. I was seriously traumatized by the whole experience, as well as the complaints process afterwards. A total of four years that made me physically and mentally ill.

I then paid for a private assessment with a doctor who was the exact opposite. He was warm, kind, compassionate, understanding and *incredibly* intuitive (seeing things about me that I hadn't recognized, but my family and best friend confirmed). We spent weeks communicating in great detail and he listened to me in great depth, giving me unlimited space to express myself and then explaining my neurology in great detail, following up with a 19-page report! (Which my lovely GP read in its entirety.) **„**

Wren, a transgender man who was assigned female at birth, tells us about his process of getting diagnosed in England when he was 30 years old:

❝ When I was 25, I stumbled across an article on late-diagnosed Autistic women. It was like a lightbulb went off. The experiences I was reading about mirrored my own so closely that I could have written them myself. I devoured everything I could find about autism in adults. Books, online articles, social media posts. When I showed my husband, he agreed immediately that it sounded like me, but I wasn't so sure. Part of me wanted to believe I'd finally found my answer, while the other part felt I wasn't struggling enough to qualify. As well, I didn't want my joy at the discovery tarnishing my relationship with my brother, whose diagnosis still held for him shame and fear.

We eventually decided to just treat me as though I was Autistic, because even if I wasn't, the accommodations we were making in our lives were helping. I stopped forcing myself to do things like go into the supermarket because 'it would be good for me' and started getting online orders instead. I wore headphones in situations with too much noise and let myself have breaks when I was getting overwhelmed. Still, I couldn't bring myself to tell people with any certainty that I was Autistic without a diagnosis, only that I thought I might be.

After my son was born, it soon became clear he was Autistic too. We knew we'd need to get him a diagnosis and I decided that if I was going to be the best parent I could for him, I needed one for myself too. I needed to finally stop questioning and have that confirmation to be able to confidently advocate for us both.

It was around five years after I read that initial article at work. I phoned my GP and was told that they didn't have any way for adults to be diagnosed, and that if my reasoning was to better support my child, then I couldn't possibly be Autistic as Autistic people don't have empathy enough for that. I was furious, but too shocked to say anything at the time. I wasn't even sure I'd heard correctly! Thankfully, my husband had been sitting in on the call and we complained to the service, requesting a formal apology and that their staff receive extra training. I also asked to be put in touch with a private practitioner whose diagnosis they would accept.

My private assessment was thankfully a wonderful experience where I felt fully respected and understood. I received the formal report a few weeks later which was registered with the GP and made for some fascinating reading. Mostly, it felt like a weight had been lifted. I was officially Autistic. I didn't need to question any more. My life finally made sense. 🙶

Linda, from Sweden, tells us about her process of getting a diagnosis when she was 41 years old:

🙸 Before being diagnosed as Autistic, I was labelled with so many different kinds of personality disorders and anxiety and depression. When the first psychologist mentioned her suspicions, I reacted with such shock and anger – total outburst – because at that time I knew nothing more about autism than the harmful stereotypical and harmful ignorance that unfortunately was, and still is, the majority of Swedish people's only knowledge. The psychologist who did my assessment, on the other hand, took his time and provided me with more 'correct' information and gave me tips on how to proceed further in my process of understanding and accepting myself (my genuine self, under all layers of masking).

However, it turned out to be a group of 'experts' who would feed me with more stereotypical info. Their main focus was my difficulties, and the knowledge they had and transferred to me was built on inaccurate, harmful stereotypes like person-first language and that I shouldn't identify with the autism because I am 'so much more than my autism and I can strive in the world *despite* having this disorder'. I felt only total confusion, desperation and such shame. Panic and emptiness because it felt like I had 'lost my whole identity', the only thing I knew. The only thing I was presented with by these so-called experts and the autism-related Swedish search results on the web was so totally dark and negative that it left me feeling: 'How the hell am I supposed to accept and love this and how am I supposed to exist and work out in this NT society now, when knowing all this?'

It took me such a long time (years) to get out of this paralyzing feeling. But then, one day, my survival mood kicked in and I paused my listening on 'non-Autistic experts' and started scanning the web – outside Swedish sources – and *finally*, I started to find accurate information, forums run by actually Autistic people, and slowly, slowly, starting with just reading, listening, processing and going through all stages of grief, denying and the feeling of being an imposter in the Autistic world, and I started to be able to grasp all this new information, not just in theory but in real life – *my* life.

Today, I am proud to be exactly who I am – with both strength and challenges (like all people) – and I grow into my genuine self more each day – much thanks to the Autistic community. I would never be where I am today without it/them/us. **"**

Here's Isabella's journey. She was recently diagnosed in Italy when she was 40 years old:

" I always had huge problems in life. I never managed to work for more than a few weeks in a row, I never managed to study, I never managed to have healthy relationships with other people, I never managed to have economic balance, I used to be homeless, I had addictions, I have been in toxic relationships. So I was wondering what was wrong with me. At 39 years old, I read about autism in adults and I recognized myself partially in some symptoms, then I read about ADHD and I recognized myself in the symptoms, so I looked for a psychologist and I told him about my suspicions of being on the spectrum and he ridiculed me and made me feel so wrong, it has been horrible.

So, I looked for another one, an expert in ADHD. She diagnosed me with ADHD and she said that if I were Autistic, I would not be conscious of it and that I do not have cognitive or linguistic delays so I could be only mildly in the spectrum. But I feel my autism is not mild! I am definitely not high-functioning. So, I looked for another expert in autism and she diagnosed me with ASD second level. 〞

Katharina was part of a parenting group in Austria, where there was an Autistic mum with an Autistic daughter. She got her diagnosis recently, at the age of 42:

❝ There was an instant connection and understanding. She pointed out often how different female autism was and so I wanted to know more and started my usual research – when something caught my attention, I wanted to know every little detail. My daughter was the absolute and complete opposite of my son (who was so much like me), but the checklist of typical female Autistic traits got longer and longer, and it slowly dawned on me. Eventually, I got a recommendation for a clinical psychologist who is specialized in female autism and who happens to be Autistic himself (and proud of it). We went through the process and eventually he congratulated my daughter on how very special she was, explained to her what her special strengths were according to her test, and worked with her on the things she still needs to learn. Once we had that squared away, I was also curious for myself, to know for sure and know the details of my evaluation. 〞

It's shocking to see that many participants have had to fight for their diagnosis. They've had to convince a reluctant doctor for a referral or have had to ask for a second opinion when the first evaluator had outdated views on autism. It really says something about the need to be assertive and combative – as well as the need for a lot of support from family – to be able to get a diagnosis. Hopefully, in the future this will change and people will no longer have to pay thousands, wait for years and be mistreated by medical professionals in order to finally hear the truth about themselves.

Why get a diagnosis?

The motivations for why a person would seek out a diagnosis are very personal. If someone has a motivation that matters to them, it is valid. No therapist, doctor or relative should ever discourage someone from seeking out an official assessment if it is important to the Autistic person themselves, even if others struggle to see why it matters to the person. Here are some of the reasons our participants have sought out an official diagnosis for themselves (or for their children).

Joanne explains:

66 Due to imposter syndrome, which a lot of Autistic people struggle with, I needed an official diagnosis to enable me to accept myself fully. It allowed me to reclaim myself, find the real me under years of masks. It wasn't an excuse for things I may have said or done, but it was a reason and that was important for me. 99

Kelly is starting her diagnosis journey because she feels it will help to have the formal diagnosis in situations where it's needed so that she does not have to keep explaining herself and justifying herself.

Jennifer has also shared how getting an official diagnosis would help others believe her:

66 Even though my family believed me, I still felt the need to go further and get an official diagnosis for myself and so that I had another tool in my arsenal to present to doctors. I already knew that I was Autistic from the extensive research I had done on the topic when I began to suspect it, but I didn't feel like anyone else, including my doctors, would validate it without an official diagnosis. 99

Karol has found it really helpful to get diagnosed before going to university:

> 66 I could ask for reasonable adjustments to be made for my study, although that makes me think it would have been better to get diagnosed earlier because then I could have had similar adjustments in secondary school and sixth form. 99

Nicky has found it hard not having a diagnosis as she has spent her life beating herself up for things that she now understands are down to her autism and ADHD. She wishes she had known years ago and been kinder to herself as a result. She adds:

> 66 That's why I feel it's important for my son to get a diagnosis while he's young so he can learn about himself and ways of coping early on and have accommodations made if he needs them. 99

Beckie has also noticed the tremendous difference getting a diagnosis has made to her life:

> 66 I didn't actually realize just how much I'd been struggling in life, just how much I don't cope in this world, how anxious, stressed, overwhelmed I am on a daily basis, that I live in a heightened state, that I'm permanently burnt out, the slightest thing can tip me over the edge. I believe it's so important to get diagnosed. All these years wondering what's wrong with you, the self-hate, becoming so mentally ill, trying to kill myself all because we don't know who we really are. 99

Sarah has also spent many years trying to understand herself:

> 66 I have always been searching for answers, since my late teens, early 20s, as to who I was and why I functioned like this. Why things were so difficult. And I soon came to the conclusion that maybe to a degree everyone felt this way and, in some ways, I'm correct. Autistic traits are raw human traits, but some of us can feel so much that everything hurts – emotionally, life hurts, being

sensitive to certain things, comments, facial expressions, tone of voice. For me, it's been difficult to trust others, especially as I've got older. I've always felt like I've been on the edge of life looking in. I've always felt like, I need to just become that little bit more mature, confident, know what to say, to be human. Now, I know I'm Autistic, and listening to other people's stories, it's all starting to make sense. I feel comfortable knowing who I am. At times, I feel I don't deserve a diagnosis, 'I fooled them', I'm really a bad, broken neuro-typical. Well, that's how I've been conditioned, I guess. **"**

Melanie reflects on how getting a diagnosis might help her be a positive role model for her children:

" I haven't got a diagnosis yet. In all honesty, I'm ok with not being officially diagnosed as I don't need to prove anything to anyone, but I think it would be helpful as far as my children are concerned. I have five and all of them are ND, but getting them any support or diagnosis has been almost impossible. My eldest feels very negatively about being Autistic and I suppose if I can show him that I am too, he'll not feel like it's a negative thing. **"**

A significant number of participants have shared that they are seeking an official diagnosis in order to be believed by others, whether it's relatives or professionals from the medical community. It says something about how intimidating it can be to tell people you're Autistic and how scary it is when people don't believe you. It is also interesting that a lot of people expressed fear of their doctor not believing them, which shows how the representation of autism among medical professionals still leaves Autistic people afraid that they won't be taken seriously.

What did it feel like to find out you're Autistic?

Let's find out how our participants felt when they found out they were Autistic. Was there shame, pride, anger, excitement, sadness, joy, worthlessness or self-appreciation?

Tanya self-diagnosed five years ago, when her son received his formal autism diagnosis:

> 66 When the psychologist read out his report, I thought she was talking about me. I cried with relief as I finally learned who I was, that there was nothing wrong with me at all, I simply had a differently wired brain. I describe it as my Elsa from *Frozen* moment where I could finally let go of the constrictions that bound me. I was not defective, I was Autistic. 99

While Mark is absolutely delighted with his diagnoses, he cannot suppress feelings of grief and anger too. He is genuinely upset when he thinks about all the people he has inadvertently hurt and all the opportunities he has missed. He feels like he's on borrowed time now, and that he hasn't got enough time to achieve everything that he has always wanted to but is only now able to.

Lorraine had initially been misdiagnosed with bipolar II disorder, so when she finally got her autism diagnosis, it was a great relief for her. She says:

> 66 I've heard it said that a diagnosis makes no difference, and for some people that may be true, but for me it explained so much. Being Autistic, I have always been aware that I am 'different' but I never understood why or how. As a child growing up with a religious family, I even thought I was demon possessed at one stage. So much pain and self-doubt could have been avoided had I known sooner in my life. 99

Beth was hoping she would feel relieved, but so far it has only increased her anxiety, confusion about the past and future, and guilt around the impact on her children and family.

Kate found it somewhat validating, but she also has had feelings of sadness for the years of suffering as a child without anyone realizing that she needed help.

C.A. shares the different emotions they went through when finding out they are Autistic:

> **"** The initial shock turned to anger. I was the way I was for a reason and that reason was withheld from me. Then I was hurt I never got the chance to know so I could change. Then sadness because this was permanent, which meant I couldn't change. I was stuck this way forever ... then came the epiphany. I understood *everything*. For the first time in my life, I *knew*. The planets aligned and everything in my life, everything about myself, every past experience, every thought and feeling I ever had, made sense. The relief flooded every sense and it washed away a lot of baggage I had been carrying with me my entire life. It washed away the hatred and anger I had at my younger self for not being able to get it 'right' ... because they couldn't. They didn't know enough. They didn't understand ... and most importantly, they hadn't done anything wrong. They did their best. They tried their hardest. They played the hand they'd been dealt ... and they'd survived. I am alive, thriving, learning this pivotal information because of their efforts. **"**

Ben felt a lot of relief and vindication. He realized he is not arrogant, lazy or broken. There is also some real pain and loss. Life could have been so much more if only people had understood.

In therapy, Marie-Laure often sees her Autistic patients going through a very emotional process when they find out they're Autistic. Many of them come into therapy asking to be 'fixed': 'I'm too emotional', 'I get angry when there's a lot of noise', 'I'm told I'm too rigid', 'I overreact for things that shouldn't be an issue' – they want to become a better, improved, radically different version of themselves. When they learn they're Autistic, some people can go through a mourning process of this idealized version of themselves. Instead of becoming an improved version, they now have to learn to acknowledge their needs, their strengths and struggles, and accept that their responsibility towards themselves is not to change their core but to actually respect themselves, *as they are.* This can be hard. When you've spent all your life hoping to be this different version of you, thinking that if you'd commit enough you'd be that person everyone expects you to be – letting go of that is *a lot.*

Then, there's usually a big relief in finally knowing oneself, rediscovering our own needs, learning to set boundaries, discovering our true authentic identity. Discovering that we're not wrong but beautifully unique. It does often help a lot to find a community because it can get quite isolating otherwise. There might also be a lot of sadness and anger for all the self-loathing, all the many years thinking you were fundamentally wrong. Often, people think about their life story and find a mixture of compassion and sadness for a younger self who was feeling so lonely and confused. There can also be anger regarding how different their life would have been had they been able to understand and appreciate themselves earlier, as well as receive certain accommodations when necessary.

Eva describes the fear of being an imposter after her diagnosis:

> **It took me some time to fully accept that I am Autistic because I didn't just want to pretend or lie about it. There is very much a sense of imposter syndrome. It feels like I am lying and even after the diagnosis, I was like, 'How do I know I didn't just say that because that's what I was expected to do?', 'How do I know that I wasn't acting like that because I know what Autistic people look like, I know what she [the examiner] is expecting?', 'How do I know that it is actually me?' I know myself: I do know that I am not pretending to be awkward and that I didn't go through my whole life being bullied and struggling with social contacts and struggling with friends and whatnot just for the fun of getting an autism diagnosis!**

Erin tells us about the major realizations she's had since finding out she's Autistic:

> **Since my self-diagnosis, I have forgiven myself for a lot of the guilt I've held onto all these years, blaming myself for not fitting in, or excelling in academics, or in my art, or writing. This whole time, I thought I was fighting my own mental health, with anxiety and depression, and now I realize I have been just fighting**

to live in a society that isn't optimal for individuals with my type of mind. My beautiful, complicated, often overwhelmed-by-all-the-things mind. I am capable of so much and it has been wasted on a system that doesn't acknowledge or encourage many of my abilities as they are not seen as 'profitable'. **"**

Now that Sarah knows she is Autistic, everything is starting to make sense to her. All those years of people telling her she was a freak, a weirdo, a nutter, it wasn't because she was any of those things. Now, she knows that she got called those names because she has a crazy sense of humour, because she sees the world differently to most, because she 'feels' everything.

Beckie says that finally finding out she's Autistic has made her whole.

Joanne was worried the people conducting the assessment wouldn't see her traits as she was able to communicate well and took part in all the activities. It was only when the report came through and she read it that she realized her traits showed more than she thought they did:

" There were things I hadn't even noticed in myself. It was so revealing and I felt like I had finally been seen. I was able to look back at my past experience from a whole new angle. Now, rather than blame myself for situations which I felt had gone wrong, I was able to see that it had just been miscommunication, or a misunderstanding based on my reactions or words. I was finally able to forgive myself and realize I was not to blame. It explained my talents, my personality, my problem-solving ability, my need for details, justice, and intense empathy. I was finally able to look for the real me and drop the mask. **"**

It has been a huge relief for Bob to know when she's struggling with something that has been dumped on her last minute – for example, being in class on her admin day – that although she's really cross about it, it's not because she's being difficult or a horrible person, it's because she struggles with last-minute changes to her routine and that is due to being Autistic. Give her half an hour and she'll be fine about it, but initially she will be grumpy!

Since finding out he's Autistic, a lot has changed for Mark:

> 66 I can finally understand why I've said and done things that most people find strange and even upsetting. I can explain this without feeling the need to apologize. I can discuss candidly things that I cannot manage, socially or otherwise, and stop pretending to hear conversations in a crowded pub when I can't, or go to local gigs when I'm feeling overwhelmed, or be unembarrassed and unapologetic if I need to take a time-out from an activity. Or have a short nap at an odd time of day in an unusual place. It's been a revelation. 99

Katharina now gets a better understanding of why she does things a certain way and why some things are significantly more difficult for her than for neurotypical people:

> 66 I understand now why people do not 'see' what I see (the pattern in everything) and it really helped me deal also with my major sensory issues. I am gentler with myself and don't expect so much of myself any more. Through my children, I have learned what overwhelms them and how to intervene early to make sure they stay well regulated. Now, funny enough, I try to treat that inner child of mine whose needs have been suppressed so much over the years like one of my children and help it early to not shut down. 99

As an intelligent, articulate, adult woman, Sarah didn't think she would ever get a diagnosis. Then, more and more stories started coming out in the media of middle-aged women getting recognized. She was eventually diagnosed as Autistic and having ADHD. She tells us how her diagnosis has been hugely beneficial for her:

> 66 I now have the full confidence that comes from having my identity validated ... that I can begin to unmask ... that I have a community and a tribe ... and that there are (finally!) answers for all my quirks and eccentricities and difficulties with the world. It has also enabled me to get Access to Work funding for support, which I'm just now starting to access. The biggest benefit is in my relationships.

> 66 My family and friends understand me *so* much more now, as I also understand myself, and I've had nothing but love and kindness from them all. And those who were in my life that weren't loving and kind, I've completely sidelined, with zero guilt. I struggled for half a century to be accepted, acceptable and valued. I have no qualms about only allowing access to me to those who love me as I am. 99

After being diagnosed as an adult, Neville found it helpful to then be given a series of workshops to learn strategies for coping and to better understand autism.

Mark says he feels empowered by his diagnosis.

Two years after their diagnosis, C.A. started advocating:

> 66 I was shut down, so I started researching and my world changed. I had accepted that I was the way I was, but never had I considered that that didn't mean there was something wrong with me. Autistic communication *was* an issue, but neurotypical communication was just as culpable in the breakdown. That realization changed everything. I've been chasing information ever since, wanting to understand more, from more people with different perspectives, from more and more branches of science. 99

Finding out she's Autistic has left Danielle with a big question: 'All I want to know is, what do I do because I am Autistic and what do I do because I am me? I will still never know that. No one can draw a line and say specifically this is why *you* are different. I think one thing many Autistics struggle with is grey areas and my autism to me is the biggest grey area I have to deal with.' She goes on to say that she still can't decide whether she would have been better off not knowing at all:

> 66 I was finally provided with a reason which helped explain hundreds of moments in my past, which has basically taken years to process, and I don't think relatives or doctors can understand what that is like. You reassess your whole life and all of your past experiences. You suddenly realize you could have actually been at fault in certain past events where before you were sure it was someone else being unreasonable. It was just the fact they didn't fully understand you. 99

Since receiving her diagnosis, Naomi has experienced several different feelings:

> On the one hand, when I got my diagnosis, it was a huge relief and I thought, 'Ah, it's not my fault!' I thought, 'I have to stop being horrible to myself, this is just the way I am. It's not that I don't make an effort, it's not that I'm ill-willed or that I'm looking for attention.' Because that's it: I've often been reproached, my own mother has often reproached me for being self-centred, attention-seeking, difficult, too sensitive in the sense of being a pain in the ass. So, when I was diagnosed, it was, 'Well, no, actually I'm just like that, that's fine, ok.' That was at the beginning of the discovery, when I was diagnosed.
>
> Then, afterwards – it's now been a year and a half – it's shifted a bit. The subject of autism and the diagnosis have honestly become a bit of a source of distress, of stress, because I no longer understand anything. When I got the diagnosis, I started reading, researching, watching videos, webinars, conferences … and I thought, 'This is it, I found my subject, I want to write about it', and I get lost, actually, it's so huge. I rushed into the subject hoping to come out of it with enlightenment, with clear answers, and it's just the opposite: I'm sinking and I never find any answers.

All of these feelings are completely legitimate. Finding out you're Autistic is such a big moment, it is essential to give yourself the space and time to explore all your emotions. Autism is a vast topic and a diagnosis can be a major turning point in a person's life. It is completely normal to have mixed and complex feelings about it. Sometimes, as therapists or relatives of an Autistic person, we can be eager to see the person reaching that state of pride and relief after being told they're Autistic, but it is essential to allow each person to feel the entirety of their emotions. It is all part of the journey of self-discovery, self-acceptance and self-appreciation. We can't rush through the process, no matter how impatient we might be to see the person finally loving themselves.

Something incredible that Erin noticed after her discovery was the ability to recognize other Autistics:

> 66 Almost like how a herd of animals can recognize a herd member who got lost along the way to the watering hole, after one meeting with someone, I could see it. You are like me, but unique in your own beautiful way. I see how you can't figure out when to jump into the conversation, I'm physically biting my tongue to stop myself from talking over everyone right now too. Even when the individual has different Autistic traits than me, I can sense it on them, they feel like distant cousins. 99

Here's how AutieMum felt when she found out she was Autistic:

> 66 I honestly felt like the weight of the world had come off my shoulders. Finally, I had an answer as to why I was different. I was no longer the odd one out. I had a community that I belonged to – the Autistic community. 99

Interestingly, while there is a huge stigma around autism (and medical professionals are often quite careful before giving such a diagnosis), most participants have felt an immense sense of relief and self-discovery when finding out they're Autistic. It is essential to perceive it as a neurotype and not 'bad news', so that people can be given the beautiful gift of finally knowing, accepting and appreciating themselves.

Self-diagnosis

Quite a lot of people within the Autistic community self-identify as Autistic, without having received an official diagnosis. This can be for many various reasons: the cost (several thousand dollars, depending on the country), the long waiting time (up to ten years, depending on the country), the lack of autism experts available in the country, all of that counterbalanced by the fact that some people wouldn't get a benefit worthy of those constraints. In most cases, people who identify as Autistic have done extensive research on autism (major emphasis on extensive – you know, deep research the way only Autistic people are capable of!) and/or have met therapists/doctors who have confirmed it is a very high probability, and/or have relatives (genetically related) who are Autistic. Therefore, a self-diagnosis is to be taken seriously. While the clear majority of our participants received a diagnosis after going through a formal assessment, we have also accepted participants who are self-diagnosed.

Charles doesn't feel he needs a formal assessment to confirm the diagnosis:

> 66 Autism is just another facet of who I am and I don't really need someone to give me a piece of paper telling me something about me that I already know. I understand that it can afford certain legal protections, but that would be my only motivation for getting one. It's enough for me to have an explanation of why I am the way that I am. The rest is for me to deal with. 99

Jodie said that in an ideal world, she would totally go through an assessment/diagnosis process, but it just takes way too long. She adds:

> 66 'There isn't enough funding, there aren't enough qualified people ... the way I see it, I don't really feel like I absolutely need it, I can live with self-identifying, so it wouldn't feel right taking up a place on the waiting list if there are others who do absolutely need it.' 99

Erin's process started with a lot of in-depth research on autism, but the financial burden of getting a diagnosis made her choose not to get an official assessment after all:

> 66 As I do with everything, I googled as much as I could about the subject and soon one webpage led to another and I found myself looking into the signs of autism and relating to *all* of them. I then started looking for information written from Autistic adults regarding what it felt like to be Autistic, what differences they had noticed between them and neurotypical folks. I felt like I had fallen into a different dimension where the authors of these

websites were writing about me, my life, my experiences. I have never in my life felt more understood.

Even though I identified with all the information I received, I was cautious, I didn't want to be an imposter and falsely take on this identity without more substantial evidence, so I spoke to a dear friend of mine who had been recently diagnosed as Autistic. She shared with me a questionnaire that the psychologist had asked her to fill out. The questionnaire was many pages and questions long and incredibly thorough, and after spending an evening filling it out, it concluded what I felt inside of me since I started down this rabbit hole. I was *very* likely Autistic, in the highest percentile of possibility according to this questionnaire.

The psychologist I found was very kind, but he also warned me right away that it does cost a decent chunk of change for an adult to receive a formal diagnosis for autism in Canada. $2,600 to be exact. I was appalled. Because our parents didn't see the signs when we were kids, we are denied access to a free diagnosis? Also, aside from the money, the diagnosis requires that a parent fill out a question-naire ... What if my parents weren't alive, or refused to help? Thankfully for me, I did have a mother who was willing to assist with this, but I eventually decided that the amount of money wasn't worth it to prove what I already knew about myself: I am Autistic.

I have always been ultra-sensitive to my environment, to noise, temperature and even the emotional energy in a room. I am sensitive to food and often find myself reaching for toast or chicken nuggets over anything more nutritious or filling. Eye contact has always felt physically uncomfortable for me, but I forced it anyway because I knew it was a thing people are 'supposed to do'. Although I have friends and have had many romantic partners, I still always struggled to understand social rules, often finding them to be archaic and serving no true purpose.

On top of all that and many other signs, I always thought I was dumb. One moment I can recite intelligible knowledge about various animals that I had recently narrowed in on, or important social issues that I am passionate about, and the next my brain has the speed of dial-up internet, unable to access any of my previous knowledge or even personal memories. I also have always had trouble staying on task with one project. I am an artist, writer, crafter, petter-of-animals, and I rarely complete a project start to finish without getting sidetracked with some new idea or inspiration, or the urge to know everything about two-toed sloths and where I can see one in real life someday. I thought I was just doomed to be sometimes dumb, sometimes smart. Maybe it was my fault for indulging in cannabis when I was a teenager, or maybe I should have just paid more attention in high school. I had no idea that what I was struggling with was just the effects of being Neurodivergent in a very neurotypical world.

Reading articles and stories written by other Autistic adults finally made me feel proud of who I am and what I am capable of. I started to see how many gifts I have received from my autism, special abilities that my neurotypical peers often lacked, and it felt as if I had just found out I was a really cool alien, from another planet, and I had just found a community of aliens from my planet that are also struggling with life on earth. Silly humans think it's impolite if you don't look directly into their eyeballs when they are speaking to you. **"**

Here's M.'s story, who is a self-diagnosed woman living in New Zealand:

" Through my life I've felt confused and deficient, not knowing why I was different, why I struggled so much and got stressed over 'tiny' things and burnt out so often. When I got an autism spectrum ('in the Asperger's range') diagnosis from an online quiz, I was shocked. I had been trying to understand my elder brother better and decided to take the test myself as a baseline. I immediately tried three more different online 'diagnostic tests'/quizzes for autism and they all gave me very similar results, definitely Autistic spectrum. First, I felt like a fraud, like my entire life and self were collapsing. But as I read and listened to Autistics and other ND people online, so many things now fit and made sense that I had to accept my ND identity and I started to feel relief. I found that in New Zealand, a formal diagnosis would take at least two years plus cost thousands of dollars, plus there's no benefit in terms of support for adults, so that gives me zero motivation to pursue an official diagnosis. **"**

Lola explains her perspective on self-diagnosis:

> **❝** Self-diagnosis is 100 per cent valid in the Autistic community.
> Nobody wakes up one day and decides they're Autistic. People
> can spend years researching before they even suggest it out loud to
> someone else. We started suspecting I was Autistic in my early teens
> and I didn't get my diagnosis until 21. It's not easy to get diagnosed
> if you don't present with stereotypical traits, and especially if you're
> not a young white male. It's hard to get diagnosed in a country
> where it's free – imagine trying to get diagnosed in America, where
> it can cost you thousands and thousands of dollars. Or in a country
> where their views and understanding of Autism are outdated
> (I'm looking at you, France). **❞**

Telling people you're Autistic

Most people who have shared with others that they're Autistic will
describe this experience as a coming out. It can be a bonding opportunity for letting others know something about yourself and giving
them a chance to know you better, but it can also be a stressful or
hurtful discussion, depending on the person's reaction. Here's what this
experience has felt like for our participants and the reactions they've
liked or disliked from the people in their lives.

Lola shares some very helpful advice on how to react when someone
tells you they're Autistic:

> **❝** People mean well but if someone tells you they're Autistic,
> please don't respond with, 'Oh wow, I never would have
> guessed', or 'You're very high-functioning though, right?', or
> the worst, 'Well, everyone's on the spectrum, aren't they?' These
> are not compliments, despite the good intentions that may be
> behind them. It feels like you're questioning my diagnosis, which
> I fought for years for, because of the massive misconceptions that
> still surround Autism. If someone tells you they're Autistic, the best
> response is, 'Thanks for sharing with me' and depending on the
> situation, 'Are there any accommodations you need?'

If everyone was 'a little bit Autistic' there wouldn't be a diagnosis. When people say this to me, they don't mean it maliciously. But it feels like they're saying, 'I don't believe you', and it invalidates the fact that Autism *is* a disability. I am disabled because the way my brain works is not the way society expects it to work. The same with telling me, 'You don't seem Autistic, I never would have guessed' or 'You're really high-functioning though, aren't you?' You may not mean it to be offensive, but it is. If someone tells you they're Autistic, don't question it. In my case, feel free to ask questions about Autism, but don't question the diagnosis. They don't hand them out like sweets – they can take years to get (five in my case).

Getting the diagnosis has been a huge relief for Bob, but she still sometimes feels a bit of a fraud, thinking, 'I've coped for so long, am I really Autistic?' Therefore, when people question the diagnosis, she finds it hard because deep inside, she questions it too, yet at the same time she totally feels that she is Autistic. She adds: 'Very confusing!'

Ben is very open about the diagnosis and some people avoid him because of that. He adds: 'I view this as the trash taking itself out.'

Milène's family were supportive throughout the whole journey and have learned a lot about autism since the day she got her diagnosis.

When Hayley was diagnosed at 19 years old, her mum wasn't surprised by the diagnosis as she had suspected it since Hayley was young. Her mum was very supportive and took the time to read up about it and learn all she could. Unfortunately, her dad was the opposite. Hayley says: 'It made me very sad and made me feel abandoned and uncared about.'

In general, what stands out from our participants' experience is that if someone tells you they're Autistic, it is crucial that you believe them. You can show interest in asking about what has led them to have that awareness about themselves, but you should always assume that they are their own expert (yes, even if you are a medical professional). Learning about autism can be a nice way of showing the person you're interested in finding out more about it.

It's ok to not be an autism expert – whether you're a medical professional, a teacher or someone from the general public – no one can be expected to know everything. However, you should make sure you don't confuse your lack of knowledge with you questioning their coming out. It would be like having someone telling you, 'I'm gay', and you telling that person, 'No, I don't think you are. I know someone else who is gay and you're nothing like them.' Always assume that they know more about themselves than you can possibly know – even if you've seen the person growing up.

Telling your child they're Autistic

It happens quite frequently that parents know their child is Autistic but will struggle to share that information with their child. They're scared due to the stigma that surrounds the word 'autism', which makes them afraid their child will feel as though there's something wrong with them. We've asked our participants what their views on this are: has it been helpful to be told you're Autistic when you were a child or was that a mistake? Do you wish you had known earlier? Would you rather never have known?

Kevin was diagnosed at four years old. He says his memories of his life mostly start at that age, so he has never known himself to not have autism:

> 66 My parents did a really good job of making sure I was aware of it, but never in a negative way, just in an 'Oh, this is who you are' way. I was formally diagnosed with Asperger's syndrome when that diagnosis was still being used in 1992. It's been mostly really helpful for me having the diagnosis. I say this because I haven't really experienced any limitations because of it. I've been able to live an amazing life and get into college and beyond. However, it has helped me be able to ask for things when I need them, ranging from extra time on tests to help finding a job when I was in high school. It was an easy, simple explanation to give people to explain all my quirks. 99

Lola, who was diagnosed when she was 21 years old, shares what a huge difference knowing she's Autistic has made in her life:

> 66 I genuinely think that knowing I'm Autistic essentially saved my life. Teenage Lola hated herself so much, in part because she didn't know she was Autistic. She thought she was broken. Please don't hide your child's diagnosis from them, I promise you, they already feel different but don't know why. 99

Gillian shares her perspective on being labelled Autistic:

> 66 Some parents don't want to tell their kids they're Autistic because that's putting a label on them. Do they think people don't give us labels? The labels that the people give us and the labels that we give ourselves are far more long-term damaging than the word 'Autistic'. Autism is an explanation, it's not a label. To me, autism is an explanation for why my brain thinks differently, why my sensory stim is heightened. It's an explanation. There's been a rise in late diagnosis. I don't think people understand the relief when we find out 'Oh! This is why I struggle with this!'. That's the same relief you can give to your child. Your child is aware that they're different. If they're not – fantastic, I'd love to be that oblivious. But most children are aware that they're different. We can help them realize that there is a communication difference, there is a different way of seeing the world. So, hopefully, they won't give themselves those labels. 99

Here's how C.A. felt when they realized they are Autistic (they got their diagnosis at the age of 27) and so is their son:

> 66 At first, I was in shock, the same for my son. I had a lot of the mainstream ideas about autism at that time. So, my immediate reaction was, 'My son is *not* going through what I did' and he got into weekly psych, OT and speech. I was of the opinion that if I had got a diagnosis at his age, my life would have been so different. I could have had friends. I could have communicated without offending people. I could have fitted in. I didn't

want him always wondering what was wrong with him and not know, like I did.

I was right, but for a different reason than mainstream understanding led me to believe. He isn't going to have the life I did not because he'll learn the skills I didn't get the opportunity to, but because he will *know himself* like I never got the opportunity to. His life will be different because he will know *why* he is different and so will accept himself in a way I never could, because I didn't know *why* I was the way I was. He will not have friends because of neurotypical social skills but because he is learning what it is to be a friend and will have opportunities to meet and know people like him, so he can make real friends rather than simply people pleasing the masses for the purposes of 'popularity' or to meet the expectation of 'fitting in'. He'll know he doesn't have to be anything other than what he is or do anything that is not natural to him. New skills and information will come from curiosity and exploration leading to problem solving and resourcefulness. Action will come from choice, not compliance.

His life will be different from mine, not because change comes more easily, being a younger age at the time of his diagnosis, but because he is learning about who he is and why every day of his life without that pivotal information being withheld from him. That understanding is a game-changer for our self-esteem, how we see ourselves and our overall wellbeing. The 'why' is everything. He got it. I didn't. *That* is why his life will be different. 🙶

Beckie, who was diagnosed when she was 39 years old, believes she has done the right thing having her children diagnosed too and openly telling them who they are. She adds: 'It's not "You have autism", it's "You have been diagnosed with this, this is what makes you *you* and you are Autistic". I don't want them struggling like I have. It's cruel.'

It's interesting to note that while many parents feel they're protecting their child by not telling them they're Autistic, our participants have shared that telling your child they're Autistic is actually key in preserving the child's wellbeing and self-esteem. It can allow them to know themselves, know who they are and start appreciating themselves and respecting their own needs at an early age – which is a brilliant skill for life, and much easier to learn early on than if you have to start as an adult after years of self-doubt, self-hatred and camouflaging.

4

Meltdowns

Joe James' experience

Let me make one thing very clear: meltdowns are not tantrums. They are a loss of control when our senses or mental capacity to cope with day-to-day life reaches a breaking point. They are the straw that breaks the camel's back. What you may see as a moment of madness because of our reaction to what may seem like a small thing is in fact the result of countless things, built up over a period of time. My meltdowns have been the bane of my life for as long as I can remember and are the one thing over all things I work on as an Autistic adult.

When I was a child, I would have these sensory overloads. I would feel like I was trapped when in a situation I was uncomfortable with, like being in a classroom while learning about something I had little to no interest in, or being forced to go to church and Sunday school, or being made to go swimming, or to Cubs (Junior Scouts), or any out-of-school club that I didn't want to participate in. I believe my parents were trying to help me by sending me to these places. They probably wanted to build my character and help me meet other kids. I hated other kids because they never accepted me, and most of the time I would end up ostracized and being hateful. When at these places I was constantly on high alert, anxiety crippling me to the point of exhaustion. I would always either be waiting for something to trigger me or have something trigger me, both being equally hard on my fragile mind. I despised being told what to do, my demand avoidance and desperate need for autonomy driving many of my emotions and actions every waking moment. It was like being driven too fast while in the back of a car and all you want is for the driver to pull over and let you drive yourself at a more manageable and sensible speed.

Another thing that would trigger me was when I felt stupid because I didn't understand certain things at school because of how they were worded and the way they lacked the details I needed. It would also take me longer to reach an answer in certain subjects, not because I wasn't good at them but because my brain did things in more detail, therefore it took longer.

Being Autistic is all about detail. We see in greater detail, hear in greater detail, learn in greater detail, feel empathy in greater detail and feel emotional pain in greater detail. We are highly sensitive beings, which can be wonderful if we are accepted and guided but awful if we are treated badly and forced to change. This greater detail is why I would so often melt down and not be able to cope around many people, because I would have to experience so much detail from so many humans around me. I couldn't block them out: every sound and smell would add up and eventually cause an overload.

My original meltdowns were more about crying – it wouldn't matter how hard I tried, those tears would flow. But I was told that crying was weak, and when I was being force-fed toxic masculine behaviour I switched from crying to punching. I would punch walls, doors, myself, other boys, pillows, you name it, I would punch it, except innocent animals. I could always tell when I was having a meltdown, although back then I didn't have a word for it. I was just a very angry child, but I had good reason to be. The major difference for me between having a meltdown and just losing my temper was always how it would manifest itself. I'm not a violent person by nature, so when I would punch something because I was so overwhelmed by anxiety and emotional or sensory overload, it would be more like an explosion. But losing my temper was more about being in total control and just being angry at something in particular. Sometimes it was a combination of both, which was when I would completely lose control and end up really hurting someone or myself. One of the biggest meltdowns was just after I discovered my brother had died – the destruction left in my wake made a demolition site look tidy.

After I met Sylvia, my meltdowns didn't stop, that's not how the Autistic brain works, but they did begin to improve. We both struggled with them, always blaming my anger at the trauma I had been through but never really knowing how to stop them. I did my best to keep them away from my children and never once physically harmed them or Sylvia, just myself and the occasional wall or door. I once threw a scale out of a window into my back garden because I didn't weigh what I thought I weighed. This was a build-up of self-deprecation about the way I looked, brought on by years of being told I was fat by kids at my school. I often wonder if my meltdowns would have been far less frequent if my trauma wasn't present, and the simple answer is of course they would. Childhood trauma due to being forced to assimilate and never feeling good enough because I couldn't left me with a feeling of inadequacy and self-loathing. So, when things don't go my way, or I make a mistake, I hate myself and snap.

Imagine you are driving, it's a nice day but you are a bit stressed and not fully concentrating. All of a sudden, a rabbit hops into the road. Without thinking, your involuntary reaction is to swerve the car around the rabbit. This results in you losing control of the car and careering off the road. Now you find yourself heading down a steep hill. You try the brakes but they aren't working. Now you panic, you are scared, confused, annoyed, angry. Then you realize you are heading on to another road at the bottom of the hill and it's very likely you will hit another vehicle. Even though it is not your fault, people blame you, get angry at you, possibly punish you, and you end up hating yourself. You over-analyse everything and keep wondering how you could have done things differently, even though you probably couldn't have. This is what it feels like when I have a meltdown, but the difference for me now is that my family and friends understand and don't get angry, but instead stay calm and talk me through it. Because of this my meltdowns don't escalate like they used to and I know how to centre myself much quicker.

I have experienced two types of meltdowns that can end up in the same way, but because I recognize the signs, I often end up not losing control. The most common is the SNAP, which is just that. I don't usually know it's coming and afterwards I feel very regretful. My latest left a dent in my fridge door, which upset Sylvia, but she didn't blame me, I just blamed myself. The other is slower. It starts with me feeling tired, then getting annoyed at little things, like dropping a spoon or spilling some tea. On their own these things are minor, but I feel disproportionally angry at each and every one. I shake from over-exhaustion and can't concentrate on anything for too long. I get very fidgety and need to release pent-up energy, so

I go to the gym or for a walk. I treat myself to chocolate and relax in a bubble bath. I play soothing music and edit my photography and create art. I do whatever it takes to calm myself, and this can take days, or even weeks. It's a horrible experience because it feels like I'm always on the edge of losing control and I can't stand being around most people, and I definitely don't want to be touched at all. During this period I can also go into shutdown, which is a common response to becoming too overwhelmed. I become very unresponsive and shut myself away from the world. I have honed the skills I need to keep my meltdowns to a minimum, but again I can't emphasize enough that had I been better understood when I was a child, these meltdowns might be few and very far between now.

Participants' experiences

Meltdowns are very common among the Neurodivergent. Most of the time, but not exclusively, they are triggered because of anxiety and the environment we are in at the time. Autism often gets the blame for meltdowns, but we would like you to consider that the fault usually is not ours. We asked our participants about their experiences with meltdowns as it's really helpful to get a broader understanding of this negative aspect of having a different brain.

Sophie James, who is also a neurodivergence advocate, was kind enough to write about her experiences regarding meltdowns. She writes about growing up as a teenage girl and how her meltdowns changed as she got older. She also has some great advice for those trying to cope with difficult situations:

> " Secondary school was when I really started to have meltdowns. When I was a kid, my meltdowns could definitely be confused or described as tantrums and they would most likely occur when something didn't go my way. My world usually revolves around me, and this was very much more of the mindset that I had when I was very young. So, when my mum took me for a girls' day out to a big shopping mall and she wanted to look at clothes for her, even though she had already bought me clothes I wanted, I had a huge meltdown and wouldn't speak to her. My brain didn't

understand why we were looking at things for her when I couldn't wear those clothes, and I developed an incredibly sassy attitude – which is funny looking back now. Other meltdowns would be caused by being told off for sucking my thumb (my personal stim for about ten years of my life) or my mum picking me up from someone's house when I wanted to stay longer. To be honest, I think they were usual reasons kids get upset and maybe that's why it was hard to differentiate me from others in terms of my neuro-divergence when I was very young.

Yet when secondary school started, that was when those childlike tantrums didn't really stop and only got more intense. Being in a judgemental, overstimulating place for six hours a day, five days a week, as well as being a hormonal and hypersensitive teenager – it's just a recipe for disaster. I remember one of the first, most awful meltdowns I had, when a boy, who had led me on for months, denied me when I finally asked him out. There were all these expectations in my head, months of dreaming and talking about it with my friends: we were going to end up together. My heart was racing when I sent him the message but racing with excitement and then ... He said no with a laughing face. He completely played me and my heart dropped, my sight went dizzy and the tears started flooding out of my eyes. This unexpected result had me feeling such extreme emotions that I wasn't prepared to deal with it and, more importantly, didn't want to. I was weeping on the floor with my best friend and dad by my side, telling me it was going to be ok. They took me upstairs to my room where I lay on my bed, face in the blankets, sobbing and whining. There really is a difference between being upset and having a meltdown – because those emotions ached my chest and they hurt my brain. It takes you to another level of frustration, anger or grief that something, which isn't that terrible, shouldn't supposedly cause. It's our hypersensitivity that is the motor to these strong emotions; although of course it can lead to meltdowns, it can also make us incredibly empathetic and passionate people.

Towards more recent years, my meltdowns got worse and worse. My grandad dying led to me having a meltdown in front of my whole school, in the middle of the courtyard, because someone in front of me killed a spider – my grandad loved spiders. Instead of an outward reaction, this meltdown was more inward, where I cradled myself into a hedgehog-like ball and stayed in that position crying, with my hands over my ears, for over an hour. Support teachers came over to try to help, but for one, they didn't have any real training on Neurodivergent people or meltdowns, and two, their way of helping was to ask me to get up. Of course, they had to wait until I was ready and then they let me go home early to be with my family because they didn't know how to deal with the situation.

My worst meltdowns have been when I have cracked my phones after throwing them in a fit of rage, or I have punched walls with my bare hands, leaving bruises or cuts. Sometimes I have bashed my head against a wall or screamed things I don't mean to the ones I love the most. The worst part is the feeling of grief or depression I feel afterwards for hurting a loved one with either untrue words or violent actions – that can be scary for them but as well as yourself.

Self-deprecation is so easy when you feel there's an uncontrollable part of yourself that can come out at any trigger. Yet right there is the first thing all Neurodivergent people should do to avoid meltdowns or work with them – understand your triggers. Make sure the people closest to you also understand them so you know what to avoid or can accumulate ways to deal with those triggers healthily. Maybe it's loud sounds and a pair of soundproof headphones that are needed, or maybe it's crowded places so a stim toy would be helpful.

As well as identifying triggers, is there a plan in place when a meltdown begins? A room? A comfort item? A way someone can take away your phone before it gets smashed, or you are safe away from a wall? Maybe it's a podcast or a mindfulness exercise that needs to be put on to guide you through those feelings. For me, I need my room, my cuddly toys or Headspace SOS meditation playing, as well as making sure I implement self-care into my daily routine to avoid burnout or being more prone to meltdowns. **"**

S. states that she absolutely gets overwhelmed:

> 66 Too many demands can leave me feeling overwhelmed, be it at work or home. I also find that too much noise has the same effect, especially if I am trying to get something done. When I am on a day off and I know I desperately need a day to myself and ensure that I do not have to leave the house, to have those plans changed can cause a meltdown. 99

Fourteen-year-old Thomas says the main thing that overwhelms him is when there's a lot of noise and people. Another Thomas describes his experience with being overwhelmed by the environment he's in and how he copes:

> 66 I often feel overwhelmed. I think triggers are when I tend to stay too long 'outside' of who I am, which drains me to limits where I can become exhausted and need urgently to retreat into a safety zone (a safe, quiet place, alone, come back into my body by exercising or stretching, for example). 99

Faith, like so many of us, doesn't always know why she is burned out. If it's been a busy week, she may not know exactly why she's feeling overwhelmed in the moment, but she is, so she will go to her room and stay there for a while until she has the energy to go out again. She adds:

> 66 Sometimes I don't figure it out, I just kind of weigh it out, other times I do. It really depends on what is going on. Sometimes there are some very specific reasons, such as the dress, the way it was lying on me, the fabric, the feel of it, the fit of it, that was why I was having a sensory overload at that moment because I don't do good with specific clothing. But other times, like if it has been a long week, I just know – ok, I don't know exactly why I am having a sensory overload, but it could be part of the reason that I had a long week. 99

M. helps us see from her perspective what can set off her sensory discomfort:

> 66 I often feel overwhelmed. This can be from physical sensory discomfort from external stimulae, or emotional stress, such as a crowded, noisy location, change in temperature, cluttered bedroom, too much social time in one day, bad news in the media, hearing something untrue or unfair, etc. 99

Linda warns us about not practising self-care:

> 66 I get very easily overwhelmed. Especially when I haven't practised self-care, slept enough or have too much planned. I am very easily triggered by noise and when things change at the last minute and I am not being given the proper time to adjust or being in an environment with a lot of people and movements and when more than one person talks at the same time. 99

Lauren explains she can often feel overwhelmed. Temperature changes and loud sudden noises can set her off in public. Otherwise, being too anxious and having a lot to do can make her really overwhelmed.
Richard speaks about his childhood and why he had meltdowns:

> 66 I have not had a meltdown for a long time. I had loads as a child. I remember punching the hell out of the school heating unit in my class. Sending dust out everywhere. I really lost my temper. This was from bullying. 99

Virginia repeats what many of us have often said: it's not that we don't want to socialize, it's just so hard to do sometimes:

> 66 I feel overwhelmed if I socialize too much, or with people I don't really know or like that much. I have to recover, even from seeing friends at a party. I have had meltdowns, which involve crying and losing a sense of where I am, but they happen less often now as I tend to be in situations I can control. I practise a lot of self-care

these days – I do basically what I want. I also make money out of doing what I like. I definitely stim, but many of my students do too, so no one cares. **"**

Melanie describes how it feels to be so overwhelmed by her environment:

" I get overwhelmed a lot. We have a busy house and noise is triggering, being touched out, spinning too many plates. And sometimes my thermostat blows. I usually blow up and scream and occasionally I have headbutted the wall. I've always been expected to keep it together and take care of everyone else but sometimes it's too much. We are currently in the process of asking for more support. We cannot manage the children's needs, plus our own and the practical aspects, without it being detrimental to our own wellbeing. **"**

Too much socialization can trigger exhaustion or meltdown in Virginia's experience, so she regulates exposure to too many humans at once.

Almost every night, Luka has a mental breakdown from too much stimulation – either from doing things he doesn't want to do or being criticized verbally, emotionally and mentally because of his differences that people refuse to accept.

When Paul is overwhelmed, he feels exhausted. This is called a shutdown, which is a type of meltdown. When Hannah is angry, her words can literally be stuck and no matter how hard she tries, they won't come out.

Bob's meltdowns come out as crying and feelings of helplessness and hopelessness, like there's no point trying to sort out the issue. When Nicky is totally overwhelmed, she will sometimes self-harm.

C.A. connects poor interoception to meltdowns, saying: 'I have no build-up feeling. I'm fine ... until the *second* I'm not and the times it has happened, I did not see it coming.'

Neville says he gets overwhelmed quite easily as a result of stress (trying to deal with more than one problem at a time), large numbers of people and unfamiliar surroundings.

Milène very helpfully describes how it feels when she is having a meltdown and what causes it:

> 66 I can get overwhelmed – this is usually a result of too many things happening at once and losing my grip on the situation. Meltdowns are usually a result of people not understanding those moments. It's when I am telling them it is getting too much and they keep talking/asking something that I just cannot answer at that moment, since everything is feeling like I am inside a tornado. The best way to prevent escalation is to leave me alone so I can give my brain the time to get rid of the internal storm. Maybe it's more relatable when I compare it to having a migraine – everything is too much: sound, lights and so on – so withdrawing myself works the same as well. When I am having a migraine, I look for a quiet space, a bit darker. With feeling overwhelmed/ meltdown, I do the same thing. 99

Mickey describes very relatable triggers, saying they can feel overwhelmed, especially if there are a lot of stimuli in an environment and if they're doing something new. Triggers are lights, loud sounds or a lot of people. Jennifer gets overwhelmed if there are too many external demands that she has not already calculated into her day or week or has been exposed to too many new experiences at once.

M. gets very easily overwhelmed and quite often:

> 66 *Anything* can be a trigger. Example: my child says they are hungry. Following thoughts occur: I'm a horrible mother! How long has she been hungry? Why didn't I pay attention to the clock? What should I feed her? No, she had that yesterday. Does she need more calcium or green vegetables right now? How much of a portion should I present? What sides should I choose? How long does this need to cook for? Which item should I cook first so everything is ready at the same time? There's more, but that should give the idea. That splintering of 50 thoughts off of one stimulus happens with every single thing, so of course I'm overwhelmed very often, several times a day. 99

Self-deprecation is very common with Autistic people. Michele describes how she feels every day:

> ❝ I feel overwhelmed not merely sometimes but every day. If things don't go exactly as I imagined in my mind, I feel like a failure. If I feel like a bad mother, fiancé, employee, coach, etc. Embarrassment or shame. ❞

Reading through these experiences will hopefully give people a little more understanding about what we go through as hyper-sensitive beings. All we ask for is patience, compassion and for people to take us seriously and not diminish our struggles simply because they don't match your own.

5

Emotional regulation

Joe James' experience

Being Autistic is very much like being on constant alert for me. I'm always aware of my surroundings, always aware of other people, always aware of every sound, smell and even taste in the air. My senses are constantly heightened due to the evolutionary development of my brain and this can cause a lot of anxiety for me. If I was living 60,000 years ago these heightened senses would be incredibly useful, but as I'm not they can often be very disabling for me in the wrong environment. When I get overwhelmed by people or my environment, I need to do something to calm myself and regain control. To do this I stim. 'Stimming' is the name given to voluntary or involuntary movements, sounds or exaggerated actions that help Neurodivergent people self-regulate. I myself like to jump on the spot and shake my hands – I encourage you to try this right now, if possible, as I guarantee it will make you feel good. I also like to look at photographs of nature, which is called a visual stim – which means, looking at something that you enjoy to self-regulate and calm you. My photography is created by me to be a visual stim, which is why it may be so popular with other Neurodivergent people.

As a society we must normalize this behaviour and stop making people like me feel bad for stimming in public. It is not weird, it is how we express ourselves when stressed or happy. It's a way of communicating our feelings without using words. This is a beautiful thing and should be encouraged and never stunted. Some 'therapies' are notorious for trying to stop this emotional regulation because people find it uncomfortable or distracting. They use phrases like 'quiet hands' or encourage children to sit still, even though sitting still may be causing them great amounts of stress. We need to grow as a society and accept Neurodivergent behaviour and not try to change it just so we fit in with neurotypicals. It is damaging to our mental health, even if you can't see it.

There is a myth that Autistic people don't have empathy, which is not only untrue but it is in fact the complete opposite. Many Autistic people have an abundance of empathy but don't always know how to express it. It can become so overwhelming at times that our brains switch it off, like an overheating computer will shut down to protect itself. If I allow myself to feel empathy to its full extent, it can knock me out for days, sometimes longer. I get very emotional and often revert to very childish behaviour in order to not have to face any responsibilities until I feel better. I will not be able to stop thinking about the thing that upset me, and I will even dream about it. I spiral out of control and start imagining terrible things happening to me and my loved ones. The only way to stop it is to go for walks in nature and do my photography or play video games to distract me. I may even watch cartoons I've watched dozens of times, as the feeling of familiarity centres and grounds me. This is my version of mindfulness and it works more often than not. I also carry a toy with me to squeeze and rub on my face, which has a soothing effect. I am never embarrassed about this and have never been challenged in public when I do it. It may be because I have a look on my face that says, 'I will punch you if you talk to me', but I like to think it's because people in general are nice and won't insult a grown man cradling a Pooh Bear plushy.

Participants' experiences

Stimming

It's honestly quite sad that so many people feel ashamed to stim. In most cases, stimming doesn't hurt anyone. It can help the Autistic person feel happiness more intensely and work through feelings of anxiety more easily. The fact that so many Autistic people have to deprive themselves of doing something healthy simply because they've learned it may be frowned upon shows how our society tends to value appearances over mental health. Our participants have described what stimming is like for them and how valuable it can be.

Lauren starts with how she stims without even knowing she's doing it:

> 66 In the past, I have had episodes where I would zone out and my hands would do weird things. This would happen anywhere but now only happens in private, mainly when I listen to music. I now know these are stims. I also bite my nails, wiggle my toes and can sway side to side. At night I rub my feet together and rock myself to go to sleep. Stimming can just feel good sometimes, and I've frequently been told to stop doing it because I look stupid or gormless. Comments like this make me really upset and angry. 99

Linda's experience really hits home how harmful shaming stimming can be:

> 66 I just realized in the last six months that I stim unconsciously and have started to explore what stims help me in different situations. Stimming really helps me to regulate when I am stressed, anxious, sad and it makes me calm, focused and joyful.
>
> I have been told to keep my feet still (when trying to soothe myself during an anxiety attack) and to stop staring out into the air (dissociating, zoning out when really exhausted and tired). Being told to stop made me feel ashamed and that I was acting non-normal, which made me really sad. Now I have started to dare to tell my close people why I do these things and why I *need* to do them, but it is really stressful because of the stigma around stimming. 99

Lorraine never thought that she stimmed until she read about it. She was never a 'turn in circles' or 'flapping her arms' type of person, but she doodles a lot. She is also able to visualize stories in her head, enabling her to 'escape' into a world that is more comfortable for her.

Bob also wasn't initially aware of her stims:

> 66 I didn't think I stimmed and at my assessment told the assessor that I don't, but I have since found out that picking is a stim – I pick the skin around my finger nails and my lips. I do it until they bleed and always have done. If there's a little bit of skin hanging off, I will pick and pick until it's gone and I've caused damage. I try not

to pick my lips because it looks awful and is making my jaw ache. I also move my jaw around and hold it in a certain way that makes it ache; I'm not aware I do it until it hurts. I didn't realize this counted as stimming. 🙶

Luka is not always aware of it, but when he stims, he violently shakes his hands and arms off and on for a few seconds. He also makes noise but is not the one who notices it, it's usually someone else who tells him to stop.

Neville, like many of us, doesn't even know he's stimming sometimes. His wife says she notices him stimming a lot, often with hand or head movements, but he's rarely aware he's doing it.

Sometimes, when Fabrizio is stressed and there are no people around, he shakes his head and moves his hand as though to cut an argument. In extreme cases of desperation, he has to hit his head to create physical pain to stop his thoughts.

One of Mark's stims is actually quite a common one:

🙶 The most destructive one is biting the skin on the tips of my fingers. I do it subconsciously when I'm not using my hands and they are a mess of scar tissue now, and I usually have at least one plaster on where I've just gone too far. I'd love to stop but I don't know how – and the main trouble is that I enjoy it, I enjoy the sensation of using my front teeth to slowly peel off a thin, hard chunk of scar tissue and then nibbling it until it goes soft, at which point I eat it. And yes, I do know that's gross, and I'm sorry. 🙶

Milène recalls a moment from her childhood:

🙶 I remember one time as a kid that I was rocking on the floor and I was told to stop and 'act normal'. Do note that I was undiagnosed back then. It made me freeze and feel like I was doing something wrong, while that actually was helping me. Sadly, that got stuck in my head for a long time, so it was difficult for me to realize that making movements that helped me was ok. Nowadays I know it's ok to just stim, my stims don't hurt anyone, it helps me and that is good. 🙶

Nia-Eloise is embracing her stimming. She finds pacing really helps and is her biggest stim. Her mum is really understanding and will leave her alone to pace and de-stress. She's trying to figure out what type of stimming will help when she's out in public. She has never done that because she has always masked, but her goal is to not mask, so she has a lot to figure out and discover.

Nicky constantly stims, either verbally or in her head, singing a line from a song or humming the same line over and over again. She rubs her feet together in bed. She sometimes claps or flips her wrists back if something pleases her, and she also chews her lip.

One of Katharina's stims is eating, which she considers to be unhealthy. A lot of people don't think of eating as a stim, but it can be. For instance, some people will tend to eat a lot in social contexts (nibbling non-stop on crisps at a party), which can be a way to deal with the anxiety induced by the situation.

Paul starts by describing how the sensation of touch can calm him:

> **❝** My stims are not too obvious. I may fidget with a pen or rub a surface, which can be the leather-like cover of my phone or the surface of a table. I can rub my own skin. (Right now, I catch myself rubbing my neck.) I can sway or rock to music (which is a 'normal' stim). Sometimes when alone, I talk to myself, occasionally in nonsense syllables, which means I am embarrassed when thinking about a faux pas I made in the past.
>
> When I had a hi-fi amplifier with a visual display with lights that moved with the music, I would fixate on it when listening to music as if I were looking at a performer. I can fixate on things visually, including the washing machine going round. **❞**

S. experiences negative reactions to stimming:

> **❝** I usually tap with my hand, my leg or play with my stress ball or fidget spinner on a regular basis like all the time. If the stressors get worse, I hit my injured shoulder. I tend to press my eyes shut for a few seconds and open them repeatedly, or start subtracting 7 from 1000, 993–7 ... Or start repeating the same things over and over again, usually things that are bothering me at the moment. I do it

automatically, I don't really control it, and people often get angry with me for it and ask me to stop, making it worse. It stresses me out, makes me angry and makes everything worse to bring up all the bad stimmers. Or cause meltdowns when they keep pressuring and getting angry. 🙷

Sarah is always jigging her leg up and down while sitting. She never really thought of it as a stim, but now supposes it is in a way. Her mum always used to ask her to stop jiggling her legs and would even ask if she needed the toilet when she didn't. To her, it was just something she liked doing. She can't even say it was a comfort, it was just something she did and still does.

Faith has had stims since she was an infant:

🙶 My parents had me at a neurologist when I was two because of the stimming I was doing with my hands, fingers and face. My fingers and hands had an open-handed finger curling movement that they originally diagnosed as 'shuddering attacks'. They usually happened when I was excited, nervous or concentrating on something like lining up my toys, waiting to be fed with a bottle or spoon, and they continued all through elementary school. The hand and finger movements were paired with a tightening and distortion of my face. When I was five, they changed the diagnosis to 'stereotypy motor movements', but it was still the same motor movement as it always was. I no longer do that stim but have evolved into other stims or tics that change. Sometimes, I throat-click, squinch my nose, blink/wink my eyes, tighten my neck muscles, flex my shoulders, pull my bottom lip over my chin and other things. 🙷

Sarah stims, mostly when she's happy. She flicks, taps and wiggles her fingers, bounces, claps, waves her hands when she's excited.

Lola shares her insight on stimming:

🙶 Stim is short for stimulation, it is a repetitive behaviour used by Autistic people to help regulate themselves. People stim for a variety of reasons: they might be happy, sad, stressed, anxious, focused, excited … it depends on the person.

Personally, I often stim when I'm experiencing negative emotions. As a child I'd blink excessively when I was anxious, or clear my throat a lot. I've always pulled on the sleeves of jumpers or hoodies, resulting in a lot of frayed edges and holes! I can also get stuck repeating the same word or phrase, which tends to get shorter and shorter until it's a repeated noise.

However, I also tend to stim when I'm concentrating. I might be tapping my fingers together or bouncing my knee, or clicking a pen, or fiddling with something. It looks like I'm not paying attention, but actually these behaviours are helping me to focus. When I worked in a call centre I had a number of fidget toys on my desk which I used when on the phone.

Stims are a completely normal part of autism and a person shouldn't be forced to stop stimming unless the behaviour is dangerous or particularly disruptive. If someone is stimming in a 'bad' way (such as hitting themselves), try to redirect them to stim in a safer way (such as hitting a pillow). "

Remember, flappy hands are happy hands!

Other forms of self-care

Stimming is the main way in which an Autistic person can self-regulate, but there are other ways we can provide self-care. Self-care is often finding something that makes you happy and doing that over and over again. It sounds pretty simple, but when we do it, it's called 'repetitive behaviour' and is seen as a negative 'trait'. This is why so many Autistic people hide their neurodivergence, because society always seems to see what we do as being broken.

Here are some of the self-regulating strategies and various forms of self-care our participants have shared that work for them:

- Using noise-cancelling headphones to turn off all outside noises
- Mindfulness
- Cuddling with a pet animal
- Learning to say 'no'
- Doing something creative (embroidery, crochet, macrame, miniatures, ...)
- Photography

- Plushies
- Blankets
- Sitting in a quiet, dark room by oneself
- Going to therapy
- Going hiking
- Reading
- Self-advocating for your needs to be met, especially around sensory stimuli (asking to dim the fluorescent lights at work, for example)
- Taking strolls in nature
- Practising yoga
- Having a bath
- Drinking tea
- Writing down your emotions in poetry
- Emotional Freedom Technique (tapping self-therapy)
- Listening to music
- Watching a movie
- Watching Twitch streams

In therapy, Marie-Laure often likes to remind her Autistic patients that the Autistic brain is a powerful one: it feels intensely, it empathizes profoundly, it thinks deeply, it observes precisely ... So, as an Autistic person, we have a responsibility towards ourselves for looking after our brain to allow it to function and recuperate according to its abilities. Self-care is like maintenance for our brain (and body!). Also, she encourages her patients to think of self-care proactively, in order to avoid reaching a state of exhaustion, rather than exclusively as a form of recuperation after having been overwhelmed.

Here's how Charles deals with being overwhelmed:

> 66 The only times I can recall being overwhelmed have been instances at work where too much has been happening at once. In those cases I react badly, either by crying, getting angry, or just shutting down by hyper-focusing on whatever my current task is. Ironically, this last method is also one of the ways I help mitigate being overwhelmed – if too much is happening around me, the only way I can deal with it all effectively is by shutting out or shutting down anything else happening around me and focusing

entirely on what I'm currently doing. Only then do I move on, prioritizing where I can or dealing with issues chronologically where I can't. **"**

Kevin also shares his ways of regulating himself emotionally:

" Lately, I find myself being overwhelmed by too many people asking me to do things. I'm a people-pleaser and I'm also a natural scheduler. I like having an exact order I'm going to do things each day and sticking to it. I'm learning to get more flexible as I get older, but schedules are still something that can cause me grief if they're not adhered to. For those meltdowns, I first sit down and try to do something relaxing for at least a few minutes. Then I try to reorganize tasks before starting, preferably picking something easier to start off with.

I am also overwhelmed by the traditional Autistic trigger of too many sights, sounds and noises, such as at a large party. I find in those cases it's best to remove myself from the situation. If I'm able to go to the bathroom, that is an easy way out of the situation for a few minutes to collect my thoughts, figure out what to do next and re-enter the fray. **"**

Screen time

Screen time can be crucial for self-care as it distracts us from a world that is often overwhelming and uncontrollable. When we play video games we can go to another world or be another person and it takes us away from the hardships of reality. When we watch movies or TV shows, YouTube or TikTok, it gives us an escape from issues causing us harm. Obviously, there is the risk that we become so distracted that we use them to try to avoid reality completely, but that is something you as a parent or a Neurodivergent individual must be wary of and balance reality with distraction. Screens can also connect us with others like us, through online video games and Facebook. We can join communities and find friends that, even though we may never meet them, will be just as good friends as those we see in person. Thanks to the internet, Neurodivergent people can thrive socially and never have to leave their home.

Our participants have shared their insights into this controversial subject. Playing video games is self-care for Lauren and she does this whenever she can motivate herself to do it. M. finds screens very important for staying in touch with friends and loved ones, watching fun YouTube comedy and music videos, plus learning and connecting with special interests, and especially photography.

Self-care helps Michele to regulate screen time. She can go down a rabbit hole of research so she tries to remind herself to set a time frame that she shouldn't go over (although she tends to). Screens are a way that Mickey can emotionally regulate by engaging in whatever media content and, overall, Mickey does relatively well at having good boundaries around screens in order not to be on them all the time.

Milène has a love/hate relationship with screens. She likes them because she can play Sims on a screen and learn how to play the piano, socialize with friends and so on. She doesn't like screens because she tends to lose track of time and get drawn into puzzle games, which makes her spend more time on her phone than she wants.

Nia-Eloise definitely spends a lot of time on screens. She feels they can be toxic because there's a lot of negativity out there and you can end up addicted to social media and waste your time on it. But they are also beneficial because they allow you to connect with others and learn about pretty much anything you want to.

Empathy

As we said before, a lot of people believe the myth that Autistic people do not have empathy – and, sadly, that includes a lot of medical professionals. However, among our participants, the responses were clear: Autistic people do have empathy. A lot of empathy, actually. So much empathy, it can be overwhelming, paralyzing, making it harder to express.

Michele describes empathy as 'heightened emotion on anabolic steroids'. She feels empathy when individuals are unjustly treated, when anyone is grieving or going through great difficulty, as well as towards issues involving the inhumane treatment of the vulnerable, including animals.

Linda explains what it's like for her:

> 66 It's like I listen to people and then my mind and body automatically 'create' the same or a version of what that person is experiencing/feeling. This can be very emotionally draining for me, especially if I feel that I cannot help that person feel better or if they don't wish or care for my help. It's sometimes really hard for me to let go. My mind and body can stay in this state of feeling very intense for a very long time. 99

Lorraine gives us insight into what she feels inside when she cannot show it on the outside:

> 66 I am very empathic. To the point I can get very upset over what may appear to be very minor to others. I have to self-censor what I watch because I can get very sad and cry over watching the news even. I am not very good at dealing with people who are upset because in my mind I want to fix and protect them, but I have no idea how to comfort them. This could seem to other people then that I lack empathy but that isn't the case. 99

M. shows how she feels and gives empathy but how it may differ from a neurotypical:

> 66 My hyper-empathy helps me connect with pets and care greatly for people but can also be a huge trigger for overwhelm. I often can't distinguish my own feelings from the feelings of others, especially if they are angry or suffering – sometimes I feel like a sponge for other people's energy. When someone was angry with me, my heart felt like it was suddenly beating at four times the normal rate. When I see sad news, I can feel the pain and suffering of it becoming a physical part of myself. I think this is not healthy, but it's difficult to switch off. It's also made it very hard for me to gain clear awareness and understanding of my personal emotions. Imagining how much they might be hurting, I'm 100 per cent there to support loved ones in hard times and offer hugs, gifts, food, sweet emojis, cute memes, a caring ear, etc. I don't always know

what helpful words to say, but I do offer empathy a lot. Sometimes connecting via devices is the most caring because then I can express empathy and people can respond when they're ready. 🙶

Mark thinks that he over-empathizes a lot and that it's closely related to people-pleasing. He adds: 'Allowing yourself to be upset that everyone around you isn't totally happy all the time isn't healthy, though a decent effort to try to understand why someone is feeling the way they do is kind and necessary.'

Jess describes empathy as an echo of what the other person is feeling. She struggles to know what to say when her friends or family are having a difficult time, but she expresses that she is there for them.

Michelle feels an enormous and overwhelming amount of empathy. She no longer interacts with the news in any way because of this. Christine's therapist has told her to stop watching the news because of her heightened empathy.

Kelly has a similar experience:

🙶 I have always been emotional, crying at sad and happy films, adverts and even when someone wins a talent show! But it's much more than this, it radiates my entire body. I feel their happiness, pain, hurt, and images can stay with me for a long time. The news reduces me to tears and I have to censor what I watch and absolutely under no circumstances should I watch anything to do with animals being hurt or neglected. If I watch a film with a dog in it, I have to know the dog lives, otherwise I won't be watching it. 🙳

Mickey adds to the growing evidence supporting Neurodivergent empathy, hopefully putting a stop to this harmful stereotype, by saying: 'I feel a ton of empathy towards other people all the time. I express empathy by validating people's experiences and asking how I can support them.'

Milène adds her experience:

🙶 When it comes to empathy, I have lots of it. I always try to help others the best I can, whether that means just listening to them or helping in any other way. Sometimes, I use an experience from my own life to show that I understand what they are going through. For example, someone says that they are feeling down because they were hurt by a friend, then I can respond with saying that I can understand because that has happened to me as well. Followed by suggesting things to do that will cheer that person up, or just let them cry and be there. Sometimes just being there is enough. **"**

In order to empathize with someone, Emma has to relate it to something she's been through to show she understands. She understands that some people think she's making it all about her, but she isn't. Also, sometimes, she feels so bad for what people are going through that it feels physically painful and she has to shut down mentally.

Nia-Eloise is a highly empathetic person although she doesn't always come across that way. Empathizing with someone, to her, is being able to place herself in others' shoes and feel how they are feeling, especially if she has experienced something similar. She expresses that by just being there for them. 'Sometimes, all you can do is sit with someone while they cry and listen to them,' she adds.

Nicky is very empathetic. She feels the emotions that others are feeling. She cries easily if someone else is upset. She is troubled if someone around her is angry. She will cough if someone sounds like they have a frog in their throat and yawn when others do.

S. adds some more valuable insight:

" I feel a lot of empathy, especially with animals and objects. As for people, I only really feel empathy for people I know or people who have been victims of violence and injustice. It makes me angry and sad and want to remove whatever makes them feel bad. I am not good at comforting or saying the right thing, so I just get them the things they like and remove all the things they dislike. **"**

While Isabella does not feel empathy for ordinary people troubles, she does feel empathy for beings being tortured or killed, as well as people dying of cancer due to pollution or killed in wars.

Sadie is affected a great deal by her abundance of empathy. She says: 'I am very empathetic unfortunately so I can pick up most things without any words being spoken, which is another reason why I don't mix with people.'

Many Autistic people feel so much empathy towards animals and Sarah tells us that she is the same.

> 66 I feel immense empathy for people and animals and can often cry for them as I can feel their pain or sadness deeply. I really do care about people and animals, and I feel that I need to cheer them up, make them smile, make them happy again. I will usually say something off the cuff to people that's hilarious and it breaks the cycle of sadness. Humour is just the best tool ever. Animals I tend to show kindness to by stroking them, talking to them and playing with them. 99

S. tells us how her empathy helps with her job:

> 66 I do feel empathy for others and this has only been enhanced since I trained as a life coach. I sometimes feel the bodily sensations that others are feeling as well as their emotions. I am always very interested in hearing things from another person's perspective. It happens most days for me given the nature of the work I do. Previous to my training, I would have shared a similar situation of mine as a way of saying 'I get it'. Now with my training I listen and validate their feelings verbally. Sometimes, all people need is to be heard. 99

Joanne says she feels the empathy but struggles with the emotions:

> 66 The reason people may not realize I notice these things or have this huge empathy is because I don't know what to do with it. I know how people feel but I don't know how to react. Unless there is an obvious fix for it, I feel useless to help. It's like I can offer practical support but not emotional support. 99

Emotional regulation isn't just about feeling better, it's about being accepted and feeling like you deserve to feel better. So many of us – to be honest, the majority of us – have suffered through some form of trauma and because we are hypersensitive it can affect us to a greater extent than neurotypicals. This absolutely isn't trying to undermine the real-life experiences of traumatized neurotypicals, it's just pointing out that we are, overall, more vulnerable, and that's an important distinction. Because of this trauma and general hypersensitivity, we are easily overwhelmed, but knowing how to manage that is integral to being happy, healthy and successful. Be kind to yourself and be kind to others who may act differently from how you would expect.

6

Masking

Joe James' experience

Masking is when an Autistic person mimics those around them in order to fit in. Many of us don't even know we are doing it but have ended up with this sort of split personality because when we act or behave in our natural way, we are treated so poorly we end up being forced by society or therapy to change. This most often brings serious mental health issues and also puts a huge strain on the individual because they are essentially having to put on a show every time they interact.

For me, like most, it started in childhood. I would have to pretend to be like others to become part of a group and I forced myself to like things like football just so I could blend in. If I did act like myself, I was badly bullied for it, not only by pupils but by teachers, parents and the public in general. I used to stim – to make voluntary or involuntary movements or sounds that express how I feel or calm me when I'm in distress. Many of these stims were very obvious and because they seemed strange, I was picked on and I ended up forcing myself to stop. I loved to flap my hands, wobble my head and make noises like a quick hum or whistle, but eventually they became a lot more subtle. Even though stopping my stimming seemed to make me happier as I was bullied slightly less, I was not happy because I was fighting against my true nature.

We stim for a good reason, and to stop us doing it is just wrong. We should be free to express ourselves in our own beautiful and unique way, and be accepted as we are, as long as we aren't hurting anyone. As an adult, my stims were internalized and because of this, I usually got angry rather than expressing my feelings safely through stimming. I was far too embarrassed to stim and thought people wouldn't take me seriously if I did it. Since becoming a neurodivergence advocate I have started to stim again more openly in public and I have never been happier. I cannot emphasize enough how important stimming is and how much people need to be more accepting, especially at a young age. We need to teach young people to be kinder and then they will become kinder adults.

Masking was always about being like others – it is a natural defence mechanism to avoid being caught out for being different. There is such a negative stigma that surrounds difference that so many children have ended up hiding who they really are. We know that the LGBTQ+ community masked, and often still mask, their sexuality and gender identity because of negative treatment, and Neurodivergent people go through the same sort of thing. Because this masking happens when we are so young, it often becomes part of our personality, so when and if we ever discover that we are Neurodivergent, we go through a serious identity crisis where we struggle to be the person we truly are. I have heard many times that after a diagnosis many people change completely and lose friends because they can't accept the Autistic person for who they actually are. My wife told me I acted far more stereotypically Autistic after my diagnosis, when I dropped my mask and became more authentic to myself.

The world is unfortunately not ready, and may never be ready, to accept Autistic behaviour without wanting to drastically change it to conform to what society deems as 'normal'. ABA (applied behaviour analysis) therapy was originally designed to fundamentally change an Autistic child into a different person. With these sorts of roots behind 'treatments' for Neurodivergent people, and many countries thinking this is the way forward, how will we ever be accepted for who we really are?

Participants' experiences

What is masking?

Let's start with some definitions. Here's how our participants describe masking:

> 'I describe it as a brick wall. I always held myself back, afraid people would not like me.'
>
> *Tanya*

> 'Masking is behaving a certain way to fit into a situation, group of friends or society. It could be by copying another who is popular, their taste in clothes and interests. Imitation at its finest.'
>
> *S.*

'It describes how I worked so hard as a teenager and younger adult to fit in and be accepted.'

Sarah

'Masking is when you hide the real you and be someone else you are not and hide your real emotions from others.'

Sadie

'Masking is altering your behaviour because you don't feel safe or accepted as you are. We present a personality to others to match the occasion.'

Paul

'Masking is essentially hiding or lessening your Autistic traits (whether consciously or subconsciously) in order to better fit in or avoid harm.'

Lauren

'I define it as putting a veil on who you truly are to make yourself more palatable to others.'

Emily

'Masking is acting in a way that is expected of you rather than as you really are in order to fit in better.'

Charles

Who am I?

While some people know exactly when they're masking and when they're being authentic, it doesn't always feel that clear. Sometimes, we've been masking for such a long time that we've lost the sense of who we are underneath the mask. Sometimes, when Autistic people learn about masking, they can feel quite some distress as they struggle to feel who they truly are. Here's how our participants have been dealing with the concept of authentic self.

M. says she definitely masks, but it's hard to tell where masking ends and the 'real me' starts sometimes. She has put her intense self aside so much, in order to try to live in society, that sometimes it's hard to recognize and pick up those real parts of herself again and embrace her whole self.

Sarah describes the impact of having masked pretty much every day since she first went to school:

> ❝ I don't know if I really know who I am. I have so much hidden trauma kept inside of me that eats me up. I have masked for the majority of my life and to be honest, the masking me is a kind of ok person. The me on the inside I have yet to let out. I know I am angry about my past and I know the person inside didn't deserve a lot of the treatment received over the years. I am just starting to understand myself now that I realize I am Autistic. Things are starting to fall into place for me. I don't know if I will ever be able to show the real me as I am so used to masking now, I feel I have become the mask. ❞

Nia-Eloise has been making a conscious effort to not mask her autism, but she's not sure who she is behind that. She has been masking her whole life, which means that she has never really been able to be her own authentic Autistic self. She adds: 'I'm excited but apprehensive to find out.'

Sarah recalls how she used to mask constantly, largely as a result of being bullied in every arena of her life. Since self-recognizing as Autistic seven or so years ago, she has been unpacking that. She is sure she still does it, to a degree, but she has structured her life to such an extent that she no longer engages with people who require her to perform for them, which helps her be her authentic self.

Growing up, Tanya recalls, she used to mask all the time, but didn't become aware of it until she found out that she was Autistic. She writes:

> ❝ I knew I was not normal as a child so I tried to pretend to be normal but I always seem to fail at normal. This was similarly the case as an adult where I tried to dress normal but again failed. Once I started being myself, the world became a better place. I started wearing retro/vintage dresses and brooches, I joined a team at work where everyone was just like me. I started being myself and could bring my whole self to work. I felt like I truly belonged. I was safe. I occasionally put on my mask in new situations and when I do it feels constrictive, I can't wait to get it off. When I wear my mask, I become very tired and drained, I just want to go to bed afterwards. ❞

Mark describes how he feels about knowing his authentic self:

> " I am a master of masking. I have a third-dan black belt post-doctoral international-authority expert level of masking. And I suspect that I will never be able to get right to the inner layers of them, the oldest ones closest to my skin that I first put on as a small boy and never took off again. But now, at least, I know that I do it and I can challenge myself to take them off. I do so, daily. I regularly feel like I am a product of my masking: if I stop, what will be left? Is there actually any real personality in there any more? What and where is the real me? But I'm content with this – I may never finally differentiate, but I can live with that and I can enjoy the new confidence and the new respect that I have for myself and that I am starting to see from others, and finally have confidence in my opinions and be able to defend them without crippling self-doubt and self-sabotage, without the dogma and the confrontation I used to generate for the sake of bolstering my confidence. "

Danielle also worries that she doesn't know who she is behind the mask. She finds it hard to establish the difference between what she really likes and what she has been led to like. She went travelling on her own a few times and that was eye-opening, knowing all the decisions she was making were entirely for her: her choices, that no one else had influenced. This is the only time she has ever felt this.

When trying to figure out who you are, it can be helpful to spend some time on your own, such as Danielle did by travelling. In those moments, you have to make choices on your own: do I want to sleep in or get up early? Do I want to eat now or later? Would I rather have a calm day staying inside or go on a hike? It forces you to connect yourself to your own needs and to the feelings in your body. For so many of us, our huge empathy and longing to fit in means that we automatically will take into consideration what other people want when making a choice. This way, spending some time alone can help you turn the focus towards your own preference, rather than prioritizing other people's feelings.

Jodie was raised in a cult, which has had a big impact on her sense of identity:

> Being raised in a cult, I came out of it very emotionally scarred. It's hard to explain cult lifestyle, it's one of those things where you can only really understand it if you have been directly part of that world. I am seeing a therapist who specializes in cult recovery. In our first session he told me about the concept or the 'pseudo cult identity', which I instantly related to. It also reminded me of masking. The kind of deep masking some of us auties do where we are almost a totally different person. There's a different mask for each and every friend, each social interaction, friends, family, romantic relationships ... The end result is usually 'Oh sh**, who the f*** am I?!' The identity crisis ... It has left me feeling like a total fraud. Not only do I not understand myself, how can anyone else understand me or truly know who I am? Well, how can they? They've only seen one version of me and that might not even be the authentic me. Would they even like me if they saw who I really am? These are questions I ask myself on a daily basis. It's complicated for me as I am trying to unlearn and unpick certain introjections placed into my brain without my consent when I was too young to fight it. Then in my teens I was mimicking a lot, trying to fit in. In that respect, knowing that I am Neurodivergent has been so helpful. It's the one thing I know about myself for sure. I have been able to meet like-minded people and it has definitely made my world feel a bit less lonely. But I still have a whole lot of recovering to do. But I'm getting there. If it wasn't for my daughter, I don't know if I could go on. But she has given me purpose and a reason to live.

Jennifer shares that, for a while, she didn't let herself have opinions, as part of her believed she wasn't allowed to. As she got older, she realized she was allowed to be her person and started to focus on things she really did like, not just because everyone around her liked them.

Christina has masked her entire life. She describes a particularly memorable moment:

> 66 I remember about a year before discovering my autism, I was standing in my garden feeling so empty. I had no idea who I was and why did I feel like a shell of a human? Now, looking back, it's because I spent my entire life creating fake personas of myself to fit the person I was around at the time. When there were several people around me where I acted differently with each of them, it caused great anxiety because I didn't know how to act any more. 99

S. finds herself masking automatically and that most of her masking simply consists of shutting up and suppressing everything, and trying to become invisible. She adds: 'I generally don't know who I am. Am I masking? Am I my autism? Or am I my PTSD (post-traumatic stress disorder)? Or is it the ADHD? The OCD? I have no clue. Do I even exist? Who is "I"?'

Unmasking

While masking can be suffocating, the good news is that there is also the possibility of rediscovering your authentic self. The action of getting in touch with your true self and learning to express yourself more authentically is called 'unmasking'. This process can be scary and distressing at times – it requires us to confront ourselves in all the times we felt we weren't acceptable as we were and all the times we've had to pretend and have been disregarding our own needs. It is also incredibly liberating and fulfilling to finally learn to appreciate ourselves for exactly who we are – not for some idealized version of who we feel we should be in order to be accepted, but truly as we are. Here's what the participants have to say about that process.

Mickey is working on unmasking in general as someone who is AFAB (assigned female at birth) who was taught to make themselves small and as least inconvenient as possible. They now want to take up space with their body and be comfortable existing. They recall having been used to masking basically all the time, but now live very authentically and only mask to certain extents around certain people.

Bob explains what unmasking looks like to her:

> 66 Yes, I mask. I cover up how I'm feeling in order to be the person people want me to be, or at least the person I think they want. Sometimes, I misjudge and get it wrong. I'm not sure what is the real me now and what is the mask. Up until now, I've not been aware of how I mask, but recently I have started to see that I cover up my real feelings and thoughts in order to fit in. I'm less willing to do this now, so I feel I may have started to look like a difficult or horrible person. I no longer agree to anything or everything I'm asked to do, but instead say how I really feel. I've not changed inside, just on the outside with what I'm willing to put up with. Getting the diagnosis was important for this reason. It explains why I get cross when plans change, when I'm asked to cover in class on my out-of-class day, etc. It's not because I'm being mean or difficult, it's because you've changed my routine. Give me half an hour and I'll be fine about it, but I need time to deal with the change. 99

Michelle masked very heavily for 45 years. It wasn't until several years after her autism diagnosis that she learned what masking is and started taking steps to stop masking. Geraldine masked her entire life, hiding like a chameleon to fit in and not be seen or judged by others. She is now getting to know her true self and feels much happier not trying to fit in and choosing to be herself in totality. Beckie says that while she can mask very well – 'us females do it best and from an extremely young age,' she comments – she tries not to. She says: 'I try to drop it so my children will be comfortable not masking who they are.'

When trying to find out who you are underneath the mask, it can be helpful to try to reconnect yourself to what is unique in you. Your passions, your insecurities, your core values, your needs, your feelings ... everything you truly care about. This says a lot about you and it is important that you learn to look at your uniqueness with kindness. For example, the fear of being rejected can mean that you care about others, that you appreciate certain people, that you are capable of taking into consideration other people's perceptions, that you cherish human contact and that you have a healthy awareness that as human beings, we all need to feel connected to others. Feeling that is a resource – keep in mind that wanting to be fully independent from everyone, never attached to anyone at all, is a trauma response. Learn to see the positive things your uniqueness says about you.

Corrinne describes what the process of unmasking has felt like to her:

" Beginning as a young child, I interpreted my sensory difficulties and aversions as fear, so I thought I just needed to overcome that fear. I also noticed that other people didn't seem to react to the things that bothered me, so I thought I was overreacting. I then forced myself to act normal and act like everyone else so I would fit in, even though inside I still felt terrible. I masked heavily as a child and into my adult years. It wasn't until I started learning about autism that I began to understand masking and better understand myself. I finally started to allow myself to unmask, which has been a process but the most freeing thing I have ever done. "

Unmasking can definitely be very intense, emotionally speaking. There is, of course, the fear of not being lovable or acceptable if we're being ourselves authentically. In that regard, it is essential to learn that we are lovable exactly as we are – with our insecurities, with our fears, with our anger, with our boundaries, our needs and our excitement. Being lovable does not mean being an 'edited' version of ourselves where we remove everything that makes us unique. Good self-esteem does not stem from being a people-pleaser. We have to learn to assert ourselves, to set up boundaries, to share our needs and feelings – and if people make you feel guilty for being authentic, then perhaps you should ask yourself whether those are really good people to have in your life. Sometimes, out of fear of loneliness, we let people be close to us even though they are highly detrimental to our sense of self-worth. This then tends to make a spiral where we feel so unlovable that we no longer have the self-esteem or self-confidence required to reach out to other people who would actually be more respectful of us.

Eye contact

When it comes to eye contact, many Autistic people have different experiences. While most participants share that they're uncomfortable with eye contact, the feeling in itself will change a lot from one person to another – and from one context to another. Some people describe eye contact as 'painful', 'a nightmare', others feel fine with it. Some tend to avoid eye contact, while others tend to stare intensely. Some are uncomfortable locking eyes with absolutely anyone, others feel comfortable looking into their partner's, children's, relatives', close friends' eyes.

Melanie hates eye contact:

> 66 I stare at people's mouths, not only because I need to lip read because I hear all the sounds from everywhere. I try to make eye contact but it's so uncomfortable and then I get fidgety and then I get uncomfortable as I'm aware I'm fidgety and then I can't remember what I'm saying and stop listening. It's horrible! 99

Linda explains that eye contact feels extremely intimate for her and that she only feels comfortable to keep eye contact with people she feels safe with. She adds that even if she feels safe with the person, she can only lock eyes for a very limited period of time before it actually starts to hurt her. She often needs to take pauses before picking up the eye contact again.

Charles shares why he sometimes forces himself to make eye contact:

> 66 I am not comfortable with eye contact, especially during situations or conversations where serious topics are being discussed. I force myself to do it, and quite often end up concentrating a lot on when to initiate eye contact, how long to maintain it and when to break it, to the point where I'm barely able to concentrate on the conversation itself. I do so because I know it's expected that there be some level of eye contact, else it appears as though I'm

not paying attention to the conversation or that I am being rude. I would rather avoid such accusations and so push myself to do so in order to avoid confrontation.

"

Karol isn't comfortable with eye contact with anyone. It was just never a natural or comfortable thing for her and she can't really fake it because of all the different aspects of conversation that she has to think about when talking to someone; adding faking eye contact on top of that would be too much.

Beth has learned to fake eye contact:

" I hate eye contact so much. But because people kept pointing out when I didn't do it, I learned to fake it. They would say things like, 'Why are you looking over my shoulder?' and 'Look at me when I'm talking to you' and 'You're lying, aren't you? I know you are because you're not looking at me.' I would sometimes just take off my glasses because then I couldn't see people so could look them in the blurry eyes better. It was so embarrassing that people brought it up so much. "

People have been using different strategies to deal with eye contact. Some people choose to remove their glasses as it is more comfortable to look into the person's eyes when they look blurry. Others choose to look at the person's eyebrows, nose, mouth, spectacle frames. Some rely on nearby objects such as a glass of water, nibbling on some food, writing with a pen and so on in order to have the option of looking somewhere else other than the person's eyes. Those options can be helpful because they can give some relief and lighten the pressure around eye contact. It can also be helpful to let the people in your life know that you are more comfortable looking away during a conversation. If they know that it doesn't mean that you are bored, and that it simply allows you to enjoy the conversation more and to focus better, they're likely to be supportive of it. Remember: you're not hurting anyone by looking somewhere else than in the eyes. You're not actually being disrespectful – on the contrary, you looking somewhere else is allowing you to actually be invested in the discussion.

S. is also extremely uncomfortable with eye contact:

> ❝ I don't look at people, not even in their direction, unless I make the active effort to try to keep my eyes focused in their direction. Otherwise, I am too consumed by my surroundings and hyper vigilant to every little movement. I find eyes to be extremely overwhelming and scary even. It causes my eyes to tear up and headaches if I try to force it because when people talk to you (expecting eye contact), they stand too close and that closeness and the trying to make eye contact causes these headaches. ❞

A lot of people feel that they have to fake eye contact or force themselves to lock eyes. It's important to remember that the option of simply not looking at someone's eyes is a perfectly valid one. Most people fake eye contact out of fear of seeming disrespectful or uninterested in the discussion. Actually, since looking elsewhere is actually helping us stay focused, it is a way of being more engaged and invested in the discussion, thus a sign of respect and importance that we grant the discussion and the person we're talking to.

Michelle has not – nor has ever been – comfortable with eye contact, but she can do it. She used to do it all the time when she masked. Now that she is allowing herself to not mask, she does not make eye contact as often any more.

AutieMum says her comfort regarding eye contact very much depends on the context:

> ❝ Eye contact is a funny one. When I am talking to my son or my partner, I don't even think about eye contact because I'm comfortable and so I just do whatever comes naturally to me. But when I'm speaking to anyone else, I try to mimic their eye contact levels as best I can. It makes me really uncomfortable and I find that I'm not actively listening to what that person is saying because I'm so focused on making the right amount of eye contact, but I do it because it's what's expected of me. ❞

Kate describes eye contact as a weird thing for her. It doesn't hurt, but it's exhausting because she's constantly over-thinking it. During eye contact, she'll be constantly thinking: 'You haven't looked at their eyes lately, look at their eyes, you're looking at their eyes too much, look away, you looked away too long, they'll think you're not paying attention' and so on. Sometimes, she fakes it by looking at their nose or one of their eyebrows.

Some people, like Virginia, have either too much or very little eye contact. M. also says that she's one of those people that tends to have overly extra eye contact instead of avoiding. Paul has never had any problems with eye contact and was surprised to discover that a lot of Autistics do. He has the tendency to stare sometimes and eventually discovered this could be an Autistic trait, so he is aware of it and consciously avoiding it. Nia-Eloise, though, describes eye contact as awful. She says:

> 66 I'm either not giving enough eye contact or I'm staring into people's souls. There is no middle ground. I'm constantly aware of it and trying to figure out what is the right amount. It's a nightmare. 99

It is quite sad that this chapter on masking needs to exist, because it is a reflection that most Autistic people have – at some point in their life – had to mask to feel accepted. Many people have been given the impression that the way they are authentically is not valid, not appreciable, not lovable. We all, to some degree, long for attachment and connection, to feel that we belong, that we fit in, that we are worthy of love, but this can lead to some people hyperadapting in order to match what others prefer. Hopefully, as more and more people decide to unmask and more discussions are redefining autism, diversity will be more appreciated and celebrated and people will learn to be proud of themselves for precisely who they are, and not for what they feel is expected from them.

7

Mental health

Joe James' experience

My mental health is a constant balancing act. If you have read all I've written so far you may understand why. I was bullied, abused by my mother, attacked and ignored by my father, left alone by a brother who died unexpectedly, forced to be someone I wasn't to the point I became a person I despised, left school without ever reaching my full educational potential, was ostracized and made to feel like I was broken, bad, unwanted and The Problem. I was betrayed by friends, abandoned by family, struggled with self-harm and almost committed suicide. I grew up angry, bitter, resentful and damaged. I truly believed I was to blame and I didn't deserve to be happy. I had no direction, guidance or help when I desperately needed it. I was seen as the freak, the oddity, the weirdo. I was hated because I fought back, classed as a thug and a waste of time. I didn't fit in no matter how much I tried and after a while I thought my future was jail or death. Then along came Sylvia. She cared, that was all she needed to do, that was all I needed in my life: to want to fight for myself, to want to love myself, to want to care. She made me feel like I wasn't the problem, but my past had slowly taken from me what I held so dear, my kindness and my trust in people.

The demons of my past haunt me, but as my life has gone on, and the more people I love and that love me, the less those demons hurt me. I sometimes struggle to be happy. Even when everything in my life is great, there is still a small part of me that feels I don't deserve it. It will always be there, but it doesn't have the power it used to. I have huge insecurities that manifest as arrogance and I still get angry when I shouldn't. But every day I'm working on it. I take my life step by step and make small discoveries about my true self all the time. I'm incredibly self-aware and love to analyse my own behaviour, but even when I know exactly why I do something it doesn't always stop me from doing it.

There are many reasons I could have given up; some wouldn't even blame me. But the determination that I hold inside me to fight, to win, to *never* give up has driven me through the hardest times of my life. My wife, my children, my friends, the memory of my brother, my morals, the pure strength that got me through every torturous moment in my childhood make me who I am. I'm flawed, but I know it and work on those flaws as much as I can. But one thing that I do know is that had I been accepted, loved, cared for, made to feel good about myself, I would not have had to fight all my life. It wasn't those experiences that made me strong, it was me, I take the credit, not the scum that hurt me, they don't deserve a damn thing. I suffer with anger issues, anxiety and occasionally depression, not because I'm Neurodivergent but because of abuse, trauma and PTSD.

Mental health problems go hand in hand with being Autistic, because of how we are treated by those who won't accept us or try to be more understanding of us. Those of you who assume you know what autism is and what Autistic people are like and how you can help them by making them more like the other kids, you are the biggest problem and you don't even know it. Every doctor, healthcare professional, ABA therapist, teacher or neighbour that has said they know about autism, then do everything wrong because they think the person needs 'treating' rather than making reasonable adjustments and accommodating that individual, are why as adults we end up hating who we are. *Accept* us, don't change us; guide us, don't force us in the direction you think we should go; watch us grow, don't manipulate us into growing at your pace; let us be who we are, don't compare us to others.

The fault of our poor mental health lays at the feet of every neuro-typical who didn't treat us like an equal. The blood of every Autistic lost in this daily fight is down to society and how it views those of us who are different and *not* broken. Change the world for us and you will have a better world for everyone.

Participants' experiences

Alexithymia

Not every Autistic person is alexithymic, but quite a few are. Alexithymia refers to the difficulty of identifying and expressing one's emotions.

This can make it more difficult to communicate our feelings to the people around us, including people from the medical field. If you find it particularly difficult to describe your emotions and feelings with words, this might be why. If you are a family member, partner or friend of an Autistic person, or a professional working with an Autistic person, and you notice them struggling to express themselves, keep in mind that it can be difficult to find the words to describe the intense emotions Autistics can feel. Try to be patient and understanding – pressurizing the person into expressing themselves will only make them feel more stressed and make it even more difficult to open up.

Just to clarify: alexithymia is the literal impossibility or difficulty of putting words onto one's feelings. It is not a conscious choice of refusing to share. For example, Danielle finds it difficult to recognize emotions other than anger, frustration and sometimes fear. Beth finds it hard to say what her moods are like because she can never put words to them. Corrinne explains very clearly how the complexity of emotions can be overwhelming, making it much harder to put into words:

> 66 My mood is often neutral or content, but also often depressed or anxious. It can change quickly and without me having much awareness of what I'm feeling and why until sometimes hours later. I also often feel a complexity of emotions at the same time, which makes it difficult to understand or define. 99

C.A. also says they have poor interoception:

> 66 Once I'm hungry, I only have ten minutes or so before I'm shaky and dizzy. I have a timer to remind me to drink because I don't feel dehydration symptoms. If I need the bathroom, I have less than ten minutes before I'm in pain from holding it in because I don't experience the steady build-up. If I feel unwell, I can't tell if it's because I need to go to the bathroom, I need to eat, I'm dehydrated, I've caught a virus, I've over-exerted myself or I'm going to be physically sick. When I am physically sick, I can't feel it coming until it's there, so I only have seconds to react. This is solely the result of Autistic sensory differences, as interoception is one of our inner senses. It is innate within our brain's development that

133

our nervous system is not the same as that of neurotypicals. Areas
of our brain are often bigger, synaptic pruning occurs differently,
etc. The result is a higher potential brain power by ways of making
faster or more creative connections others may not see, but it
comes at the price of those connections in our own body being
missed or not fully made. I like to joke that my life would be
perfect if I could just be my brain without this dastardly
corporeal form. **"**

Danielle gives some great examples of how alexithymia can be triggering
on a daily basis:

" I would love to know if I actually have alexithymia as I am
really unsure that I relate well to what I am feeling. I don't
like emotions and I don't understand them very well in myself.
I absolutely hate it when people ask, 'Are you ok?' If a friend texts
me this, I will ignore it. If my boyfriend asks me, I will be angry with
him (it's like he still hasn't learned though as he still occasionally
does it). I don't know why it makes me angry but I think maybe it's
because I don't know the answer. It's a stupid broad question and
I don't know if I am ok. I guess sometimes it broaches how you are
feeling, which again I *hate* because I don't know. I don't know
how I am feeling, apart from angry that you are asking. **"**

Having a word for it – alexithymia – and being able to explain
that to the people around you can make a huge difference. It
might mean that if people ask you questions regarding how you're
feeling and you tell them 'I don't know', they will be more likely
to understand that that's a real and valid answer, rather than an
invitation for them to insist.

Anxiety

Anxiety is a theme when talking about Autistic people's mental health.
Most of our participants have experienced anxiety in some form, be it
phobias, social anxiety, panic attacks or nervousness. The frequency

and intensity can vary from one person to another, as well as from one point in time to another. Here's the way our participants have described how it impacts their lives.

Richard is feeling very anxious about his Autistic son moving into a residential college:

> ❝ My Autistic son is moving into a residential college and I am struggling with this because I know the transition is going to be hell. His comprehension is that we are literally leaving him. It's going to be heartbreaking. But we know it's the best thing for him. And once he gets used to it, he is going to love it. Sometimes, the right thing to do is so hard. I've never suffered with depression because luckily my brain seems to offload and move on very quickly. But I am going to be pushed hard with my son moving so far away. There is a guilt to it because of his comprehension, he won't understand. ❞

Emma explains the impact of internalizing the anxiety:

> ❝ I internalize all the anxiety until I get to the point it triggers a meltdown and quite often what I am supposedly losing my mind over isn't actually the real cause, it's an accumulation of multiple factors. ❞

Jennifer was diagnosed twice with generalized anxiety disorder. She was having a lot of trouble placing the source of her anxiety. She later realized that the trouble placing it was due to alexithymia and that her anxiety was stemming from her sensory overload and Autistic burnout. Beth has made a list of the biggest triggers to her anxiety: 'mess, deadlines, driving, being in a place full of people, people not wearing face masks any more, changes to routine or plans.'

Lauren says that anxiety definitely stops her: it stops her from leaving the house, socializing, engaging in special interests. Anything can trigger it, but usually being outside of her comfort zone (which is essentially her home). She used to have frequent panic attacks, but now it's rather in the form of persistent underlying dread.

Charles has a lot of anxiety when it comes to social situations or going into new situations or places. He goes on to say:

> 66 I definitely feel like it has stopped me from doing things I want to do, or being the kind of person I would like to be. My anxieties take the form of extreme nervousness, adrenaline spikes and a much-increased heart rate during these situations. If I am with others during new situations I am not comfortable in, I can be short and snappy with them. 99

Paul shares how he's been working on reducing his levels of anxiety:

> 66 I always had a high level of anxiety, but since diagnosed with autism I started training in emotional freedom techniques and later mindfulness, and these were very effective in reducing my levels of anxiety. Anxiety never stopped me from continuing with life, but I would overthink and ruminate a lot. Much of my anxiety was about money worries and sometimes health, and sometimes about whether a romantic relationship would develop with someone. However, nowadays, I am typically calm and feeling fairly content. I feel a core sense of tranquility even though I have problems to solve. 99

S. says that her anxiety has absolutely disabled her in every way. She adds: 'I constantly need support and there isn't much I can do by myself.' Karol also describes how present anxiety is in her life:

> 66 My anxiety absolutely stops me living the life I want to live. It basically controls my life. It decides what I do and what I don't. I always try to make sure I don't increase my anxiety but that basically means I don't do anything. For example, I don't really go outside unless I have to because of all the unpredictability and the possible sensory overload in the outside world. My anxiety is usually meltdowns, nervousness in a lot of situations and a few panic attacks. The meltdowns are particularly bad because sometimes I'm so overwhelmed that it stops me processing any new information and a few times that has put me in dangerous situations. I have nearly walked in front of moving cars a few times in the past. 99

Sarah explains how she has had anxiety every single day:

> ❝ I have always had anxiety and that has never left me and I doubt it ever will. I don't even know when it is going to hit me hard but it always does and it comes out of nowhere! Sometimes, I have been physically shaking because I am so anxious. I constantly feel on edge if I go anywhere outside of the house. My house is my safe zone. ❞

Depression

Depression is not simply sadness, it's a cumulation of sadness, shame, despair, exhaustion, discouragement, self-loathing, loss of motivation, loss of pleasure and so on. It has a neurobiological impact, which means that your brain is literally reducing your ability to feel pleasure, motivation, energy or enthusiasm and is instead causing you to hate yourself and to have darker thoughts.

Loneliness has been a major trigger to Sarah's depression:

> ❝ All through my life I have suffered with anxiety and depression or low-grade depression fairly constantly, with a few episodes of depression lasting a few weeks, months. Life can feel lonely at times. This was probably my main trigger, although I wasn't always alone, maybe just more I felt misunderstood as I can find it hard to express what I am thinking and sometimes it's hard putting my thoughts into words. Again, when you don't have that small talk ability, it's more difficult to express all the time, in the neurotypical world. Now, I'm learning it's ok to do things in short bursts. It's not always easy, although sometimes it is with those I am close to. I know my limits now with socializing; however, I also know how much my connection to others improves my mental health. We have to find a way to balance and pace ourselves. This comes with accepting who we are as well. ❞

Hayley's depression has been especially hard in the last three months. She tells us:

> 66 I've been in a deep depression where I've attempted suicide, ended up sectioned and on psych wards, self-harming, not taking care of myself, etc. My self-esteem is at an all-time low. I hate the way I look and behave, I just hate everything about me. I would like a break from myself but I'm stuck with me. I can't get away and that just makes me hate myself even more. I suffer really badly from anxiety and again I'm on medication for this. I get panic attacks often and I feel like I'm constantly nervous and on edge. Trauma has ruined my life. If I hadn't experienced the trauma that I have, I don't think I would suffer as badly mentally. Not being able to communicate very well didn't help as I couldn't really tell anyone what had happened to me. 99

Jodie describes how having a clear plan regarding what to do in case of suicide ideation can actually save you in the moment you might be at risk of hurting yourself:

> 66 One morning after school run, I just felt ... unsafe. So, I called my GP surgery and booked an emergency appointment, saying I was having a mental health crisis. I then called in sick to work. I had to take that opportunity before that ideation became a reality. I had a crisis contingency plan stating I would reach out to my GP if I felt I needed help, so I followed the plan. I asked J. to come to the appointment with me, partly for emotional support and partly because he also needed to know where I was at. I needed him to look after me when this instinct to look after myself had passed. And he did exactly that. He called my best friend and asked her to come over, which she did. He did all the right things. I didn't know it, but he did talk me off that ledge (figuratively) and I will always be grateful for that. I'd probably say the last year or so has been generally more positive. I do feel a lot more motivated. 99

Milène has struggled with depression in the past and it is definitely not a place she likes to be at. Now, she tries to be optimistic as much as she can and has learned to enjoy the little things in life. She adds: 'Yesterday for example, I saw an orange-tip butterfly for the first time! It was adorable.'

> Seeking out professional help (talking to your GP, a psychiatrist, etc.) can help you understand what is causing your depression, how to work through those feelings and figure out if some changes need to be made in your life to help you feel more balanced. A healthy person is not someone who will never feel an ounce of sadness, anxiety, self-doubt, anger, etc. but a person who will be able to experience the whole variety of emotions, the ones we enjoy as well as those we sometimes dislike. Working on your depression means understanding yourself enough to know what you actually need and to be able to feel emotions in a wider spectrum.

Tiredness

A huge number of participants have described their usual mood as 'tired' or 'exhausted'. Sadie, like many others, has said that she always feels tired, regardless of whether she's had few or many hours of sleep. Melanie also describes how tired she feels:

> 66 I'm tired, exhausted, frustrated by the lack of support and feeling in a constant state of overwhelm. I don't feel as capable of managing things as I did before I realized I was Autistic and I think it's because I understand myself much more now and simply can't pretend that I'm someone I'm not. It's like I've allowed myself to be my authentic self and that means things now bother me that didn't so much before. 99

Anger

In therapy, Marie-Laure often hears patients saying how scared they are of their anger. Many people are aware that they could technically get really angry if triggered – or have been in the past – which makes them very careful not to let themselves go there. To a certain degree, that makes sense. Uncontrollable rage can be hurtful to the person as well as the people around them. It can lead to a lot of shame and self-loathing. But dismissing your anger and judging yourself for it isn't helpful. It is important to understand what the trigger is, as well as why that trigger was so important to you. Dismissing your anger could lead to you bottling things up and means you might be just one trigger away from a really big explosion. Finding safe spaces to explore your anger can truly make a difference, whether it's by writing about it or talking about it to a safe person (friend, partner, relative, therapist, for example).

Katharina recalls that as a teenager, or even before, she had an incredible amount of anger inside, eating her up, together with unbelievable impatience, not being able to wait for anything, even for a second. Her impulse control was very low. Now, people say that she has the patience of an angel, but she sure does not feel this on the inside.

Sarah says that in her twenties, she became verbally angry very quickly, more with family but easily with friends and strangers alike. She adds:

> **❝** Like a volcano erupting, always regretting my actions after, but I found it difficult to control. Despite how I may have appeared, I mostly always felt lost, low and confused about life. **❞**

> Keep in mind that even if the way your anger is not to your/ other people's liking, it is still worthy of being heard, understood, processed and acknowledged. Often, anger can be completely legitimate: it can show someone may have disrespected you, overstepped your boundaries, or that your needs simply weren't met. You can read more on anger and meltdowns in Chapter 4.

Trauma

Almost all our participants have experienced trauma one way or another. A lot of it comes from bullying (at school or at home), invalidation ('no, that noise is not too loud'), suppressing emotions ('stop crying or I'll give you something to cry about'), and generally feeling like the person's authentic self isn't appreciable. As a therapist, Marie-Laure has often seen other therapists struggling to recognize the Autistic way of functioning of a person because the patient's PTSD symptoms were getting in the way, being more obvious to some therapists than autism. Since a lot of Autistic people have experienced trauma, it is important to keep in mind that our global and medical representation of autism is that of a traumatized Autistic – many people (especially doctors) struggle to picture what a non-traumatized Autistic person looks like.

Trauma affects Jess's life every single day. It has made her afraid of people and leads her to making friends cautiously. She adds: 'I will never be the person I could have been.' Kate feels that her history of trauma – including sexual, physical, verbal and emotional abuse – has permeated who she is as a person. She says: 'I can't really imagine living in a way that wasn't impacted by trauma.' S. has been dealing with her trauma since she was 13. She comments: 'I don't remember how it was without it, I don't remember how peace felt.'

Isabella said something very powerful, which is that she thinks her biggest trauma has been being Autistic without knowing it. Just to put a bit of context around this sentence, showing how powerful her words are: this comes from a woman who has experienced being homeless, has been in abusive relationships as well as in danger on many occasions.

Noah describes how hard trauma is, saying it is all-consuming sometimes, making it hard to trust people or himself. It brings triggers and such deep pain; it comes in nightmares, disturbing his sleep; it interrupts friendships and his ability to ask and feel worthy of help or kindness or friendship.

AutieMum struggles with her mental health, saying:

> 66 I think a combination of childhood trauma, teenage trauma and my autism have meant that I struggle to control my emotions and my mood can change drastically in the space of a few seconds. I don't just feel happy or sad, I'm either ecstatic or I'm suicidal. If I'm neither of those two things, I'm just numb (I think of this as survival mode – just getting through each day as it comes). I have zero self-esteem and have also been diagnosed with an eating disorder in the past. I have attempted suicide multiple times and begged to be

sectioned/admitted to a psychiatric ward, but I've never been taken seriously. I've tried anti-depressants, anti-anxiety medication and counselling but nothing really helped. I find the only thing that helps me is keeping a check of my thoughts and as soon as I feel remotely suicidal, I tell my partner. We talk about it and then we spend the next few days/weeks just waiting for it to pass while keeping me safe. I shouldn't have to rely on my partner to keep me alive, but if the National Health Service (NHS) doesn't care, who else is there? **"**

S. suffers from PTSD induced by human violence:

" Strangers and people generally cause me fear – my hyper-vigilant brain takes notice of everything and everything is like a threat all the time. It causes constant nervousness and panic attacks, a phobia about being touched, phobia about men (stranger men), being trapped and trauma-related topics just send my brain immediately down a spiral of memories and flashbacks leading to panic attacks. **"**

Katharina explains how thinking about trauma can be so hurtful that it can feel re-traumatizing, in a way:

" I am still trying to figure out how trauma actually affects my life, but then again thinking back does not help and revisiting such events is not helpful at all I believe. For an Autistic it is like fully reliving that experience again and without proper guidance to put it in perspective, it is only harmful. I am old enough that I don't want to be bitter or suffering from my past but focus on the good in my life (my family, my job, my good friends) and look to the future. I cannot change the past and dwelling on my trauma brings no good except bad flashbacks. I am trying to learn and do better for my kids. **"**

Last year, M. was diagnosed with stress disorders and sleeping disorders from trauma. It really undermined her ability to work and live her life and stay healthy, but she can also feel proud that she has overcome these traumas and disorders for the most part and found a lot of courage within herself and learned to be more assertive in advocating for herself and setting boundaries. Sarah has also worked incredibly hard on owning, unpacking and healing from her trauma. It's something she is immensely proud of and she feels that she's generally very well balanced emotionally.

Mood changes

We did not plan to have a section on mood changes. We did not even ask our participants specific questions on that topic. However, in the questionnaires we've received an overwhelming number of accounts spontaneously describing how quickly moods can change.

Linda, for instance, experiences moods that switch from one extreme to the other:

> My mood is highly variable, depending on my current energy level, amount of stress and above all if I have prioritized self-care (meditation) or not. It can vary from one minute to another – especially if I am not grounded. It's *so* draining to be thrown between these extremes.
>
> I feel and express myself very strongly: when I am happy, I am super-positive, jumping energetic, chatty and giggly. Nowadays, I am very enthusiastic very often. When I am sad, I am so low and often crying. When I am angry, I can be extremely loud, argumentative and really have to find (healthy) ways to let those overwhelming toxic feelings loose or it feels like it consumes the whole me – I *hate* anger, frustration and irritation.
>
> My mood the last six months is the most 'stable' and harmonic I have experienced in my whole adult life. I still experience these high and low feelings and express myself as before, but now I feel it's not frightening – it doesn't consume me any more and I now like that I feel and express so much.

Nicky also notices that her mood changes hour by hour. She can be very happy, but a small thing could spoil it and make her sad or angry. S. also says that her mood changes faster than she can keep up with. She adds: 'I get angry very fast, then I get excited over something, sad over another, then stressed, angry again … It's beyond me.'

S. has become aware of the triggers that affect her mood:

❝ My mood is generally stable where I feel calm and content for the most part of the day. I find that auditory issues are what usually change my mood. I can pick up on other people's moods and energy, so this can affect me, but I have learned to take time out and shake it off, literally. I find I get irritated when there are too many noisy distractions. Sometimes a visual thing can cause great irritation, for example I caught sight of someone outside my office continually bouncing their legs under a table earlier today as it was in my eyeline just past my computer and I could feel anger building in me and I couldn't wait for them to leave. ❞

Happiness

This section may not be very long but that doesn't mean Autistic people don't experience happiness. If you've read the previous section, you'll see that a lot of Autistic people describe that they feel happy for much of the time, even if a trigger can make them switch to a different mood quickly. We're sharing many stories on topics that bring us joy, in the chapters on special interests, couples and self-regulation. Often, Autistic people feel emotions intensely – be they enjoyable (joy, excitement, enthusiasm, appreciation) or unpleasant.

Charles' mood changes depending on who he's with; some people, like his partner, are able to make him feel happy simply by being there, and taking part in activities he enjoys can cheer him up a lot. However, he says that he usually returns to a darker mood once he's on his own or after an activity has ended.

Isabella said something so delightful we just had to mention it: 'I love life so I am happy to be alive every day.'

> Finding our tribe, knowing who we are authentically and exploring our special interests definitely improve our mental health and bring us great joy.

Self-esteem and self-confidence

Self-esteem and self-confidence may be developed over the course of many years. They are sometimes confused and though they can be intertwined, they each refer to a specific aspect of how we perceive and present ourselves. Self-esteem refers to the appreciation a person has towards themselves, how we perceive ourselves through self-love and self-respect. Healthy self-esteem is not based on achievements or strengths, nor on being a fabulous people-pleaser. While it is important to be aware of your resources and to feel proud of yourself, a healthy self-esteem implies full acceptance of who you are, with the parts of you you've always loved and the ones you've felt were harder to love at times. It means being on your side unconditionally and not having to prove that you're worthy of being loved.

'Self-confidence' refers to how much you trust your own capability to achieve things, whether or not you will dare to try to do something you wish to do. It means believing in your ability. Healthy self-confidence means believing in yourself sufficiently to try to do the things you wish to do (preferably the ones that are healthy for you, but we're not here to judge), while being ok whichever outcome there may be – whether the task is the success you were hoping it would be or it did not work that way. Basically, it means being your very own, believing in your abilities, but (ideally) in a pressure-free way!

Lauren describes her self-esteem and confidence as ok now, though she has struggled with them in the past. She adds: 'Now, I pride myself on being odd and a bit more out there.' Dear Lauren, you are an inspiration to us all!

Having good self-esteem and self-confidence, people have often accused Ben of being arrogant. He replies: 'I'm not. I just feel like every person has inherent worth.' Not only do we completely agree with him, we also hope each of you will someday see your own worth – it is there, even if you are not aware of it right now.

Richard has pretty good self-esteem and confidence, inspired by his grandfather:

&& I have good self-esteem and confidence. I've always thought that when things got tough, I had me in my corner. And I am a pretty good ally to have. My grandad once said, 'If you can't rely on

145

yourself, who can you rely on?' That stuck with me. He also said, 'A calm sea never made a skilled sailor.' So, when things got tough, I knew it was making me better at handling things. **"**

Isabella has learned in time to see what a fantastic person she is:

" Yes, I think I am beautiful and very intelligent, brave and incredibly full of resources. I think I am one of the best people on earth (among few others). I used to think I was inferior to others because others were seemingly so sure, self-confident and successful, but after some years of living and observation, I found out that most people are way more stupid than me (sadly, it sucks...). **"**

Linda tells us about all the hard work she has done:

" My self-esteem and self-confidence have been totally absent most of my life. I work *really* hard to 'build' genuine self-esteem and self-confidence from scratch by self-healing from trauma. Mindfulness, meditation and returning to my genuine interests, attending forums and webinars for/by other people in similar situations and bonding over exchanging experiences, support and tips is the key for me. **"**

Maddie feels that her self-esteem is a lot better than it was, but is still not high. Going to the gym has really helped her, as well as practising both phone and in-person conversations more and more.

The important thing to remember is that self-esteem and self-confidence are learned skills like any others. This means that self-hatred is learned one way or another (bullying, abuse, nasty comments), but can also be unlearned. If you currently do not appreciate yourself or feel extremely insecure, it does not mean this is the only possible version of you. Just as can learn to walk, talk or write, you can also learn to appreciate yourself and to believe in yourself.

Milène calls her self-esteem and self-confidence a 'work in progress':

❝ I am doing better than a few years ago, so that's good! I think part of it comes from always feeling different and being left out. I rarely got invited to go somewhere (that is still rare). So that made me feel like I wasn't worth it. Also, the fact that pretty much everyone I know has their lives with a partner and I don't is something I can struggle with. But I keep on hoping. ❞

S. has been working on her confidence and self-esteem over the last few years:

❝ My confidence and self-esteem before I had my initial counselling were rock bottom. This has changed over the past seven years and while I still have wobbles now and again, I now live by the mantra 'feel the fear and do it anyway'. It isn't 100 per cent all the time but it's nowhere near rock bottom. There are areas in life where my confidence and self-esteem aren't great, but they aren't connected to work. It has more to do with dating, etc. ❞

Paul feels that he has never had good self-esteem but has been moving into self-acceptance. He thinks his self-esteem problems largely stemmed from his difficult relationship with his parents and extended family, since he never felt really fully loved and accepted. He adds: 'I never felt I fully belonged.'

Kevin recalls that things got really bad when he was 18 years old:

❝ That was when I first became aware of how my autism affected others and how far behind my communication skills were, and I constantly wondered if I could ever 'catch up'. I realized that my life was not going to reach the ideal that many other people reach and that made me sad. I do need to be shown that I'm valued and loved on a regular basis or I won't necessarily believe it myself, but I now feel like I have that in my life. ❞

Karol describes her self-esteem and self-confidence as 'very bad', due to years of trying to be 'normal':

> 66 I have a very low and negative view of myself. I think it's partly the bullying I endured at school but mainly because of an idea of 'normal' that I've been striving for my whole life. So much so that I was willing to completely erase myself to be a more socially accepted neurotypical version of myself and I guess that wasn't too hard to do because with all the things I did 'wrong', I grew more hesitant about myself and hated who I was. 99

Danielle also describes how trying really hard to 'appear normal' leads to a lot of stress:

> 66 If something unexpected happens, I can really struggle with that and I put pressure on myself to be prepared for all scenarios. When I am not prepared it's almost like my brain can't accept it and goes into a continual loop that keeps misfiring as it cannot compute. I do not know how to cope with these situations and I fear them the most. I also fear I will not be able to act in the way that I should and be able to maintain my usual show of being normal. 99

Noah's struggles with self-esteem or confidence especially come up around interactions or life decisions. He feels he's always doing or saying things wrong. Danielle also struggles with self-confidence socially and will constantly analyse conversations she has had to try to figure out if she did well or if she got it right.

S. explains that she has zero self-esteem and little self-confidence. Years of bullying, being made fun of by teachers, classmates and parents, do that to you. She tends to blame herself for everything and can't stop herself from looking at herself as a failure and disappointment to everyone.

Charles says he has very bad self-esteem and self-confidence. Winning a game or painting a figure that comes out looking particularly well can raise it somewhat, but compliments make him somewhat uncomfortable as he has a lot of imposter syndrome going on inside.

Beth shares that she has terrible self-esteem:

> I've been working with a mental health charity to try to improve how I think and feel about myself. Thanks to a wrong diagnosis of borderline personality disorder where medical professionals told me to 'stop being dramatic' and 'attention seeking' and that 'there are people worse off than you', it made me feel like I was an awful person. That alongside a string of failed jobs just knocked me off my feet and made me feel like a failure. I'm slowly building it up and trying to believe in myself more, but it's really difficult.

Many participants have described that knowing they're Autistic – and actually learning about neurodivergence – helped them understand themselves better, how to respect their own needs and how to appreciate themselves more. Virginia, for instance, believes that the diagnosis improved things for her as she now takes more care of herself. Knowing herself better has allowed her to have fewer panic attacks and less depression.

Emily explains what a tremendous difference learning she's Autistic has made on her sense of self-worth:

> I'd say the single biggest thing that's improved my self-esteem and confidence is realizing I'm Autistic. Suddenly, I make sense as a person. I'm no longer broken but I'm a fully fleshed-out human who was hanging out in the wrong places, with the wrong people. Understanding yourself and finding your clan makes a huge difference to how you feel about yourself. Getting older helps too – you run out of f**ks as well as collagen when you hit middle age.

C.A.'s self-esteem is much higher since their diagnosis and their self-confidence higher since they became a teacher. They add: 'My self-esteem, my internal sense of self, was something I didn't gain until after my diagnosis, once I understood myself and learned enough about who I was to accept and embrace myself.'

Mark has been on quite a journey, from suicidal thoughts to starting to like himself:

> **❝** The autism is harder to pin down in terms of mental health. It is a huge relief to just know, finally. I can start to under-stand myself and my history at last – and I'm not going to try to suggest that completely reinterpreting your own opinion of yourself in your fifties is an easy task, because it isn't, it's beyond exhausting. The constant intrusive memories and harmful self-analysis are reducing – not all of them, and not all the time, but I can definitely see an improvement.
>
> Having a chunk of the ADHD symptoms reduced – in my case, specifically the executive dysfunction, rejection sensitivity, social anxiety and so on – has been hugely helpful in allowing me to get the measure of the Autistic traits that I've probably got for life. The inability to understand exactly what people mean, rather than what they actually said, is a constant challenge. And the regular periods of becoming overwhelmed by sensory inputs: with me, it's mostly noise and crowds, but I can also become very anxious as a result of being put in an interminably boring situation that I have to remain in out of politeness. I have accepted that my need for short naps during the day is ok rather than feeling guilty about it like I have since I was a child; they work incredibly well as a soft reboot option on my issues of overstimulation.
>
> So, previously having spent long periods in a deep depression, with my suicidal ideation only not being acted on because it was too much effort (the irony does not escape me), and generally very low self-esteem and poor self-image and no self-confidence whatsoever, I'm now largely the opposite. I feel valid, I feel generally content (although I can still be pushed into a sad mood by really quite small incidents, like a thoughtless or dismissive comment from someone I respect and care about) and I feel productive. I am not working what society would call a full working week, there's far too much sitting in coffee shops and reading a novel in the sunshine for that, but it's vastly better than it used to be. I know when to remove myself from anxiety-initiating situations

and to not feel shame in doing so. I can see a point on a distant horizon, for the first time in my life, pretty much, where I might actually like myself a little. **"**

Gillian has described how learning about neurodivergence has made a tremendous difference with regard to her self-esteem:

" I had really bad self-esteem for a very, very, very long time. One thing that helped was learning that it wasn't a 'me' thing. Learning that 'Oh, you're not a broken neurotypical person. You're actually a pretty common-regarded Autistic person. You're not even an exciting Autistic person, you're just an ordinary Autistic person!' It's like, 'Oh, this is just a common thing. This thing I thought was a weird thing I did. Turns out you all do it!' That's a really important part of the community-building as well; it's that people go 'Oh! There's a word for this! It's so common that they even have a word for it!'

That's been really helpful for my child. She was talking to me about not knowing how she feels. And I said, 'Well, actually, there's a word for this, it's called "alexithymia", and I explained this and I could see that it helped. Imagine having that information as a child. I have terrible interoception. Absolutely awful. I rarely feel thirsty. I go from not having to go to the toilet to 'I need to go to the toilet right now or I'm going to wet myself'. I go from 'I'm not hungry' to 'I'm starving' because somebody has drawn my attention to it. I sat on a fork for 45 minutes once before I noticed! My body gives me no signal, it's shocking. But having that word helped, I could be like, 'Oh, this is a thing!', and I can help my child.

The more I learned about neurodivergence, the more self-accepting I became. All the things I used to give myself such a hard time for not being good at, or not being able to do, or 'Why can't I do this?', it's like, 'Oh, I'm actually disabled.' That self-acceptance of knowing 'It is too overwhelming for me. It's ok for me to say it's too noisy for me in here, I have to leave, or I have to get away from that smell, whereas before I would have tolerated it and just been like a ball of stress, a ball of anxiety. Now, I'm just like, 'No, you know what? I don't like that!' and I'm gone. Also, I have a lot of rejection sensitivity. Just knowing that term is a protective thing. It helps to have a word for it. **"**

One major tool when it comes to improving your self-esteem is learning to assert yourself. Sometimes, our low self-esteem makes us think that if we become a complete people-pleaser, others will like us for it. The issue is that as long as we do that, a) people will never get to appreciate the real us, with our opinions and character and personality – and they might actually dislike us for seemingly lacking personality – and b) we will never learn that we are actually lovable just the way we are – with our triggers, our flaws, our shame, our insecurity … all of it! Learning to stop being a people-pleaser and starting to make choices based on what feels right for *us* is an essential step in building healthy self-esteem.

Gillian tells us the difference this has made in her life:

" I had a very big Autistic burnout when I was 22. I was diagnosed with complete physical exhaustion. At that time, I was working three jobs and was in college, so that led to the burnout. Also, at the time, I would have been a real people-pleaser as well. That people-pleasing thing of 'If I just say "yes" to everything, then everybody will like me because I'm doing everything for everybody'. I do still do a lot, especially with advocacy, but I've got better at saying 'no' to things I can't do. The big difference is that now, I'm choosing. Before, I would have said 'yes' to things for other people. Now, I say 'yes' to things for myself. **"**

8

Interactions with medical professionals

Joe James' experience

Within the autism community it is common to find us speaking about two different types of autism. I'm not talking about low- and high-functioning, or classic and Asperger's, I'm speaking about the medical model of autism and the neurotype autism. The idea of autism being a medical issue is engrained so deeply within society it's hard to imagine another way of seeing it. It is referred to on the NHS website, charities have been created to help people 'suffering from this infliction' or to try to cure it or treat it, and these organizations try to bring attention to this awful 'problem'. I'm hoping you can see where I'm going with this, as it's pretty obvious to me and most others within the community that describing autism as a medical condition or disorder is incredibly harmful and hurtful to us on a grand scale, even if you believe it may help an individual person. I'm all for treating people as individuals. If someone has actual medical needs then by all means help them, treat them, try to cure them, that's what medicine and the medical community do, it's their job. But to describe an entire minority of people, no matter what individual medical needs each one may have, under the term 'autism disorder' isn't just wrong, to me it's lazy. When we treat every Autistic person, no matter who they are, as disordered, or suffering from a medical condition, we are not truly helping them because them being Autistic isn't the real problem, the fact that they are not being treated as an individual is. We are constantly stereotyped by charities, the media, doctors and other medical staff, teachers and society in general. Just because someone is different, it doesn't mean they are broken; not all Autistic people are struggling in the same way, and in my experience what we most suffer from is anxiety, depression, hypersensitivity to our environment and people not making reasonable adjustments when we need them.

The other major issue I have with the medical community is the lack of understanding of what makes someone Autistic. So many people are denied a diagnosis based on old-fashioned ideas that have been debunked for years but are still believed by professionals. These include but are not limited to eye contact, friendly behaviour, smiling, having a vivid imagination, being articulate, having friends, being sociable, enjoying imaginative play and having empathy. Many of us can do these but are still Autistic, but according to some assessors we are not. Autism is a neurotype, not a simple list of traits that equals a deficit.

This brings me to what autism really is. It's a neurotype, a different type of brain evolved side by side with a typical brain. Autism exists within our species to change it, to advance it, to help it thrive, and what has happened is instead of that difference being respected and appreciated, psychologists and other professionals have labelled us disordered and now the world views the word autism to mean broken, suffering, needing treatment, incapable and not as good as neurotypicals. Why some of the medical community continue to insist that we all need therapy from the moment we are 'diagnosed' (another term that makes my skin crawl), and that as soon as we can be manipulated to change the way we do things, the better our lives will be, is beyond me and can only be described as cognitive dissonance. Here's a thought. How about you let us grow at our own pace and stop putting expectations on us to reach your targets and goals, as if children were gladiators and only the strong will survive? How about changing the education system, changing the way subjects are taught, or is this too much work? Instead of trying to force different minds to work in the way you expect them to, is it not worth the time and money to find out how to work with different minds and see them as potentially brilliant rather than as a medical burden?

We need to start looking at autism as neurodivergence and not an infliction 'caused' by something. It is genetic, it is hereditary and the only thing that causes it is procreation. Enough of the clickbait science that keeps insisting we are things to be researched and prevented. Without us you wouldn't have computers to write your articles on in the first place. Let's start at the very beginning, and I'm hoping this book will be that beginning. Because the *only* way to learn about autism is from the individuals who have Autistic brains.

Participants' experiences

This chapter is one that Marie-Laure finds incredibly important because it gives hope that medical professionals might someday update their understanding of autism. It's one thing that the general public doesn't know much about autism, but it is sad to see how little doctors know about it. As a psychotherapist, Marie-Laure often interacts with other medical professionals and almost each time they show how little they know about autism. It's simply not taught in much detail during their training. In Marie-Laure's experience, over the course of five years of university plus five five years of psycho-therapy training, autism was mentioned only once, during a 1.5-hour lecture (which wasn't even only about autism). Basically, unless the professional finds interest in neurodivergency and seeks out the infor-mation by themselves by doing additional training and reading about it, they simply won't know about autism. Medical professionals are expected to be familiar with many different subjects, so of course they can't specialize in everything. Unfortunately, it means the Autistic community is often wronged by the medical community's lack of knowledge on the subject.

Here are the stories of our participants' interactions with the medical system, describing what makes a doctor neurodiversity-friendly, as well as the mistakes medical professionals should make sure to avoid. Keep in mind that these stories come from people from various countries, these issues being vastly represented throughout the globe.

Interactions with general physicians and nurses

In many countries, our general practitioner is supposed to be the first doctor we meet when we're struggling with our mental and physical health. They can be the medical professional who has known us for the longest time and who will be referring us to different specialists. That doesn't necessarily mean that visiting them is easy. Beth, for instance, finds going to the doctor intimidating as well as overwhelming. She explains: 'The rooms are very brightly lit with white lights, it's noisy and people don't respect social distancing any more, which makes me feel anxious.'

Another Beth, from England, recalls that during a medical appointment, she had a quite significant panic attack and was sat on the floor to avoid passing out. Her doctor then touched her several times and asked her to get up. Beth adds: 'Just a complete lack of awareness of potential sensory sensitivities.'

Hélène describes that that's precisely what makes physiotherapist appointments difficult:

> ❝ The physical proximity to the physiotherapist in addition to the body manipulations are highly uncomfortable to me, they stress me enormously, especially since they're trying to be bonding by chatting, which adds the discomfort of having to talk and seem friendly. ❞

The difficulties around being touched also happen with nurses, as Karol, from England, describes:

> ❝ A few weeks ago, I also had to have a blood test done and because in the past I would feel very faint or nauseous after those, I was really nervous. The nurse couldn't find a vein so she asked two other nurses for help and one of them saw I was nervous and asked if I wanted to hold her hand. I don't like people touching me (and one of the other nurses was already touching my other arm to take the blood) and I needed my hand to stim, so I said no, but she held it anyway. She meant well and wanted to help. It was also in a way so that I could still move it so I could stim, but it made me feel really anxious to be touched by not one but two different people. It felt rude to tell her to stop so I just went along with it. ❞

Wren, from England, went to visit his doctor over the course of his first year of university, due to anxiety:

> ❝ I could barely leave my room other than to force myself to go to lectures, where I felt safe sitting alone at the back of the hall. Once, I almost collapsed in the kitchen of my student house, having been so afraid of having any social interaction that I hadn't cooked or eaten properly in days. The GP was completely unhelpful. My memory of the appointment is, again, foggy, but I believe I was

given a phone number and told to come back if it was still a problem after some group talk therapy. Group talk. A perfect solution to social anxiety. Of course, I never called. 🙉

Our family doctor is often one of the first medical professionals we'll talk to about being Autistic. They're often the ones who will get us a referral to have a professional assessment made by a specialist. Unfortunately, this does not necessarily mean that they have an accurate understanding of autism. Mickey, from the USA, remembers that when they first brought up to their doctor that they thought they might be Autistic, the doctor told them they couldn't be because they could make eye contact. Of course, that's absolutely not a reason to say anyone's not Autistic, but it is quite an indicator of that doctor's (and many others') understanding of autism. Emily, from the UK, describes that being fobbed off, told that there was no way she could be Autistic, was probably the lowest point. She remembers: 'I felt like I'd told someone a truth about myself and then been condescended to and told I was making it all up.'

Danielle, who comes from England, puts off going to the GP as she absolutely hates going there:

> 🙉 I don't like appearing needy or wasting anyone's time and I would hate it if they thought I was doing so. When I did go, my expectations were correct: they had no clue how to deal with me. They only had procedures for dealing with children with autism. I would love to discuss my condition in general with a medical professional and have often thought about asking to talk about options for drugs that may help me be more normal, but I am too scared to go because I feel I will been seen as a time waster. I am just not that person and I don't want to be seen as someone who is too self-obsessed. 🙉

Michelle, from the USA, prepares for about ten days before going to her doctor, writing down everything she want to talk to her about. She and her doctor have negotiated her wait time, as it is easier for her to wait in the lobby rather than the exam room, so that helps.

Interactions with psychologists and psychiatrists

We've asked our participants to share their experiences with psychiatrists and psychologists. Experiences were mixed, some people having expressed what a positive life-changing experience it has been, while others pointed out that it had been completely destructive. We do want to make one point extremely clear: we do not think medical professionals (including psychologists and psychiatrists) should make it a therapeutic goal to make the person's Autistic traits less perceivable. If the patient were to be able to camouflage their Autistic identity, they would pay a very high price by sacrificing their self-esteem, needs, self-confidence, and would probably feel incredibly anxious as a result. However, therapy can be helpful if the goal is to help the client become an expert in themselves, which means learning to not only accept but also appreciate themselves as they are, to know their needs better and learn to be more assertive, to heal past traumas, etc. Therapy should always seek to help the person be more respectful of themselves. Therapy can be helpful to many people, whether Neurodivergent or neurotypical, but many participants have noticed that seeking therapy from a therapist who has no proper understanding of neurodivergency can be extremely harmful. Melanie, from the UK, is currently having cognitive behavioural therapy (CBT) for anxiety and says it's been the most negative experience she's had so far:

> 66 My therapist is nice but keeps on with the 'ifs' regarding me being Autistic. So, I'm telling her that I rehearse conversations as part of my autism and she's dismissive of that and says that's just anxiety. It's hard enough to continually feel imposter syndrome but then to have a medical professional add to that. The CBT has only been half helpful too. What she considers to be unhelpful thinking, I consider to be very helpful thinking. But my anxiety has improved through having to assert myself, so maybe that was the whole point. 55

Here's WolfRahm's experience with psychotherapy, which illustrates very well the misunderstandings that can occur between neurotypical and Neurodivergent ways of communicating:

> ❝ She [the therapist], by agreeing to dedicate her time and attention to me, made me feel like not everything had to go wrong for me. Having been completely ignored by the staff of the school that I went to, this was a nice change. I had severe avoidance issues and going there, physically entering that school's premises, going through corridors there to get to her office and then waiting outside her office for when she finished her preceding appointment and became available, especially when I encountered other people by the time I finally entered her office and closed the door behind me, was an anxiety-inducing challenge each time.
>
> At some point, it just became too much for me anxiety-wise and I started skipping the appointments almost intentionally. I say 'almost' because I really wanted to attend, but if the meetings were not on the days when I would go there straight after lessons from the location of the school that I went to, when I had to go there from my home, when I saw the planned estimated time to leave draw closer, it was like simmering in fear waiting to go, as physically walking in the street to get to the location of the school caused additional stress, and that plus the stress of entering the premises of that school became just too much to bear at some point. So, I would be at home waiting for the time when I was supposed to leave and the stress would just build up. It would build up so that when the time of my planned leaving came, I would just not get up and go but instead still be sitting there, as if hoping that giving myself another minute or two before leaving would alleviate the stress. But it didn't, the stress was still there and even stronger, and then having been sitting like that for yet another few minutes I was realizing that if I didn't get up right then and go, I might be late for my appointment, so that caused additional stress on top of that because I didn't want to be late, and I kept sitting and simmering in my stress, anxiety and fear until I realized that it was way too late to be going at all because by the time I would have got there, half of the appointment time would already be gone.

That resulted in more stress – stress over facing the psychologist and what I was going to tell her regarding my tardiness. So, I ended up not going at all. [It's also possible that I did go and was late to some appointment(s) and got told off, and then I was scared of being late again, so I started skipping the appointments altogether – I don't recall.]

After each of those times, I then found it stressful to go there again because I had to explain why I hadn't attended our former appointment, but I did. And unfortunately, then, it happened again. On one of those occasions, when I then went to see her, I met her outside the school's building and she told me off for that pattern of behaviour, telling me that she had waited for me and that I didn't respect her time. I completely understood her perspective and was deeply ashamed.

I also went to see a psychologist in my late adolescence. I tried to explain to her my problems with social anxiety and agoraphobia. Back then I didn't know these terms, so I explained as best I could that I had a problem – felt unwell – when walking in the street when there were other people in the street, and the psychologist told me that it was normal and that some people liked being around many other people and some didn't, and there was nothing abnormal about it. I had no choice but to believe her, as she was the qualified one, not me. But on some level, I did know, deep in my mind, that the level of distress that I experienced when getting from place to place, walking to school and back, going to the library or to church, really going anywhere when and where there were other people, was anything but normal. Only due to her lousy explanation, I started believing all the more that I was abnormal on the whole, that I was the only one like this. There was no point continuing the appointments with her because according to her, I had no problem(!), so not only would I get no help from her but I also felt like she might feel that I was imposing, making appointments with her out of whimsy because I had nothing better to do or was seeking attention, that she would perceive me as a nuisance who would deliberately waste her time, and that I wasn't welcome there. Because of my lack of knowledge on the matter, not being familiar with the terminology, and my difficulties in verbalizing my problems, I didn't successfully convey what mental states befell me while walking the street when there were other people walking there too, but I did express that there was a problem.

I experienced my third depression in summer time. So, then I accessed mental health services at the university. That day, I hadn't eaten at all until the time of the appointment. I was hungry. So, I went to that counselling appointment and while waiting to be called, I opened one of the boxes of chocolates I had bought earlier and started eating them. She called me in. I had not eaten many of the chocolates and was still hungry, so I continued eating them, and when the counsellor and I entered the room, I asked her if she would like some. Her response to my gesture was nothing that I would have expected. She then went on to tell me how inappropriate and unprofessional my gesture was. I got confused. I wasn't getting it. I was shocked. She also referred to my action as 'giving gifts', which surprised me since the box of chocolates was already opened and I was eating them, I wasn't offering her a whole unopened box, I was offering her some of those that I was already eating. Her tangent went on for about 15 minutes out of my approximately 50–60-minute session. She made me feel really bad.

I felt so bad that I even considered leaving that room there and then and never returning. But I didn't listen to my feelings. I didn't know the code of conduct. Now, from the time perspective, I reflect and know that exactly would have been the appropriate response: to just storm out of there and not go back. But I stayed and proceeded with the session instead, despite how bad she made me feel, because I thought that leaving would be inappropriate. She even asked me if I still wanted to proceed with the session. I should have said 'no'. I couldn't focus on the session and of course from that point on I couldn't honestly open up to her because I no longer trusted her as a therapist, so that session was an utter waste of time, both mine and hers.

After the session, I had to call my surrogate brother for moral support because that's how bad I felt and I couldn't shake it off. He explained to me that what the therapist had suggested was basically that I had tried to bribe her. 'No, thank you' would have completely sufficed, she didn't need to make me feel like I did something bad when I intended to do something good. I was meant to have more sessions with her, but after that incident I just couldn't. It didn't feel right to me to continue having therapy with someone who made me feel so bad over nothing, over having offered chocolates. I asked the department if they could allocate a different therapist for me, but it wasn't possible, so I quit. I felt scared and embarrassed going to their department for my other appointments and even going anywhere near the location of their department because I was scared and embarrassed to meet this lady somewhere. I didn't know how I was supposed to behave when seeing her somewhere, what her feelings towards me after my request/complaint would be, what the code of conduct in that situation was, so I didn't want to see her at all. I felt like I had done something wrong, they were conflicting feelings because in my heart I knew that I hadn't, but because of her reaction on that day when I offered chocolates. ”

As a therapist, Marie-Laure thought that WolfRahm's testimonial was very helpful. It is true that in psychotherapy training, therapists are encouraged to interpret a lot of what is said and shown by the patient. WolfRahm's story is the perfect example of the devastating impact it can have when psychotherapists try to over-analyse a certain behaviour by seeking the implicit meaning (as neurotypicals often do) – coming from someone who uses direct communication (as Autistic people often do), the therapist can derive a completely wrong understanding of the person's intention.

In Tanya's experience from Australia, finding a therapist who specializes in autism has made all the difference:

“ From the age of 13, I saw counsellors at school as I struggled with peer relationships. There was something wrong with me but the counsellors never knew what it was. I finally got diagnosed at 21 with generalized anxiety disorder and depression. After that, I regularly saw psychologists and psychiatrists to help 'fix' me. Every time, I felt like a mental defective who could not be fixed, I wasn't normal. Currently, I have a psychologist who specializes in Autistic women. The experience has been amazing. I feel seen, I feel heard.

She uses techniques that benefit me as an Autistic person rather than making me feel like a defective. I leave sessions feeling positive as my toolbox of self-care has been expanded. This is a stark contrast to the counsellors I saw in my teens and the psychologists that were 'helping' me during my years at university. Therapy can definitely be beneficial when it supports an Autistic person to be their true authentic self and thereby enables us to flourish. **"**

Sarah recalls a session she had with a counsellor in England in 1994:

" I spoke to him about my difficulties with relationships, feeling alone and not feeling I can communicate like everyone else. I remember him saying, 'But you do communicate well, there's not really anything wrong with you.' After that I just carried on, thinking I was ok and that eventually everything would click. Well, I'm almost 50 now and I'm still waiting ... **"**

Gillian from Ireland also explains how dismissive and invalidating it feels when a therapist tries to normalize someone's experience:

" I met a first counsellor. She and I were speaking in two completely different communication styles. She was a really lovely woman but she wasn't listening to my words, she was listening to what she was thinking. She was trying to be nice to me, like, 'Oh, everybody feels that way!' and I was like, 'No, that's not helpful. I know you're trying to be nice, but that feels really, really dismissive.' Especially as I didn't know I was Autistic and one of the things I was really struggling with was this 'Why am I finding this so hard?' I have misophonia and hyperacusis, so I'm very sound-sensitive and I can't bear touches, and so there was a lot of sensory overwhelm going on, but I didn't know any of that. I knew I was struggling but I didn't have the terminology or the knowledge of why I was finding it so difficult. So, when I went to her, she was trying to make me feel better, but she wasn't understanding why. Hearing 'Oh, everybody's like that' wasn't helpful because I knew not everybody was like that. Not everybody's having the same difficulties! **"**

As a therapist, it can be tempting to try to normalize the patient's experience, hoping to alleviate the feeling of shame. However, there's a thin line between normalizing and dismissing the person's experience.

One of our participants, Maisie, who grew up in Indonesia before moving to the USA, has worked in the USA as an ABA therapist. She no longer works using the ABA method, but she has shared what that experience has been like and what made her decide to move on to different methods:

> **"** Most of the pre-school-aged Autistic students I met during my field work received ABA therapy through the Young Autism Project, a research pilot led by Dr Ivar Lovaas, the founding father of ABA therapy. To achieve optimal success, Autistic children participated in a 40-hour-a-week intensive one-to-one in home therapy provided by trained students. The team met regularly with a senior therapist assigned to each case, along with a monthly meeting with Dr Lovaas at UCLA. At that time, I worked with Autistic children between the ages of three to six, with various degrees of support needs. My day consisted of going to school and therapies at my clients' homes.
>
> Did I like working as a behavioural therapist at the time? I enjoyed being with my clients, sitting on the floor playing with cars and trains, singing songs and taking walks around the neigh-bourhood. For each session, I followed a checklist of carefully designed 'drills' I was trained to deliver. My job was to follow the training protocol, to ensure that my clients could consistently produce correct anticipated responses. For each correct response, I would praise or give my clients a reward, such as M&M's or favourite toys. I was also trained to tally and log the number of correct, incorrect or no responses after each completed drill.
>
> The best part of working with my clients was all outside of 'the sit-down' times, it was when we ate lunch together, blew bubbles, played outside or bounced on a giant ball. I realized those were all moments when my clients and I were being our authentic Autistic selves. They trusted me and I learned from them just as much as they did from me.

I did not like the times when my little clients were not able to perform according to the prescribed methods, even though on other days they were able to complete the same tasks without problems. When my clients were 'off', they were not capable of working for the rewards they chose, nor caring about my repeatedly saying 'Good job!'. I now understand my clients were possibly going through a sensory burnout phase where they were in an extreme need of a physical, mental and emotional break. I often questioned whether I was offering the right support approach during these sensory burnout periods, but we did not have any other solutions at that time. The best thing to do to help someone experiencing a sensory overload or burnout is to take a pause to give them space and unconditional understanding.

For a long time, I complied with instructions given by my supervisors to push through and implement 'planned ignoring' when clients were crying or lashing out. Planned ignoring is called an 'extinction' method, where trained adults would completely go about their business without saying a word or even glancing towards a distressed child. There was an expectation that an ignored behaviour would dramatically increase before the undesired behaviour became less frequent.

The fact is, ignoring someone in distress is not only cruel and traumatic, but the method also prevents a person from developing self-belief in their own decision-making abilities. Almost all forms of 'inappropriate' or 'challenging' behaviours we witness are in reality communication attempts. Can you imagine growing up thinking that even if you feel cornered or desperate for help, others will give you the silent treatment? Ignored Autistic children grow up believing that they are the ones to blame when they need help for something beyond their control.

I was determined to figure out how to best design a more wholistic programme as I moved my way up as an ABA clinician. I learned from other experts, trained myself using different approaches and partnered up with professionals with backgrounds in speech and play-based therapies. I used to believe in providing early intervention programmes to increase my clients' positive long-term outcome.

With each certification training, I continued to feel dissatisfied. I felt that I was missing something very important, but I couldn't pinpoint what it was. I wanted to know how to help my clients to live their best lives and none of these programmes gave me a clear answer. My 'Aha!' moment came when I realized that Autistic minds do not need to be 'fixed'! Autistic individuals have a different developmental trajectory, so all attempts to 'reprogram' Autistic minds are barriers to cultivating the best part of Autistic interests and traits. You know that saying 'Great minds think alike?', well we need to reframe that into 'Great minds think differently!'.

To better understand and support Autistic people, one really needs the right kind of 'manual', and each Autistic person comes with their own unique handbook created over time by meeting the person where he/she is at throughout their lives. Parents of Autistic children frequently lose their ability to intuitively guide their Autistic child because of reliance on professional advice. Families could spend years trying to 'fix behavioural problems' instead of figuring out the best sensory and communication support at home. Many hours are spent in the car going from one therapy to another, and in addition to school hours everyone is beyond exhausted.

More and more Autistic adults are working hard to speak up about their traumatic experiences growing up immersed in a pathology or a deficit model of intervention. In this model, Autistic/Neurodivergent people are blamed for functioning differently than the neuro-majority. Unfortunately, most interventions and educational programmes available for Autistic individuals are based on a deficit model, with the main goal of 'fixing' natural Autistic expressions, such as stimming and echolalia.

Autistic advocates, including non/minimally/unreliably speaking individuals, have started to publicly share that autism and other types of neurodivergence are simply part of natural human evolution. I have personally experienced working with Autistic people not using 'mouth words' to communicate and I found them to be very thoughtful, creative and innovative thinkers. 🙶

Doctors' perception of autism

In an ideal world, we should all feel perfectly safe telling our doctor or therapist that we're Autistic – it might be helpful for them to have that information and it should help us get support in the way we need it. Unfortunately, the sad reality is that many doctors still have very outdated views on autism, meaning that they might not have an adequate or respectful response. Naomi from Switzerland recalls two shocking experiences when she told her gynaecologist and her doctor that she is Autistic:

> It's quite alarming to see that doctors don't understand. When I tell a doctor that I'm Autistic, they don't see it. It's obvious that it doesn't show in me, they're completely taken aback by this information. I told my gynaecologist that I'm Autistic. I asked him if I could remove my contraceptive copper IUD to have kids one of these days. He said yes, no worries, and asked me if I had any diseases in the family. At that point, to test him a bit – I wanted to see where he was at on the topic of autism – I said, 'No, no, no illness, but there's quite a lot of autism', just to see how he would react (I hadn't told him I was Autistic yet). He said, 'Ah, yes, that... Unfortunately, we don't have a test for the fetus', meaning that there is no test to be able to abort in time in case the kid is Autistic. Of course, that's not at all what I wanted to say, but I said to myself, 'Gee, that's bad!' I said, 'No, no, don't worry, I'm Autistic and I have no problem having an Autistic baby.' And he was a little bit like, 'Ah, yes, damn, ah, yes ok ...' And then he said, very embarrassed, 'Ah, at the same time you're lucky, my daughter is really bad at math' and I tell him 'But I'm not good at math at all ... not that you think, I don't know, that I count matches on the floor, it's not like that!' Anyway... And my GP, I vaguely told him once and he really didn't get it. He frowned a bit, then he changed the subject straight away. It's like it's not interesting to him. It was like I said, 'Hey, I adopted a cat recently.'

Jodie, from England, tells us about the first time she told her GP she was Autistic:

> 66 I took myself to the GP (after months of psyching myself up, of course) to be told by a GP that I can't be Autistic: 'You're making eye contact!' Oh, for god's sake. Enough with the eye contact thing, seriously! I actually need eye contact so I can assess people's body language, facial expressions, etc. as it helps me figure out what the bloody hell people are talking about. Anyway, yes, the GP was obviously not up to date with his Autie knowledge. 99

Joanne from Great Britain has noticed that since getting her diagnosis, medical professionals have started telling her less, writing things in discharge letters that they didn't even discuss together. Eva from Denmark also said that as soon as somebody knows you are Autistic, they start talking to you as if you were a child and they don't take you seriously. The last time Maddie went to see a doctor, which was in the USA in 2020, her mother went with her. She noticed that the doctor did not really listen to her, but only listened to her mum, even though she was 21 years old at that time.

AutieMum in the UK has also noticed how doctors who know she's Autistic will treat her differently:

> 66 I find that any doctor who knows I'm Autistic will either speak to the person who's with me as if I'm incapable of understanding or they will ignore it and get impatient when I ask questions because I struggle to take in verbal information. The doctors that don't know about my autism treat me pleasantly but then I feel like I have to mask, which means I don't actually take in any of what they're telling me. 99

Wrong diagnosis

Many participants have described how before finding out they were Autistic, they had been labelled by many different diagnoses, simply because the medical professionals did not recognize the Autistic traits. In addition to the person being fed false information about themselves, it has huge repercussions on how medical professionals will consider them and treat them. For instance, Amélie from Switzerland was initially diagnosed with borderline personality disorder (BPD) for 15–20 years. She explains that despite having a new, accurate diagnosis (autism), the BPD label is still stuck to her. She says: 'Because of the BPD, I'm seen as a crazy woman with psychosomatic issues, a hysteric, etc. I have no valuable medical care and it is even harmful.'

Beth in the UK was also misdiagnosed with BPD:

> ❝ I was misdiagnosed at 29 with borderline personality disorder and put on very strong antipsychotic drugs after I had a 'breakdown'. Now, in hindsight, it was a meltdown that they tried to medicate. The health professionals treated me at arm's length, saying things like 'Don't be dramatic' and 'No, we're not reviewing the diagnosis because it's right'. In December 2021, I was finally diagnosed as Autistic with ADHD and the health service still refused to acknowledge they were wrong. Only in February 2022 did they take BPD off my medical records. ❞

Lorraine, from England and South Africa, started seeking help at the age of 25 and was eventually diagnosed at the age of 46. In the intervening years, she was misdiagnosed with depression and with bipolar II. She explains: 'I was given an array of anti-depressants and mood stabilizers – all to no avail and even with them making me feel worse, as evidenced by three unsuccessful suicide attempts.'

S., from Morocco and Switzerland, feels that all her diagnoses (PTSD, ADHD, OCD, panic disorder, social anxiety, insomnia and depression) are mistaken and could be summed up as her being Autistic and struggling with a neurotypical world.

Maddie, who is now 23 years old, finally got her diagnosis a year ago, in the USA. She recalls: 'Before being diagnosed with autism, I was diagnosed with severe clinical depression, generalized anxiety disorder, social anxiety disorder, bipolar I and II, avoidant personality disorder, eating disorder not otherwise specified, substance use disorder (other), opioid use disorder.'

Imagine spending years being told something about yourself that doesn't feel quite right. Imagine the amount of self-doubt, of feeling unheard, of feeling lost and confused. Also, the years of taking medication that may simply not be necessary or adapted to your needs. Of course, there can be human errors, which means, sadly, there will probably always be a small percentage of wrong diagnoses. However, what was noticeable in our participants' stories was that this is a recurring theme for Autistic stories.

Marie-Laure also finds this in session, where a lot of the Autistic patients she sees have been previously labelled 'chronically depressed' or suffering from 'generalized anxiety', bipolar, hypersensitive, etc. by other therapists or doctors they have previously met, without the word 'autism' having once been mentioned to them. Or she sees patients being sent in by their doctors to get tested for ADHD or giftedness without once having been told about autism. It leaves people lost for years (often even lifetimes), being deprived of words and communities that could help them understand themselves and make sense of their lives.

Being taken seriously

It is shocking that this section of the book needs to exist. It is sad that so many of our participants have shared countless stories of how doctors fail to take them seriously or speak to them respectfully once they know they're Autistic. But there were so many testimonials around that recurring theme that we simply had to bring attention to it.

Anissa from New Zealand tells us about the long-lasting impact of not having been believed:

> 66 I experienced years of people not believing me when I said my ears hurt, disbelieving that I had a stomach or headache again or putting it down to 'a nervous disposition' or an imagined physical sensation to get out of various events or things I was 'too shy' or 'too sensitive' for. After years of hiding who I was and confusion as to why I would spend days in darkened rooms and being gaslit about my lived experience, post late-in-life diagnosis I still find myself second guessing how I feel. 99

When WolfRahm happens to get a doctor that s(he) finds really good, s(he) tends to stick to that doctor and only wants to be seen by that doctor:

> 66 I'm socially anxious, so having to interact with a doctor, whom I don't interact with often anyway, is stressful, even if it's a doctor that I find to be good and choose to be seen by, and when it's someone new, or someone I have been seen by in the past and haven't found good, it's even more stressful. I'm always worried that my problem won't be taken seriously or that I won't get it adequately addressed. It happened quite a few times. This is the reason why when I get to have a good experience with some doctor, I then cling to that doctor. 99

Karol from England and Czech Republic started by saying that most doctors are very nice and make jokes, which makes her feel more at ease. But sometimes she feels they don't take her seriously:

> 66 It's really difficult for me to assert myself and I just tend to listen to them being dismissive about my issue and just leave it, I guess. Almost two years ago, I tried to end my life and they thought I was doing it for attention and didn't really listen to me when I said I don't think I can keep myself safe. Nine days later, I made another attempt on my life but I didn't tell anyone about that. I wasn't doing it for attention, so why would I go and get help? Now, I'm really scared about getting help for any injury related to my mental health because I'm scared I'll be judged and they'll think it's because of me wanting attention. 99

Joanne from Great Britain has had many interactions with the medical profession:

> 66 The main thing I remember was a feeling that I wasn't believed. I found it difficult to explain how I felt. I often laughed when I was in a lot of pain and my mum often said she knew it was serious if I cried with laughter. I learned to hide my pain. I was often told the pain I felt wasn't possible, symptoms were brushed off and

ignored. I tried to ignore it, thinking it was all in my head. It wasn't until I was 30 that I finally found out the cause of a lifetime of pain and hidden symptoms. I was diagnosed with hypermobile Ehlers-Danlos syndrome (hEDS) and the diagnoses kept coming: fibromyalgia, IBS, postural tachycardia syndrome (PoTS). Everything I had been told was in my head or not possible suddenly was there in black and white. **"**

Bringing up topics in therapy

In psychotherapy sessions, Marie-Laure has noticed that some of her Autistic patients can struggle with bringing up topics. Sometimes when she has asked at the end of the meeting 'Is there anything you'd like to add before we end the session?', she's been surprised to hear the person has had an entire topic in mind that they hadn't mentioned. We therefore included a question about that in the questionnaire we shared with our participants and realized that a lot of people truly struggle with bringing up a specific topic in therapy sessions.

When asked whether she found it difficult to do so, Michele said:

" God, what a relief that you are asking this because I did not have the words to identify it. *Yes.* If I don't go in with a piece of paper or a written list, I get extremely upset that all my boxes were not checked during the session. **"**

Eva also struggles with this and explains why that is:

" I know I don't want to be rude and I would have to change the subject from what she [the therapist] is saying or what is being said and it doesn't feel natural and it feels uncomfortable and rude. It happens quite a lot ... unless I specifically say what I want to talk about or unless I start off straight away with it. A lot of the time I say 'Hi, hello' and 'How are you', 'I am fine', and she will ask the question and I'll answer that and then, it just moves on and it is really hard to just talk about what I would like to talk about. **"**

Kate struggles with being concise enough to get information out and often has to prioritize what she wants to talk about first so that she doesn't get too deep into an alternative topic and run out of time. Nicky would often find she ended up talking about something different, but she thinks that was more driven by her not realizing what was important or troubling her before she went in. Geraldine tends to either go off topic or not know what she wants to talk about.

Explaining how you're feeling to the doctor (pain scale, performing pain, alexithymia, time)

Being understood by a medical professional isn't always an easy task. Several obstacles can get in the way, according to our participants' experience. One that was frequently mentioned was pain scales. Sometimes, doctors ask you to evaluate your pain from 1 (low pain) to 10 (high pain).

Gillian from Ireland struggles with pain scales and tells us about performing pain:

> I have never had good experiences of going to the GP and being taken seriously. I now know it's because I have things like alexithymia, so I couldn't describe properly what I was experiencing. And pain scales made no sense to me. I was like, 'Well, what's your baseline? What's zero? I don't know what zero is! I don't know what eight is!' I thought, 'It would not have been a ten, ten would have been like death, so it can't be a ten...'
> I remember when I was pregnant and the midwife said, 'That was a contraction,' and I said, 'Oh, really, was it?' and she was like, 'It was a really big contraction!' I was like, 'Alright,' and she just couldn't get over it because I was like, 'Oh, that's fine.' I felt it, but I was just like 'that's manageable'. I wasn't performing pain. I wasn't performing pain like they expect you to perform pain. If I went in and said something was really painful, I didn't look like I was in pain. I don't know what I'm supposed to do – like, what is the neurotypical response?
> Now, I've come up with a pain scale where I consider 'number two means this' and I go into my doctor's office and tell them, 'I'm gonna tell you using this because this makes sense to my brain.

Me just telling you a number two or three makes no sense.' I get migraines and I was trying to describe my migraines and I just couldn't be taken seriously until I said, 'This is where I am! Eight or nine is where my migraines are.' And they were like, 'Oh, god, that's terrible!' Up until that point they thought I was just getting bad headaches because I couldn't describe it in the way they expected it. Also, with the ADHD, if it's not happening to me now, I have no idea, I can't describe it because it's in the past and I live very much in the present. **„**

Eva from Denmark and England also suffered from a doctor not understanding how much pain she was in:

„ I am being investigated for rheumatism or arthritis or fibro-myalgia. I was set a medical appointment and he was doing pain checks on me and he thought I wasn't in particular pain and he wrote in his notes, 'Not in as much pain as most people.' But I am in pain! I was induced with my third child with no pain relief. I had piercings (for migraines), I just closed my eyes and breathed through it. I didn't make a noise. And I said something to my daughter afterwards about the pain and she said, 'I didn't know you were in pain.' And of course it hurt, they made holes in my body so of course it hurt, but I didn't say it. So, I said to my husband, 'How did that doctor know whether or not I was in pain?' My husband said, 'The doctor was probably looking at you and looking for signs, like you making noises. Also, you didn't say you were hurting.' And I said, 'Well, the doctor didn't ask me.' I think I said 'that hurts, that hurts', but I don't think he understood. I think he didn't understand that the way I express pain was different from other people. I don't go 'Ow! Ow!' because it feels weird. So, what, was I going to pretend 'Iih! Ahh! Uhh!'? How could I do that? So, I just keep a straight face …

Also, I think I have a higher threshold for pain than other people. I ran a half-marathon on a broken leg. But when I went to ask the doctor to check because it hurt and I said I think it is broken, they didn't believe me because they didn't think I could walk on it. And I ran on it but I still think it was broken and they didn't believe me and sent me away and I had to go through a whole hoop of things to actually be seen and have a CT scan for them to find out that it was broken. It was like, you know, I could have told you it hurt, it just didn't hurt that much. Then again, I think that Autistic people can have a different experience of pain than other people. So, I think that most professionals don't know this and they need to check with their patients how they perceive pain. If you have an Autistic person coming saying they are in pain, they need to check when they say from 1 to 10, what's your 10, what's your 1? And it is the same if they say, 'Is it a dull pain or a sharp pain?' and I say I don't understand that question. What do you mean by a dull pain or a sharp pain? It's pain ... And I would just say sharp because they refuse to move on until you give them an answer. I am not really sure what is meant, a pain is a pain, what the hell is sharp or dull?

One important factor to take into consideration is alexithymia, which refers to the difficulty of identifying and describing emotions and feelings. Katharina from Austria explains how it makes it harder to be understood:

> Many of us are alexithymic (having a hard time assigning words to emotions, which can also cause meltdowns). Contrary to common belief, I am sure that Autistics do feel emotion very deeply but expressing them in a 'neurotypical' way is the hard part. It is often so hard that it comes with a time delay and the preference is to deal with these feelings alone. However, the typical therapy approach is to talk about 'How do you feel now?' and 'What emotion do you want to move to?', thinking that this move from one emotional state to the other will bring an improvement of the mood. But if you can't name your emotions in generally understandable terms, how are you supposed to move from one to another? Supposedly, there are therapists out there that do have the skills to adjust their language and therapies to instead of working with emotions, explain the various situations that we struggle with through cause and effect, connections and logical pathways. This is a concept that I could completely work with

because I always look for logical explanations for everything. So, while we have come a long way already on some people understanding that eye contact is not needed or that sensory overload is real and painful, we still need to find ways of dealing with these emotional processing differences. **"**

Another important factor to take into consideration is the time issue. Lauren from England describes feeling things either very intensely or not at all. Therefore, when in session, chances are she feels ok and can't remember what may have caused a meltdown the night before. So, she can go to a session knowing she has so much to talk about, but can never address it because she's not 'in the moment'.

Joanne, from Great Britain, also expresses her difficulty coming from being very focused on the 'now':

" If I am feeling ok, I can't remember how I felt when I didn't feel ok. I couldn't even really put a time scale on things and say when I felt different. Time seems very hard for me to process. Days can feel like months and months like days. Hours can pass in a heartbeat or drag on for an eternity. I remember things vividly from many years ago like they happened yesterday and yet not remember what I did yesterday. This is a really important thing which I feel the medical profession needs to think about when treating Autistic patients. **"**

9

Special interests

Joe James' experience

My special interests define me as a person. They are as integral to me as breathing is to living. Without them my life would be very boring and I would really struggle to keep myself happy and my depression at bay. You may consider many of them to be hobbies and you would be right, but the difference is that I obsess over them and tend to hyper-focus completely on one at a time and become so engrossed I often get lost in them. This can be incredibly annoying to the people around me and may even affect my work. This book is a good example, as I've really struggled to keep focus on it ever since I got back into fitness after a back injury, which also became a specialist interest while I healed from it. In fact, it's because my injury became my main focus that I was able to heal so quickly, with no thanks to the professionals I must add. (Many of my special interests come and go with the wind, which is great because it makes me a more interesting person.)

One of the most notable special interests I've had, and still have but to a more subdued degree, is photography. When I first started taking photographs, I would take thousands at a time and practise every time I went out. I am completely self-taught and picked up the skills to create a professional-looking image very quickly. This is because I took photos at every opportunity and it even ended up in arguments with my loved ones because they got so annoyed at my obsessive behaviour. Now I'm a renowned photographer they realize how ridiculous they had been (joking, they still blame me for ruining many family days out). The point is that my ability to delve into a hobby means I can become an expert, or as near to it as possible, far quicker than most people, which to me is definitely an ability that can become disabling at times.

My other notable special interest is neurodivergence (autism, ADHD, dyslexia and many other neurological differences). I have studied and researched these differences ever since I found out that I am

Neurodivergent and have been an advocate for positivity and change for over four years at the time of publishing. I have become a specialist in this subject and my opinion is valued by many professionals and the community I represent. I'm even able to write a book about autism alongside my co-author and that's not something most specialists can say. I know that special interests are what we are evolved to do. Autism can literally be defined by this one thing that we all do. It is what links us all: not our inabilities, but this wonderful, world-altering, game-changing, incredible part of neurological difference.

How does the world treat these abilities? It takes a big fat dump on them. We are looked at as freaks, abnormalities that don't conform to social expectations, learning disabled because we struggle to focus on things that don't interest us. Over and over again we are expected to reach neurotypical standards rather than society, especially education, adapting to suit us.

We tree learn, neurotypicals forest learn. So, if a neurotypical sees a large group of trees, they assume it is a forest, then move on with their day. If an Autistic person sees the same large group of trees, they will spend months gathering as much information as they possibly can, counting trees, discovering what animals live there, how the different seasons effect the environment and so on. The Autistic person will then conclude that it is a forest, it will just take them much longer. The advantage of this different way of learning is that the detail in which we have learned is far more vast. The disadvantage is that we aren't given the time we need to learn and are forced to learn things we are not interested in. We can't change the way we learn, so it is up to the education system and any other training to adapt to us.

When we find our passion, whether that is rocks, animals, postcodes, toys, sport, art, photography, the universe, dinosaurs, video games, science, invention, innovation ..., we flourish. It's magical, and I wish more than anything that neurotypicals could understand this.

History teaches us so much about how Neurodivergent people's special interests have shaped the world we live in today. Einstein, Darwin, Tesla, Madame Curie, Newton, Elon Musk, Edison, Andy Warhol, Sir Anthony Hopkins and millions more Autistic people are responsible for advancing our species. Yet we are treated as though we are broken, less than human, like we need changing, moulding to conform to social norms. It is one of the greatest injustices of human kind, to mistreat those who do not match the majority, those who stand out, those who go against the grain. We have suffered and continue to suffer persecution on a global scale, despite having committed no crime, other than to think outside the box.

I have many special interests, other Autistics may have only a few, some have only one which will dominate their life and make them absolute experts in that subject. But because the education systems around the world don't often suit us, we never get the chance to reach our potential in that subject. Instead, these amazing Autistics are seen as oddities and mocked for their 'obsessive' interest. In my opinion, an Autistic person with a special interest can often match or surpass the expertise of someone with a degree in that subject. If you don't believe me, then I challenge any autism 'expert' with a degree to a debate and we shall see who knows more.

If we want to make this world more inclusive then we must encourage these special interests from a young age. At the very least the child's mental health will be better, and for many of us that is the biggest issue we face as adults.

Participants' experiences

What are our special interests?

There is a bit of a stigma around special interests, where people often think it means a person exclusively loves trains and physics. While some people do love trains and physics, a special interest can actually be quite anything. As a therapist, Marie-Laure sometimes meets people who feel they don't really have a special interest. In many cases, those people simply did not realize that their strong interest in their spouse, their child, societal topics or other people (knowing how others feel and function, understanding others) actually counts as a special interest.

Here is a list of just some of the very, very many special interests our participants have shared:

> " Learning, my child, babies, the environment, history, arts and crafts, medical field, human relationships, ancient Egypt, books, board games, photography, collections (sneakers, stamps, etc.),

politics, serial killers, bird watching, sci-fi, firearms, animals, music, autism and neurodivergence, society, reading tarot, boats, cranes, dance, hair and makeup, clothes styling and designing, science, law, economics, cars, celebrity or real-life crush, feminism, evolution, singing, nature, *Star Wars*, escape rooms, Legos, family history, etc. 🟥

Hélène made a very interesting comment regarding terminology, saying 'special interests' might actually be described more accurately with the term 'intense interests':

🟦 I have several intense interests or preoccupations. I prefer to call them 'intense interests' than 'special interests' because they are not as specific as often described, but they are intense and repetitive. 🟥

Jess also made an interesting comment regarding the distinction between special interest and hyper-fixations:

🟦 I distinguish between special interest and hyper-fixations. I hyper-fixate on things regularly and will obsessively do them (reading a book, playing a game, researching a topic) for a week or so, then lose interest. My special interest is always fascinating to me and I constantly engage with it. 🟥

> Quite a few people have described having some major special interests – these will be the passions they've had for quite some time (years, often), as well as smaller interests that they will hyper-fixate on for a short while (a few days or weeks usually) until they get bored with them and move on to a different one.

How much space do they take up in conversations?

There has been quite a lot of diversity in the answers we've received from our participants. Some people have said that it is incredibly difficult for them to talk about a different topic, while many have said that they're fine talking about a subject they're not passionate about.

However, most people have said they really dislike small talk and need to find the topic somewhat interesting to remain engaged in the discussion.

For instance, Charlotte often brings up certain interests in conversations because she has the most to say about them, though she can talk about other things. She also finds some other topics interesting and can enjoy learning a little about them, although they won't be a strong focus for her.

Nia-Eloise doesn't find it boring talking about other things and really enjoys learning about people and their interests. But she also enjoys talking about her interests, as she knows a lot about them and enjoys them, so she wants to share her knowledge and joy with others.

Kevin used to always find himself driving the conversation towards his special interests, until he realized it annoyed people, so now he overcompensates and often won't share how deeply he is interested in something until people really press him about it.

Linda loves to talk about her interest but is cautious not to 'info dump' too heavily if she senses the other person doesn't find it interesting at all. She adds: 'But if I really get going, it can be difficult to stop!' When others are speaking, she goes all in and engages 100 per cent in whatever subject they are talking about, regardless of whether she finds the subject interesting or not, to keep focus and create an interest, as well as to show respect for the person speaking. She really hates small talk and needs to feel genuine engagement in each conversation or she will zone out.

AutieMum struggles to listen to other people talk about their interests and personal lives. She says, 'As much as I may love that person, I really couldn't care less. I try to care, believe me, but I just don't. I can feign interest for about five minutes and then I end up changing the subject or walking away ... oops!' Dear AutieMum, on behalf of all the people who have found themselves stuck in an endless and tedious conversation: we hear you!

Richard's wife has told him that he will hijack a conversation and talk about what he wants. He says, 'I was not even aware of it!' He finds small talk hell and gets great pleasure in talking about what he's actually interested in.

M. has noticed that 'people' is a lifelong special interest for her, which makes her a good listener. That can be quite convenient when it comes to making conversation!

Hélène doesn't necessarily bring up her favourite topics, but she feels this wonderful excitement one can experience when we finally get to talk about our special interests:

> ** I don't particularly try to bring up my favourite subjects (I'm not very good at talking about them, I prefer to do it alone), but if one of my intense subjects is brought up, I'll have a hard time channelling myself: I will talk a lot, bring up the subject when it stops, etc. I'm not interested in subjects that are not part of my sensibilities, I find it hard to develop a conversation about them. **

How much space do they take up in our lives?

Making life decisions around our special interests – studies, jobs – can be a bit of a gamble. For some people, it will lead to a wonderful sense of fulfilment, doing something they are passionate about, for others, it can be quite difficult. S., by studying her special interest, has managed to find an environment in which her amazing passion and knowledge of the field are appreciated – which isn't always easy:

> ** My special interests help me a lot with my university life. I chose to study English Literature, which is basically two of my special interests combined, which makes my performance outstanding. Outside of that, people usually just frown and ask me to shut up or simply say they are not interested and that I bore them to death. That makes me sad. **

Noah has tried to study one of his special interests, but unfortunately the interest didn't last through the studies and it became the least motivating activity he has ever had to do.

Emily has tried to make one of her special interests a job, which has been financially complicated:

> ** For years, I've struggled to make ends meet doing my special interest as a job and doing too many favours or not charging

enough because I liked the project. Economically, making my special interest my job has been catastrophic. I'm hoping I can be a really great lawyer, then I can be useful to people, scratch my social justice itches *and* get paid a sensible wage. **"**

Faith explains how her special interests can become an important part of her life:

" There is one topic that is my favourite part of being Autistic: it is my special interests. I love my special interests. Over the years, they have evolved quite often and quite drastically. It is never something small, it is always something big. So, for a while, when I was little, it was like little pet shops, starting off small. And then, it was like a little puppy; that's a big jump. So, we got the puppy. I get stuck on it and I can't help it, I just keep talking about it. Then, my special interest was a Jeep; I now have a Jeep. I've had two dog special interests; I got a dog both times. And now, my special interest is Nike Jordans, the shoes. I know all the names of all of them, I know the colours, I know what size I am in men's, women's and youth, I know what websites to go on if I want a cheaper pair. It is stressing me out right now because my dad told me: 'For your graduation gift, I am getting you Jordans' and I was ecstatic about it and I found this pair that I wanted but they are over $200, so I said, 'I will pay the difference.' But I miscalculated how much money I have and I was $20 short and I was supposed to have these shoes about a week ago and it is stressing me out and I think about it every day. 'I could have my shoes right now', that is what I think. I get stuck on it and I don't stop talking about it until I get them and I will get upset if I don't receive the object and I am not meaning to get upset in a kind of selfish, bratty, spoiled way – I am genuinely upset because I am stuck on this item and I can't have it. And it stresses me out because I don't know what to do. It is like I need it, I really need this right now. If I get it, it is almost like nothing else can ruin my day because I have received something within my special interest. **"**

Melanie has many special interests but little time in which to do them. She often feels guilty about indulging her special interests as she's a busy mum and feels as though all of her time should be centred around her children. She is aware that this can lead to burnout, so she's working on it.

Kevin has found a wonderful way of incorporating his special interests into his daily life:

> **"** While my special interests used to change sometimes, they have remained relatively static as I age, largely because they are heavily integrated into my life. I'm part of a Discord server that watches *The Price Is Right* together every day. It's great to have that hour of community time together with other people in the middle of my day. Likewise, I have seen the band Umphrey's McGee 36 times. I am active on a message board and I use shows to connect with people in person. I find connecting with people online through shared interests and then meeting with them in person afterwards to be much easier than beginning connections in person.
>
> I try never to let 'online' things affect 'real-life' things when I can though. If I have an online game night and a gathering of church friends scheduled at the same time, for example, I will always choose the church friends. I've gone through too much of life where I didn't have any in-person connection that I never take it for granted when it comes up. Meanwhile, I've been online and active in community groups since 2000 and know that is something that will never be hard for me to find.
>
> It absolutely helps my mental health to do my special interests. For two examples, I eat lunch and stop working completely at 11 am every day to watch 'The Price Is Right' and it definitely is a nice break that really helps me dive in and focus in the afternoon. Likewise, I listen to music for an hour before bed every night just to decompress and end the day doing something I enjoy as well. **"**

When we see how essential those special interests are to our mental health, we realize how important it becomes that we make time for them. When possible, it can also be nice to build a community around that special interest – it can help to find people around us who are interested in our passions, so we can feel that wonderful excitement of talking about our favourite subject in the world. If there is an Autistic person in your life, make sure you maintain a positive way of referring to that person's passion – it may not be *your* favourite subject in the world, but they should still be allowed to see how amazing it is to have a passion.

The importance of our special interests

Many participants have described that it is essentially vital for them to find and dedicate time to their special interests. It helps them with their mental health (several people reported it making them feel less depressed, less anxious, as well as improving their self-esteem and self-confidence). Overall, it just brings a sense of joy and excitement that can be felt with such delightful enthusiasm. Having the ability to feel such intense passion truly is one of the perks of being Autistic.

Danielle describes herself as minimally speaking. She explains what that means:

> I can verbally communicate concrete and simple answers, but not for my deep thoughts and feelings. I am much more expressive and communicate best through typing. Typing is the method I use for in-depth conversations. Sometimes I find it impossible to speak out loud. I feel scared and frustrated in those moments. During those times, access to my keyboard with someone who is comfortable with it helps, as well as written choices. Sometimes I just need some time to relax. Finding a good way to communicate needs to be the main focus for adults when we are young.

However, the fact that she's minimally speaking doesn't mean she can't communicate. One of her passions is writing, which she does thanks to a tablet and keyboard:

> One interest and passion of mine is writing my thoughts and hopefully helping others by sharing some of my life experiences. Learning how to type to communicate gave me confidence

to tell my stories, some with videos. I created a YouTube channel that I sometimes post to. Engaging in these interests helps me organize my time and body. It often gives me a sense of calm and helps me find my peace. Additionally, engaging in these interests gives me opportunities for success and interaction. With my writing, I can communicate more and reach more people. **"**

Charlotte describes that being involved in doing either research or projects related to her interests is important to her sense of wellbeing. She says she wouldn't feel useful otherwise and adds: 'It's difficult to judge how they impact my "life" because I can't see a life that has any meaning without them.'

Karol describes how her special interests bring a sense of calm in the otherwise chaotic world we live in:

" When I build Lego or do maths it makes me feel calm and focused and I'm in the zone. The chaotic world that we live in kind of stops existing and it's overtaken by a calm and logical world where everything makes sense and it all fits together. The Lego pieces go together so well and so neatly to make something and the maths formulae and the different numbers work so well together and things start getting cancelled out so eventually you get one answer. It's like an anchor for order and logic in the world of chaos and obstacles. **"**

Thomas, who is 14 years old, really enjoys gaming as there is such a wide variety of things to play. He says these affect his social life in a good way as he can connect with others from all over the world.

Fabrizio has notices that it definitely helps him to follow his interests as they distract him and keep his brain occupied when he is alone. They help him not to think about the many concerns or worries he can experience otherwise.

In the words of Emma: 'My special interests keep me sane.' Honestly, that sums it all up, we couldn't have said it any better!

Olympics

One of our participants, Michele, has had an incredible experience regarding one of her special interests – judo. She competed in the Olympics as a teenager. She was kind enough to share her story with us, telling us about her passion for judo and what the Olympic games were like for her as an Autistic person.

She started by telling us about the moment she decided to practise judo intensely:

> 66 I did my first tournament and I have like that dark memory of losing and the pain of the crying. There was a puzzle that my brain was saying, 'I want to figure out this puzzle now. I don't like that feeling of losing.' So ever since that point, I think my brain kind of flipped a switch of trying to figure out the complexities of the sport. I think I enjoyed judo from the start. I enjoyed the mentorship. Judo players are very vulgar, but what comes with that vulgarity is blunt honesty; they are so rough around the edges. So, I think my passion coincided with the puzzle piece, meaning with judo and also the human element of judo. 99

She shares how participating in international competitions has been a goldmine for someone like her who loves to observe people:

> 66 At the Pan-American games, you have a variety of cultures (the Pan-American Union, North America, South America, Central America and the Caribbean). The Olympics is like a United Nations meeting and you have all these different cultures and you kind of sit back and observe how they interact with one another. If anybody likes to study human behaviour, it's like a dreamland. So, I was very inquisitive about how all these teams interacted with each another. Even the famous individuals like some of the icons that were there, to see how they reacted. Let's say if I asked them for a picture or an autograph, I liked to kind of figure out those puzzle pieces. I remember wanting to take a tennis woman's picture and she said 'no' and I wondered, 'Is she being selfish? Is it a good selfish or a bad selfish?' People said she was such a jerk, but I was

wondering if she was trying to focus. But then, why was she at the opening ceremony if she wanted to focus? I remember being very confused. It's a treasure trove of information. **"**

She then goes on to describe how her teammates helped her navigate through the social aspect of the Olympics, and her discovery of how sexualized the athlete's experience can get:

" You realize that there are condoms everywhere! I had one team mate who was a very strong mentor for the majority of my life and I love that lady. I think she kind of grasped that I was a little bit different, a little bit naïve, and she really took fantastic care of me as a teenager. So, she would take me to see the condoms and then she would say, 'Let's go the next day and see how many are gone!', trying to show me what the Olympic culture was. It is very interesting to see all that hard work that leads up to this moment, it was very interesting to observe.

I was too young to be engaging in all of the acts but as long as I was with my team mates, I felt safe. They actually coached me on how to party, like 'don't drink too much', 'drink some water'. They tried to teach me how to be in those environments. Sometimes, players from other countries would trick me into coming into their hotel room, you know, for 'team training', back massage when nobody else was there … They couldn't fill in all the little gaps, but for most the part they would coach me, explaining, 'Ok, if you go to that hotel room and something feels awkward and there is nobody else showing up, he starts turning the lights down, get out of there.' And that saved me a lot. **"**

She then comments on the sensory aspect of this sport at such a high level:

" When I was very young, I had a hard time with processing sensory issues. Post-puberty, I became a lot more sensory seeking; I wanted to learn, to see things, to absorb as much as I could. That is an element of sports that I actually enjoy. When a crowd is loud, so loud that it feels like parting your brain, I shut off and it becomes just a tunnel and it becomes one noise and buzz in the background, but it is not overwhelming. You can be in your own tunnel. But then, if I was at the cafeteria, the noise was hell for me. Whereas if I was at a sporting event, it was background noise, there was no pressure to have any discussion, it was just the pleasure of watching and screaming at the game, you know. **"**

Michele also shares how one of the aspects helping her feel safe in that environment was to be spending time with one of her team mates, whom she felt safest with:

" One of the bigger factors for me was who I was going to bunk with. So, if I was with my emotional support team mate, I was very at ease, mainly anywhere, I was safe and I knew what to expect from her. A lot of the difficulties I had came when I ended up with people I did not know. The team mate that I am speaking of is someone with whom I know what to expect and I know that she is not going to get upset. I know what her routines are and there is a level of confidence. As long as I was with her, I would be ok. **"**

She also shares the type of pre-game routines she had:

" My mom had to do my hair in a specific way, I had specific sounds that I was listening to by repeats. At a certain period, I would just lay down and meditate on what I was supposed to be doing. I would maybe run over some tapes of the person I was fighting. I did lots of stimming with my hands or my feet. In judo, you can pace and pace and pace and people think you are warming up and trying to get into the groove. You can suck your fingers and people think that you are just trying to get your hands ready for the tournament. So, a lot of pacing! Also, you would certainly roll your feet, roll your hands prior to getting on the mat ... everybody does that as an athlete. That is probably the most Autistic trait that athletes have, their pre-game routines. Some athletes wear socks, stinky socks, for three weeks or something and they won't wash their socks. For me, those pre-game routines were there to calm me down. The pre-fighting is very difficult for me. Part of my routine was usually the wrestling. I would probably be on the toilet five to sixteen times prior to fighting my first match. Then, I asked my coach to be left alone, sit in a corner, think about my next match, warm up a little bit more and then free my digestive system. I would have diarrhoea, really bad stomach issues due to stress. **"**

Michele recorded the whole event on her camera, which was very important to her. Here's how that went:

" I had my camera the whole time and I documented everything. Then, at the closing ceremony, someone was running and my camera was knocked off my neck and I was hyper-fixated on that. After the closing ceremony, everybody was like 'Come on, let's go out!' and I sat in my room and I was saying, 'I'm not going anywhere', and I went in there probably crying and hyper-fixating and went back over and over. I thought, 'Maybe I can just go back into the stadium and maybe they've found it. Are they closed now? Do I have time in the morning before we leave?' That was one of the hardest moments. As silly as it sounds, because it was just a camera, but it documented my whole spirits from my own point of view. When I was growing up, and even as a teenager, I loved watching video tapes of myself, not just judo tapes but all those videos of myself. I would go back and watch the tapes and compare them to my brother's tapes to understand why I was crying and he wasn't, trying to compare it from an analytical standpoint. And so, having that video was important to me because I wanted to not only see my memories so I can like re-feel them and relive these moments, feel like I am physically in that moment again, I also wanted to watch the tapes so I could see the jokes people would laugh at or see what kind of things I might have said that were caring, or like evaluate my own self within the pinnacle of my mind as a 17 year old. So, that was a very difficult moment for me, losing that camera. Thinking about it, I still want to cry. Not because I am sad at that point any more, but I can physically feel how I was feeling in that moment. **"**

She also shares how observing others has been an essential component of her masking:

> 66 I have masked most of my life. Between judo and consistently observing and noting the behaviour of others (and observing myself via studying family home videos), I came to a quick conclusion that being goofy will inevitably shield me from the discomfort. I had no idea what it was doing to me because I do not believe I have a real identity. Occasionally, I used to accidentally switch social situations around. For example, in the judo culture, there is a weird pattern of commenting on each other's weight or calling each other chubby. The reason for it is actually flattering because if you are good at judo, people want to keep track of what weight class you will be fighting in. One time, I used that comment on someone who was not judo-related, however. I was still on autopilot from a judo trip. As a result I was kicked out of the birthday party I was at. I tried to explain myself, but it was no use. 99

After the Olympics, she started teaching judo:

> 66 I recently had a judo club and I really don't have good social skills and when it comes to people of my own age or older and it comes to conflicts, it gets very difficult to cope for me. There were always some older judokas that would come to the practices and I was very naïve and I didn't realize they were actually there just to steal people from my class and they were criticizing my teaching methods and it was a hard place for me to be in. So now, I only teach judo individually to disabled people on various levels and I love it. 99

She concludes by saying how essential it is to find your passions and for the people around the person to truly encourage them and show them how wonderful their passion is:

> 66 I think that for people, having something that you are confident in, having something that you are good at, for the neurodiverse mind is one of the most important things. Also, to be validated by

191

others that what you are doing is of value and is working and is functional and is providing something for yourself and for society. I think that everybody's brain works differently for a reason. There are some kids I work with who have some special interests that just blow my mind! It is to me very crucial for their self-esteem. If I didn't have judo, I really don't know what sort of person I would be today. Those passions are important for one's self-esteem. **"**

10

Friendships

Joe James' experience

I think in my life there has been nothing more confusing and challenging than friendships. From my earliest memories I can remember trying desperately to make friends, and even more desperately to keep them. The first friend I had was a boy named Phillip. We were both four years old and lived across the road from each other. There weren't a lot of children on our countryside estate and none that were our age, so it was almost inevitable that we would become friends. We were very close growing up and often spent time at each other's houses, but preferably we would stay at his as he didn't like my mother. As I got older, I made many friends over the years. It seemed I could charm most people over a short period, but it was over time that my mask would drop and the real me would reveal itself. I wasn't like most kids, so they didn't really know how to handle me. I was over the top with energy and often very clingy to a single friend, overwhelming them and pushing them away. I didn't know or understand where the boundaries were and would usually just say what I was thinking, which at times would upset people and get me into trouble. I spent so much time apologizing for my actions, it made me think I couldn't do anything right. On top of that I would also be very trusting of people who were nice to me, hoping they would be my friend. Those people hurt me the most because many of them were just using me or teasing me and I didn't find out until it was too late and I had already told them secrets and inner thoughts. I was so trusting and they turned against me, either to protect themselves or simply because they were nasty.

Over time, I became dubious about anyone wanting to be my friend, but no matter how many times I got hurt, I kept going back and trying. I was determined to find the perfect friend, but it never happened until I met my wife.

As an adult I still longed for acceptance, finding friendships and getting hurt, over and over again, like a boxer who kept getting knocked out but kept returning to the ring. I did have good friends, but we would fight and not speak, then make up, then repeat the process. It could be very toxic for both parties and my mental health suffered every time. I wanted to give up more often than I can count, but there was something inside me that truly believed I could find a friend who wasn't Sylvia, who truly understood me. My nephew Jake was like a younger brother to me and we were very close, but I was more of a father figure to him, like my older brother had been to me. We are still very close, but even we fell out and had many issues. My search for this perfect friend was a thorn in my side and it was holding me back from letting myself get too close to people. I would look for flaws so I had an excuse ready for when they inevitably hurt me and I could tell myself I didn't care. But those flaws would be something I would hyper-focus on and then try to change even if the friend didn't want my help or didn't feel like that flaw was a flaw.

After I discovered I'm Autistic, I decided that perhaps I would find a friend who understood me by being friends with another Autistic person. I didn't realize my wife was Neurodivergent, so it hadn't occurred to me that I had already found a Neurodivergent friend. I went to a local meeting for Autistic adults but it was a monumental failure. I didn't fit in there either, as most of them were not interested in the things I liked and they irritated me because my expectations had been unrealistic. I left with such an empty feeling inside me, truly believing that that had been my last chance at finding someone. I didn't feel like I belonged anywhere. The world didn't seem to accept me for who I was, and these Autistic adults seemed so sheltered and mollycoddled, they just frustrated me. I felt like I was part of both worlds but couldn't fit into either. I even started doubting my own diagnosis, thinking how can I be Autistic if these people were also Autistic? No one had explained autism properly and to this day no one has still.

I stopped searching then and just concentrated on my family and being the best dad I could be. In 2018 I met Sam. Sam was diagnosed ADHD and we hit it off immediately. Our kids were best friends and still are and they were convinced the two of us would get on. Sam and I ended up doing so much together and he was a huge reason I became an advocate and shared my photography. He and his wife really encouraged me in those early months and even helped me get through my depression. After posting on Facebook and becoming more known in my local area, many other Neurodivergent photographers reached out to me and wanted to become friends. I met so many new people and a handful of them became friends. Not all those friendships have lasted, Covid put a real strain on so many people, but I never actually fell out with any of them, we just drifted apart.

One friend I met, though, would give me everything I had dreamed of and became a brother to me in an incredibly short period of time. Richard and I met and became friends over Facebook and got to know each other over Messenger. It took a while before either of us felt trusting enough to meet, but when we did, we knew we had found the missing piece we had both been searching for all our lives. Richard had experienced very similar disappointment when it came to friendships and our love of photography bonded us, but our shared neurodivergence solidified that bond. It wasn't long before we had organized a photography road trip to Cornwall and were driving off towards sunsets for a week. It was a proper bromance and we have never once looked back. I now have many really close friends and am even finding it difficult to find time for all of them. All my new friends are late-discovered Neurodivergent, so it wasn't that I couldn't get on with other NDs, it was just that I didn't get on with *that* group of NDs, probably because unlike me they had been brought up Autistic, not neurotypical, and didn't have to find their tribe later on in life. It is most often our life experiences that bring us together, and many of us have very similar experiences, not because we are Autistic, but because of how undiagnosed and even diagnosed Autistic people are treated.

Friendships are always hard, no matter what your neurotype is. I think the key is patience from all parties and accepting that some differences may not always be negative. If you are Neurodivergent or suspect you are, try to find people who share your passions, your special interests and your unique way of experiencing the world around you. We can all get along, but it takes both neurotypes to put in the effort.

Participants' experiences

What's friendship like in practice?

The experiences regarding friendships vary a lot from one person to another. Some people do not really have any friends, while others have quite a lot of them. Uh, interesting, it's almost like Autistic people aren't all exactly the same and that a stereotype does not actually represent accurately the diversity within diversity (to all our sarcasm-impaired friends, that was sarcasm!).

Sarah shares how difficult it can be to make friends when you feel so different from others:

> ❝ I have always felt different from an early age. It's never been easy feeling connected to life or to people. I always found it difficult, or that it took a lot of effort to fit in and be like others. Small talk is difficult, my mind often goes blank. I mean, I can do it to a certain extent, I've learned over the years what to say and how to say it, but it doesn't come naturally. Don't get me wrong, I do have a small selective handful of friends and family I love dearly. I've lost many over the years too, either through conflict or lack of maintenance. Groups can be tricky too, I don't necessarily think because of anxiety but actually because the taking turns in conversation thing is difficult. I have difficulty with concentration, catching what's being said, losing track, hearing the wrong words and more. Of course, I can in certain situations, maybe where I feel more comfortable, but it can be tough. I've discovered that I love to talk about certain things I'm passionate about, but this is a little overbearing for some. I'm learning also that my problems aren't necessarily due to me being Autistic but from trauma in social situations over the years of being 'weird', a bit 'off', being 'othered, rejected' and saying things that just aren't what is the 'norm', whatever that is.
>
> At times, life has been hard because I just felt I couldn't connect. I mean, sometimes I did (masking), but it's always been difficult to build relationships, friendships. In my 20s and 30s, I would often think, 'Gosh, if I could just talk to people or connect with others just like everyone else does, I would never be depressed again. What do

those who can connect with others have to be depressed about?'
Sometimes I was obsessed about finding an answer to why I was
different, looking to how I could fix this. This was pre-internet days.
There were times when I thought I'd cracked the code, at last.
'Got it! U-bloody-reka!! I can do it, I am like everyone else, there's
nothing wrong with me! Is there?'. I often felt, and still do now,
overwhelmed and drained during socializing. Close family and a few
friends are the exception, although maybe that's because I can be
more myself with them. I now know it's exhaustion from masking.
One of my assessors said I was very good at it – even they found it
difficult to decide as to whether I was Autistic or not. I mean, I had
developed a mask for every occasion, taking on mannerisms, accents,
body language from others I observed, like a chameleon. I know
now, this can be common in Autistic woman.

Hannah says that social media often leaves her feeling left out. She
adds: 'Just because I say I don't want to go somewhere, it would still be
nice to be asked, to have a feeling that you would like me there.'

Kristel finds getting close to people difficult as she feels so different
from others and she also finds it difficult to trust people. Friendship can
bring a lot of heartache – she seems to be more caring than others and
it's not always reciprocated. She enjoys going out sometimes and can
have a good time but at other times feels very lonely in a crowd.

Until two years ago, Mickey had just a couple of close friends, but
they have made several close friendships recently. They have a very
healthy rule, where they almost exclusively spend time with people
who are soul nourishing instead of draining. That's such an important
criterion when deciding whether you'd like to meet up with a given
person or not, and whether or not you have the energy for that meetup.

Some people are aware of certain preferences that make it more
likely for them to enjoy interacting with their friends. For example,
when Milène hangs out with some friends, it is usually one on one or in
a small group. She prefers the one-on-one interaction since there's less
risk of becoming overwhelmed or overstimulated. Charles finds it easier
to communicate via messaging. Some of those friendships have been
based on playing video games together, others primarily on messaging
apps where shared interests have kept the friendship going. He has one

friendship that is primarily based on sharing memes with each other. Let's be honest: that does sound like the dream!

Sarah usually likes to invite friends over to her house as it's where she is more comfortable, so she tends to do the entertaining by asking them around for dinner, or a coffee, or a drink on a weekend.

Mark describes that he now sees that he has friends, though he did not see it when he was struggling with depression:

> 66 I do have some friends. I felt for a long time when I was depressed that I only had friends who were the partners of my wife's female friends, but I think that feeling was a product of my own insecurities and that isn't fair to them. Now I feel that I do have at least some friends, though I'm still not the guy who arranges anything. I'll go to the pub to meet up and I'll be pleased to be asked, but I think I've suffered so much rejection that for the moment I don't have the confidence to reach out. I had a few occasions – at school and again at university – where I suggested a meetup and everyone agreed and then a specific plan was subsequently made and no one turned up. 🙶

Faith has some wonderful friends that she very much appreciates. She tells us what made her decide to tell her friends about her autism diagnosis:

> 66 At first, for a few months, I kept my diagnosis to myself because I was still trying to figure it out myself and kind of realize 'Yeah, this is true!', but eventually I slowly started to tell my friends because I wanted them to understand for instance that when I say 'no' to hanging out, it is not because I don't want to but just because in that moment, I can't. You know, if I ever come across mean to you guys, I do not mean it in any way, I am just presenting the wrong emotion without knowing that I am. So, I wanted them to get a better understanding of why some of the stuff I do happens and that I can't always control it so that they are not getting mad at me for having an attitude that I don't know I have. That did happen many times. I still struggle with that.
>
> One of my bigger struggles is presenting emotions. So I will say something to my mum where in my head it sounds perfectly fine,

like I am not being mean, but it will come across as I am really mad at you now and I don't mean for it at all because I can't read the tone of voice that I am presenting, so she will be like 'That was mean' and I wasn't meaning to be mean. There have been different times where I said something or I had been very straightforward on accident or said something in a way that sounded rude, like the context of it, when really that is not what I meant and it has upset people, and I am like 'I didn't mean that, it is not how I meant it to come across'. For example, the other day, I was a little frustrated because my friend wanted to come over and I decorated my car for a senior parade and she was like really late and we were already halfway done with my car and I was a little bit frustrated – but not enough to like care about much. And when I called her, I said, 'Are you ever going to show up?' and then she was like 'Hey!' and then I felt really bad because I didn't mean it like that. **"**

Lola confides that she used to suffer from major social anxiety. At school, she never kept a friendship group for more than a couple of months as suddenly she found herself being the annoying one who was considered to be deliberately upsetting people. She adds: 'Top tip to neurotypicals out there: if someone asks what they did wrong, don't respond with 'You know what you did'. I never had a clue what I'd done!'

Making friends can be difficult, it's true. The more we grow, the more mature we get, the better we know ourselves, the more our self-esteem improves, the more likely we are to find out what we need in terms of friendships. We all have different needs when it comes to finding the right balance between needing some alone time and needing to be with others. Sometimes, the social pressure gives us the impression that we should necessarily have many friends whom we see frequently. That is especially the case in our teenage years, where fitting in can sometimes feel like an absolute priority. It is important to make the distinction between what societal pressure is making you feel you should enjoy and what actually works for you. There is no right or wrong in that regard, only contexts that tend to make you feel good about yourself, your day, improve your mood and energy levels, and others that don't. And those will be different for each person and at each moment in time.

Are you an extravert or an introvert? (Spoiler alert: or an ambivert?)

The stereotypical representation of autism is that of a highly introverted person. However, we have found that our participants' responses very much varied in their responses. Some consider themselves to be very introverted, others extraverted and quite a few are ambiverts.

Let's start with our fellow introverts. While not all participants related to being introverted, quite a few of them did. We feel that those voices are extremely helpful because there is a bias in society where people are often encouraged to act more in an extraverted way. As such, being an extravert is neither better nor less than being an introvert. It is just as essential a skill to be expressive and connected to others as knowing how to enjoy your own company and to spend some quality time by yourself. Of course, there is a bias because extraverts tend to be louder so we tend to hear them more frequently and they are therefore overrepresented in public spaces and discussions in general. But being an introvert is just as great as being an extravert – all that matters is that you allow yourself to make choices that are healthy for you.

Fabrizio describes himself as 'an introvert, an extreme introvert'. He likes to be around people who get him, people with whom he can discuss his topics and not be misunderstood: scientists and people with some culture. Sometimes he organizes parties at his place with a maximum of eight people. They are close friends because they are on the same wavelength, speaking about the same subjects, attuned to the same scientific topic, one completing the ideas of the other, working together to publish good scientific works, and beyond that they wish the best for one another.

Christine calls herself a 'hermit', explaining that she prefers to be totally alone. Nia-Eloise says she's definitely an introvert, to the extreme. She adds: 'I could be alone for months and I wouldn't care or be lonely.'

S. is an introvert and a misanthrope. She hates having people around. When she's feeling social – which is every once in a while – she likes to have her close friends around. After a few hours, she will still need a break and to be alone again – except from her safe person, whom she can be around all the time.

AutieMum is a 'mega introvert' and struggles to express herself outwardly. She much prefers staying in alone to going out to meet friends. Sarah also likes being on her own a lot, she is happy in her own company. She finds it quite draining and tiring to be with other people. She hypothesizes: 'Probably because I have to mask?'

Sunny is an introvert and has a small social battery. She spends a lot of time reading and thinking, which recharges her. She prefers quiet environments and will get overstimulated easily in large or noisy groups and with high-energy friends. Some people take little or no energy to be around, depending on how similar their personality is and the ease of communication.

We also had some participants who described themselves as extraverts. Thomas, for instance, says that he has a ton of friends, who are all highly Neurodivergent. While Faith considers herself to be very extraverted, she makes an important distinction between finding it easy to make friends versus wanting to hang out with friends:

> Since I was very little, I have been very verbal, which is part of the reason why I was diagnosed so late, because I talked so much. I never had a hard time making friends but I definitely had a hard time hanging out with friends. I would love being with them at school, but it was not very often that I wanted to be with them outside of school. Now, since high school, I am quite opposite: I love being with them. For me, making friends was not hard; I have always been very extraverted, so going out to meet people was very easy. I think the fact that I now know why I had such a hard time hanging out with people, that makes it easier to hanging out with people because I know my limits.

Many people will say that they can either be an introvert or an extravert, depending on the context. We call this being an ambivert. This means that while we can be extremely quiet in a certain context, we can also be very chatty in a different one.

Geraldine can be either an introvert or an extravert depending on situations, people and context. She is a complete extravert when she is dancing, performing salsa burlesque shows and teaching ladies' styling dance classes. She is more of an observer and mute in new situations where she doesn't know people. She then tends to actively listen more and ask questions.

Emma says that she has a small group of very close friends who know her inside out. The majority of those people are also Autistic but two of them are not. To these people, she is extraverted. She also has a group of acquaintances, for example people she works with, whom she likes but isn't closest to. She notices she is far more introverted with them.

Jodie has often been perceived as shy, though that's not exactly an accurate description of her:

> 66 I would say I'm more of an introverted-type person ... the quiet observer type. All my life people have said I seem shy, which I find absolutely hilarious! If I'm not talking to you, it's probably more to do with me not having anything to say to you. I do have my quiet moments, especially if I'm anxious, but once you get to know me, and when I feel comfortable around you, I am probably one of the mouthiest ***** in the room! 99

Naomi has actually made a very similar observation:

> 66 People have always said to me, 'You're shy', but I've never understood that word, it doesn't suit me at all, in fact. Of course, from the outside I can seem shy because I don't talk easily to people, but in my personality, I can't keep things inside, I'm quite external, bubbling. It depends on the people I'm with. With the people who are a bit sensitive, nice, whom I can trust, I'll be able to go out more, to be more open, and depending on the people, depending on the combination of people, I'll often close myself up. I'm hypersensitive to people's dynamics. If there is one person more or less, it changes everything, it changes how I am going to be with these people. It will disrupt the whole balance if one person leaves or arrives. It's really complicated. That's why I like events where people are sitting – I hate parties where people are standing and the dynamics can change very quickly. 99

Isabella is an introvert who can be very extraverted at times. She likes situations of freedom like nature, festivals and alternative people.

Hélène would say that non-Autistic people see her as an introvert, whereas Autistics and people she's closest to see her as an extravert.

Kevin has noticed how even while being an introvert, he can still be chatty in the right circumstances:

> ❝ I would still consider myself an introvert, however not strongly so. I've noticed in the past couple of years that I can often be the chatty one when I'm out in a small group setting and I don't mind that about myself. If you put me in the right group, I can be more extraverted, open and free-spirited. I have to feel comfortable around the people, though. If I'm in a group of mostly new people, I will be quiet, especially at first, every time, and I will need some recovery time to 'decompress' after I get home. ❞

Lauren says that she's probably an introvert who can be very good at appearing to be an extravert. She likes to be quiet sometimes, but in the right group of people, she can be very loud and funny. She adds: 'I really enjoy my own company.'

Sarah considers herself an ambivert. She truly loves her friends and close family and loves to spend time with them, but only for so much time and she needs decompression time to recharge afterwards. In fact, she needs at least two hours of decompression time every day or she will burn out or melt down.

C.A. describes how their way of socializing has changed over time:

> ❝ I was highly extraverted as a child. That changed with the social traumas, especially going into high school with the multiple school changes. I gave up trying because I felt there was no reason anything was ever going to be any different. Now, I just have so many more things worth my time than socializing. While I loved being with people and socializing as a kid, in the school holidays I never went anywhere. I didn't crave wanting to go anywhere or see anybody. I'd stay in my room, read, write, watch cartoons. So, I guess in that sense I was a far more balanced individual prior to this apathy setting in, but at the same time my experience of friendship now is deep and real rather than the shallow caricatures I craved in my teen years. ❞

When Linda decides to go out and socialize, she makes sure that she is prepared: well grounded, having rested and eaten, and then she is very naturally open and sociable and loves to interact with people. When she is in a setting with introverts, she becomes extra extravert!

Charles is primarily an introvert, though he can be extraverted around those he is comfortable with. He likes being around those people, but not for extended periods – having some time to himself, alone and doing nothing but what he wants to do, is near essential to allow himself to 'recharge'. After working a series of shifts in a row, he always strives to set aside his first day off as a 'nothing day', where he does nothing and goes nowhere in order to recover from his shifts. He is perfectly comfortable in my own company – he worked for five years at a site where he was a lone worker, which suited him just fine for the most part.

Jess likes to see her friends every few days, but she prefers to spend evenings alone or with her partner. She considers herself an 'extraverted introvert'. When she is in a social group, she is chatty and funny and the 'life of the party', but she would not like to be in a large social group more than once a week.

Mark would have called himself an extravert a few years ago, but now he is not so sure any more. He has a quick mind and can make a conversation interesting, and he still sometimes feels the need to bolster his self-image by talking too much socially. However, he thinks that when all the masks come off, he is quite introverted in reality. He likes to be by himself. He genuinely enjoys his own company, whether that's quietly creating at home or in a coffee shop reading and people-watching. He is at his most comfortable when he is safely by himself.

Whether you feel that you are more an introvert, an ambivert or an extravert, what matters is that you can make choices based on your actual needs – not on what you perceive to be societal expectations or what others think is best for you. You are your own expert – no one other than you can decide what you need at a given moment. And keep in mind that it's completely normal that your needs can change depending on the context. Allow yourself to decline an invitation if you feel it will not bring you any joy and will be painful instead (maybe because you're feeling overwhelmed that day, or because the plan has changed and no longer suits you, or because you know you need to be alone or at home for a while). Also, when you feel that you long for more contact, try to reach out to people who make you feel safe – people you appreciate and who appreciate you authentically. If you're always waiting for others to invite you, you might unintentionally give people the impression that you do not want to see them that much – leading to them not inviting you that frequently any more.

Are your friends Neurodivergent or neurotypical?

There is a notion that Neurodivergent people tend to find each other – whether it's in friendships or couples. Let's see what our participants have to say about that: myth or reality?

Since Sarah has recognized her neurodivergence, it's become increasingly obvious that absolutely everyone she values in her life is also Neurodivergent – and nearly all of them have recognized it too, often as a result of her being open about her journey. She attributes much of this to communication similarities and the differences that cause problems with neurotypicals. She feels that the people she is comfortable with, and has stuck with, are those with similar communication styles.

Linda often feels another type of connection with Neurodivergent people, as though they are talking and understanding each other on a different level. There is less empty small talk and no strict communication rules – you can be up front and discuss whatever subject in a very opened, focused and intense way without it feeling strange. She feels it is much easier and quicker to get to know someone this way and to bond with each other.

Another Sarah has realized that she seems to be drawn to other Autistic people like a magnet. It is only recently that she has become aware of this. The majority of them don't even know they are Autistic, but she can see it as clear as day now.

Gillian has noticed that the vast majority of people that they are friendly with now either knew they were Neurodivergent before they became friends or discovered they were Neurodivergent as they've been friends. They add: 'So, that whole "We find each other" thing absolutely has proved to be true for me. We just gradually flocked together.'

Thomas has also noticed that his friends are all Neurodivergent and that he's able to detect those 'special' people in a huge crowd, he feels drawn to them – and it often goes both ways.

Jodie describes how she has found acceptance in the friendship she has with an Autistic person:

> **❝** After I left college, I very soon drifted away from people, I found those friendships ... tiresome. I don't think I knew why at the time, I just didn't feel like I really connected with anyone. When I realized I was Autistic, it all made sense. The one close friend I've stayed in touch with is also Autistic and I think that's why we've stayed friends. We just get each other in a way other people don't. People probably find me a bit weird but my Neurodivergent friends are just so accepting. Or they are just as weird as I am! **❞**

Najib also feels closer to Neurodivergent people because he feels that they understand his struggles better than neurotypicals do.

Richard shares that after years of finding it difficult to have close friends, finding out about his neurodiversity has allowed him to build very authentic friendships for the first time in his life:

> **❝** I've never had many friends. Always maybe one as a school kid, a small group in my twenties. Then, one main friend, which switched to another. But they always stopped making an effort and I got the message after trying. Now, knowing I am Neurodivergent and making friends with another Neurodivergent, I have made the best friend I have ever had. Someone who gets me, does not judge apart from in a jokey way. We can take the mickey out of each other's quirks in a way that only has love behind it. It's not stressful, but comfortable and easy. We can be ourselves and not care. Completely unmask! **❞**

Milène's friends are mostly Neurodivergent and she thinks that is partly because they let each other be and don't have the 'basic social expectations' that society tends to have (like weekly drinks somewhere, etc.).

Paul did clarify, however, that just because someone is Autistic doesn't necessarily guarantee a good friendship. He recalls having one Autistic friend who dropped him because they were too demanding and Paul couldn't give them enough time and attention.

S. is only surrounded by neurotypicals, but they are all very understanding and supportive. They help her understand the world and guide her through her fears and issues. They say that she gives them a different view on their problems, a break and simplicity.

Karol's friends are all neurotypical. She used to work with someone on the spectrum but when she left the job, they didn't really know each other well enough to keep in touch. She attributes that to the fact that they were both socially awkward.

C.A. says that they do not have a lot of friendships, but the ones they do have are good ones and most of them are Neurodivergent too. 'It's just so much easier being around people who understand you,' they say. C.A. doesn't have 'acquaintances', meaning that 'you're either everything to me and I am invested in anything you do, or you don't even cross my mind'. They hypothesize that that's why neurotypicals seem to have so many friends: they're not 'friends' per se, just acquaintances that they can exist around comfortably without actually being close to them. That's simply not something C.A. feels they could do.

Melanie has never had any close girl friends. She says she's not the 'sleepover' or the 'wine night' type, it really isn't where she's comfortable. She has always preferred her own company and doesn't like the drama friendships can bring. She feels that it's too complex and she doesn't understand the rules. However, she does have a few newer friends who are struggling with undiagnosed Neurodivergent conditions and anxiety and they feel comfortable with one another. They can chat, stare at each other's chins and talk about a million things all at once. And no one gets annoyed if they don't contact each other for a few weeks.

Emma gets on far better with neurodiverse people as she considers them easier to understand. She finds it hard to get on with or relate to neurotypical women as she can't understand their social rules and they often seem two-faced or have an agenda. With her neurodiverse friends, it is possible not to speak for months and then just go back to chatting like they only talked the day before. It's so easy!

It sounds like there is this tendency for neurodiverse people to be friends with other neurodiverse people – even when both people are unaware of the fact that they are Neurodivergent! Friendships between Neurodivergent people and neurotypical people seem to work well mostly when the Neurodivergent person feels confident, comfortable and safe enough to be authentic, to unmask and to invest themselves in the relationship in a way that is respectful of their own needs.

How frequently do you like to contact your friends?

Some people feel that a close friendship should mean frequent contact. The reality is that for many people, calling each other just to see how we're doing, or meeting up frequently when we do have a lot of other distractions in our life, can be difficult. In therapy, Marie-Laure has heard many Autistic people feel guilty about this, fearing that they're terrible friends because they do not reach out to others as frequently as they expect the norm to be. It is important to respect your own needs in terms of frequency and to find friends who understand and are respectful of what works for you. You can be a wonderful, caring, invested friend even if you only see the person once every few years, just like you can be a wonderful, caring, invested friend if you see the person every day. To many people, the frequency of contact is not necessarily correlated to the importance the friend has in their life.

AutieMum describes how her need to speak to her friends can very much vary in terms of frequency:

66 I'm the friend who will text you a thousand times in 24 hours or not text you for a year. I don't care any less, I just don't have the energy or the inclination to strike up conversation. Most of the people I enjoy spending time with the most are parents of Autistic kids. I find that they accept me for who I am and they don't judge me for being a sucky friend at times. 99

Charles tends to find it difficult maintaining friendships and if he doesn't see someone regularly in real life, they tend to fall out of touch (except for online friendships). This is partly why a lot of his friendships revolve around work – he sees them regularly at work so it's easier to maintain the friendship. Danielle says that keeping friends is hard work, she has to think to text them regularly. She won't do small talk so she has to think of things she can say of interest. Sometimes she forgets to text people when she should. Sometimes she really doesn't feel like meeting friends even when she has made a plan to, but she usually tries and makes the effort anyway and usually ends up enjoying it.

Hélène says she has about five true friends, but feels it is not the same as what she would consider a 'standard friendship'. She describes the interactions to be very spaced out over time – she can sometimes go three to five years without so much as a phone call.

Noah states that he has the most incredible friends. He adds, 'It's strange because I don't really miss my friends, but I appreciate them.'

Sarah explains how the frequency of her contact with her friends tends to vary:

> 66 I tend to go through phases of contact with friends. Sometimes I will speak to just one friend for weeks on end and then that will die off and I don't contact them for months. There's no reason behind it, I just get caught up doing other things or I may have a little project I'm working on with my craft or something and I zone in on that instead and forget everyone else. 99

Milène prefers to have a small group of friends than a large one because she finds it difficult to keep in touch with a lot of people. She simply forgets and time goes by faster than she realizes. The people she is friends with either have the same issue or don't mind when she doesn't speak to them all the time.

Nia-Eloise describes how frequent interactions with friends can be exhausting:

> 66 The only person I feel close to is my mum. I have people I call friends but I'm not emotionally close or attached to them. I could see them once a year and that would be fine by me. I don't like people

who text all the time, I find that so exhausting. Unfortunately, most neurotypical friendships demand that you meet up regularly and text a lot and that's just way too much for me. "

Karol says that since she tends to attach herself to one friend, she sometimes worries she might be too much, so she might just not talk to that friend for a few days, but then she gets worried that she hasn't talked to them in a while and that they'll think she's a bad friend for not talking to them.

It is essential to be clear about the difference between how much you appreciate someone versus how frequently you contact them. There are people we truly appreciate but we simply do not feel the need to contact or see them frequently – and that's ok. Being a true friend does not necessarily have to mean frequent interactions. It is such a wonderful feeling when you get to see a friend you haven't seen in years and then it feels so natural, like no time has passed, where you still have that connection. It can help to inform them that even if you're not the type of person who will reach out to others regularly – this simply doesn't work for you – you very much appreciate them and are enjoying seeing them. Let them know that to you, the frequency of contact is not a correct scale of how much you care about someone.

Fusional friendships

While some people prefer to have many different friends at a given time, many Autistic people have described that their natural inclination would be to have one rather fusional or exclusive friendship. However, quite a few people have been hurt by this friendship mode and have decided to protect themselves from it. Christine says that she been attached to one person in the past but was 'burnt' by that, so now she does not attempt to attach to anyone. Ben also describes that he has over-attached to people in the past and he now avoids it.

AutieMum finds that she tends to attach herself to one person and constantly seek their approval, which normally ends with them getting tired of her or her losing interest and not messaging them. She will stay friends with the person but will no longer be attached to them.

Hélène feels that one relationship is enough for her. When she develops a feeling with someone, it can become 'total', so she tries to watch herself in order to stay within social conventions and not be in a 'too close' dynamic. If she invests herself, it's fully. She thinks she has often driven people away by being too invested, too whole in a relationship, and she has seen many relationships fail in this way. She adds that she already has trouble finding enough space to invest herself in one friendship, so she can't have several at the same time, otherwise she immediately feels overwhelmed with stress and cannot cope.

S. has realized that while she used to attach herself to one person pretty quickly, those were also the people who ended up hurting her the most. They abused her good nature and now, looking back, she can see that those relationships were very toxic. It took her and her current best friend a few years to get really close, as S. was quite wary of people by the time she met this friend. She then says that they've been besties for about seven years now.

Charles feels he can seem clingy at times:

> 66 My tendency is to focus on one particular friend at a time, but I am very aware of how clingy that can make me appear and so I try to be careful to not allow myself to cling too much to them and to limit interactions so I don't appear too eager. It's something I also find I have to stick to when meeting new people on dating apps, as very often being too eager can drive people away. 99

S. tends to get fixated on one person, but feels that luckily her need for alone time gives them a break too.

Emily used to focus on one person quite intensively but is now too busy to overwhelm anyone. With work, children and social life, she doesn't really have the time to bother one person to the point where they get fed up with her. And if there was, it would just mean they're not emotionally healthy enough to set boundaries they could both work with, so she wouldn't be bothered by them shedding her.

Linda, earlier in life, had been 'all in' with one person – very intense and giving her all to that person – which didn't lead to a healthy relationship at all and always ended with the person leaving. When meeting people now, she has a more patient approach and wants them to get to know each other and find out if they are a good match before she engages too much.

Exclusive friendships are not necessarily unhealthy. It's a perfectly valid preference and it's wonderful when you get to have one person who knows you really well and appreciates your authentic self. It is simply riskier because if the person ever loses interest or isn't a healthy or kind person, then the risk of being hurt is quite big. It's important to make sure that the friend you're attaching yourself to is truly well intentioned, meaning that they contribute to you feeling good about yourself, showing that they accept and appreciate you as you are and that the relationship goes both ways: they are supportive and interested in you, just like you are.

11

Couples

Joe James' experience

My wife is my hero. She is the air I breathe, the sun that warms my face and the glue that holds me together. Many wonderful things have been written about one person's love for another but there are not enough words to give justice to the way I feel about Sylvia.

We met not long after I was forced out of my home at the age of 17 and I was living with a family friend, who I didn't really like or understand. Sylvia was from Poland and came to England to learn English and to get experience as a beauty therapist so she could get a better job back in Poland. My grandad was Polish so we had lots of family and acquaintances from Poland, which is how Sylvia found out about the job my birth mother was offering. Sylvia was also employed as a cleaner and taught my young sister Polish; my birth mother liked to get as much as she could from her free labour.

When I first saw Sylvia, I was taken aback by her beauty. She looked like a Baywatch babe and I believed that I had absolutely no chance of ever being with her. She had heard rumours about me from people in Poland – my reputation for being a troublemaker and a weirdo had spread across Europe, apparently. She didn't want anything to do with me and ignored me whenever I returned home to see my sister and dogs (I missed them so much and hated living alone with a stranger, in his filthy house).

One day my birth mother mentioned that Sylvia was homesick and missing her friends. She asked me if I could take her to the local pub and introduce her to my friend so we could all hang out. I reluctantly agreed as I didn't think she liked me, and my instincts were spot on. She didn't want to go but had agreed because she was scared of my birth mother. My friend never turned up as he was ill, so it ended up being just the two of us. We got a few drinks and that helped calm our nerves, and not long after we were joking and laughing, mostly at the expense of my birth mother. In an ironic way, if it wasn't for her, we would not be together, and she loved to remind us of that over the years, almost using it as an excuse to manipulate me.

Over the following months, Sylvia and I became best friends, regularly going drinking and playing pool. She became part of my small friendship group. One day we were all out having fun and Sylvia had drunk a little too much. She didn't want to go back to my birth mother, as she was worried about being judged for being tipsy, so I agreed that she would come back to mine. We all ended up back at the farmhouse and continued to have fun. But Sylvia wasn't well, so I went and looked after her. Out of nowhere she kissed me, I kissed her back, and from that moment my life was on a path to being the happiest I've ever been.

We started dating and we became closer and closer. Neither of us knew where it was heading. To me it was serious, but Sylvia wanted to return to Poland and saw it as just a romance that would end when she left. I knew it was down to me to convince her I was worthy of her, but that was hard as I didn't believe I was. I spent so much time making her feel special, but my darker side was always there, bubbling away, occasionally spilling over. What was amazing about Sylvia, even though she found me difficult a lot of the time, was that she could see the real me and always knew I was just grieving and in pain. I was still damaged by the loss of my older brother and traumatized by the bullying and abuse I had been through. I confided in her and she believed me because she could see how my birth mother treated me and she hated it.

Sylvia's time in England was coming to an end, but Poland hadn't joined the EU yet and I was desperate for her to stay. I knew if she went back, I would likely never see her again, and that wasn't an option I could face. In the few months we had been together I had improved so much. I had a reason to live, to grow, to find my way, and I feared without her I would be lost again. I asked her to marry me in a desperate attempt to convince her how serious I was about her. I had never wanted to get married after seeing how unhappy my parents were, but I knew if I didn't marry her, she would leave. I never expected her to say yes. She missed her family and friends in Poland so much and had planned her future there. She was going to open her own beautician shop in Gdansk and live with her parents until she could afford a flat of her own. But here I was, throwing a huge spanner in the works, and she didn't know what to do. Days later, after much discussion, she agreed to give me a chance. She loved me for sure, but was scared about what a future with me might be like. I got a job and did everything I could to convince her I could grow and be the man she deserved.

A month later Sylvia sat me down and told me she was pregnant. At first, I was terrified: how could I possibly be a dad at such a young age? I knew she wanted children and I had wanted a son, but I was 18 and not anywhere near mature enough to take on that responsibility. But I decided very quickly that I was going to do everything I humanly could to be the best dad I could be and not let Sylvia or my future child down, and that's exactly what I did.

The years were rocky and we had many ups and downs. I won't go into details about parenting as that is another chapter, but suffice to say, it wasn't easy. I grew very quickly as a person and took my responsibilities very seriously. I always provided and gave my family the best life I could possibly give them financially. But I was still very much a broken man and there was no quick fix for that.

Luckily for me, Sylvia is the most patient person I've ever met. She nurtured me and showed me how loving and kind humans can be to each other. She took care of me and made sure I felt loved and appreciated always. I often tried to push her away, thinking she was better off without me, hating myself at times and wanting to leave so they could be truly happy. My self-doubt would often rule many of my decisions and we found it difficult to be romantic as I was so standoffish and she had so much anxiety.

Over time we found a balance and compromise became the cornerstone of our relationship. We both had to pick our moments to bring up certain issues up, and when we did clash it wasn't for long and we would forgive each other very quickly. There was an understanding between us that I couldn't explain, but after my diagnosis it would make sense.

After I discovered I'm Neurodivergent I went on a whole new journey of self-discovery and understanding. I improved so much after finally having answers to so many questions in my life. Sylvia became even more patient with me as I found my feet as an Autistic person and delved into the world of autism, wanting to learn everything I could about how my brain worked. I never saw it as a disability, only something that caused me to act differently, which in turn caused others to treat me cruelly.

Sylvia has always had severe anxiety and my unpredictable behaviour made it worse. She didn't like how I would act in public a lot of the time and would be embarrassed and hide away. It wasn't her fault, her upbringing was more regimented and she cared what strangers would think of her, whereas I didn't care that much. She had many issues with the way she looked, even though to me she was a goddess, but she was also bullied as a child and that had given her many mental health problems that I wasn't aware of.

Sylvia and I are inseparable and spend most of our time together, either having days out or snuggled on the settee watching movies and TV shows. We love playing video games together, even though she's not very good. We love our food but have had lots of issues with our weight, so try to eat as healthily as we can, but often succumb to naughty meals and snacks. But at least we always are there for each other so emotionally we are supported. We love to joke around and tease each other, although sometimes Sylvia takes it too far and touches a nerve. I always forgive her, but she doesn't like admitting she is wrong and is incredibly stubborn.

After I became an autism advocate and researched neurodivergence to an expert level, I noticed many things about Sylvia that made me highly suspicious that she was also Neurodivergent. Her anxiety, her lack of friends outside our relationship, her demand avoidance, her obsession with having the house cleaned and tidied in a certain way, her routine and dislike of that routine being broken, her strange rules that she mentally could not cope with if they were broken, like going under the quilt cover if we napped during the day – she insists we use a blanket and even told me off for using the throw on our bed, saying it 'was for decoration and not for sleeping'. She loves animals more than people, doesn't like parties or gatherings with strangers, hates to touch certain fabrics, is sensitive to light, has super hearing, and doesn't feel temperature like anyone else around her. She is very easily distracted and cannot hide how she feels as it always shows on her face. But the main reason I believed her to be Neurodivergent is that she understood me at a deeper level than just knowing me. We have this unbreakable bond and more often than not know what the other is thinking. It's really strange and we cannot explain it, but it is one of the most beautiful parts of our friendship.

Neurodivergent people it seems are drawn to each other even when we don't know we or the other person are Neurodivergent. As previously mentioned, all my friends are Neurodivergent and some didn't even know it until after meeting me. I believe a relationship is far more likely to be possible for us if the other person is ND and this may explain why we struggle so much with relationships and friendships. The world may try to understand us, but society will never truly know what it's like to be one of us. So instead of trying to understand us, just be understanding of us and that will be enough to make us feel welcome and give us a better life.

For anyone reading this who may potentially meet a Neurodivergent person and perhaps want to begin a relationship with them, please don't underestimate them, don't assume you know anything about them because you've read about autism, or know another Autistic person, or worked with Autistic people – the person you are with is an individual. Be patient with them, guide them, learn from them about a different way of thinking and seeing the world around you. If we feel loved, we will share that love, but remember, it may just be that we show it differently from what you expect.

Participants' experiences

Communication

Richard shares that he is married and has been for 20 years. He confides:

> 66 She is my best friend and absolutely gets me. I can tell her anything and she never judges me. She is always supportive and makes me better. We hug all the time, and initiated by us both. But especially when I see she is upset about something. When we do fight, it usually ends with us laughing. But I need to resolve the issue and move on. She thinks she is neurotypical. She has quirks and she loves to be organized with her lists. She had a chaotic childhood and developed coping mechanisms to have control over what she *can*

control. Which is great for me, because I am disorganized. She is patient with me when I need it and we rarely argue. I'm not afraid to show my emotions in front of her. And we have had many of those since I was diagnosed with cancer. I've been in toxic relationships. One particular one turned me into someone I just didn't recognize. I hated myself then, looking back. I got out of that relationship by moving country. No joke, I actually moved country because of a job offer. She was not a good person to me. She was selfish, never had my back. Would take other people's side no matter how bonkers it was. She treated me like an accessory. **"**

Richard has shown how much it matters to him to be able to share his emotions and feel safe with his partner. Of course, it can sometimes be difficult to share openly, as we're often feeling very vulnerable when it comes to sharing our emotions – to the point where we can feel completely overwhelmed and unable to communicate any more.

Hélène describes that communication in her couple depends very much on the subject. She explains:

" We can discuss various topics really well, especially when it comes to our Autistic perspective, we have the opportunity to have deep discussions and exchanges. However, we can't discuss political topics, it's too much emotional involvement to handle and we don't appreciate debates about ideas. As far as topics involving the couple are concerned, as I have difficulties in asserting myself, it only works on subjects that he is willing to discuss. On those that unsettle him, I avoid expressing myself, which is not ideal. I would need to talk about it, but the fear of conflict makes me introverted. However, there are very few arguments, we tend to take it easy and put things into perspective to overcome the tensions and frustrations that we can't resolve through communication. We are both aware of the luck and improbability of our meeting, which makes us get some perspective on the 'discomforts' we encounter together. When I was younger, I couldn't deal with this, I would let my emotions overwhelm me and then I'd have a fight. I don't cry in front of him and rarely get angry openly, nor does he talk to me about his frustrations or dissatisfactions as a couple. In the few crisis situations we've had, I've withdrawn, the emotion being too strong to handle through communication. 🙄

> Withdrawing is a perfectly understandable reaction when feeling overwhelmed. It can often stem from an underlying sense of guilt or shame triggered by the feeling of having upset or disappointed our partner and not feeling sufficient for them. Another typical reaction when facing a conflict in our couple is to freeze, which can frequently happen to people who are afraid of conflict. Given that Autistic people tend to feel emotions and empathy at a higher intensity than neurotypicals, the emotion felt during a disagreement with our partner can be intensified because it simply becomes too much to process, we're too far out of our zone of tolerance.

Sadie describes this very well, saying that if a conflict occurs in relationships, she will shut down and zone out. It can then still look like she is paying attention, but in reality she is no longer there, in order to protect herself. It definitely is a way of protecting ourselves when we're submerged by emotions. A little advice to all the people who tend to withdraw when there's a conflict with their partner: it helps to let your partner know that if you withdraw, it is because you're feeling overwhelmed – because you care so much. Otherwise, they might think that you're avoiding them or not reacting because you don't care about them or the relationship any more, and that can make them panic and get in the way of leaving you some space to regulate yourself. If you can, just let your partner know how you function and that you still care, even when you're not responding. You can even add that it's precisely because you care about them and that they mean so much to you that each conflict becomes immediately overwhelming.

Corrinne describes clearly that her go-to reaction in conflict is to shut down and go mute. She adds that she has difficulty saying anything for fear of being misunderstood.

Charles says he's had eight relationships, of which he's had two sexual partners and another occasional sexual partner. Here's how he describes his relationship with his current partner:

“ Communication with my partner is fairly good, though serious issues tend to be addressed via text/email as we both find it easier that way. We don't really argue. I have confided in her a lot more than I have anyone else, and we occasionally have deep conversations about ourselves that sometimes lead to revelations. I don't like to cry, at all, but have cried in front of her a few times, usually out of anger or frustration (not with her, with a situation where she happens to be there). She is very supportive of me and I try to be very supportive of her too.

My go-to reaction when there are issues tends to swing from anger to withdrawal. The few times we have had difficult conversations face to face have tended to end up with me staring at the table, not looking at her, with my jaw set, wanting to say something but not being able to. We have found it's easier for us to articulate ourselves and resolve any issues by text and/or email and so that's how we've done it for years. My parents always had a philosophy of never waking or sleeping on an argument, something I think is admirable, but that can also lead to more conflict, and having some time to cool off from an argument has been beneficial for me, as it allows me more time to really think about the issue and why I reacted in the way I did.

When my partner is upset, which doesn't happen a lot, I try to make her feel better by giving her a hug, getting her something like a chocolate bar, or, if she's communicated it via a message, with a kiss emoji/hug gif (providing it's not me she's upset with, then it's a whole different set of responses). We're not a particularly affectionate couple, nor are we lovey-dovey. We rarely say 'I love you' to each other. I think we show our love by making each other laugh, keeping ourselves entertained and doing things for each other, sticking to the unwritten rules that every relationship has (certain chores, making sure things are done, giving each other space, not allowing things to become problems, etc.). ”

Emma has come up with a helpful strategy for communicating on sensitive matters, where she and her partner send each other text messages to overcome the block in speech when it's hard to talk.

Thomas tells us how he and his partner have learned to step away from withdrawing and instead to share:

> 66 My last relationship taught me how to make it work, very
> loving and patient. We are involved in a conscious process
> and a conscious relationship, meaning we share everything. The
> beginning was tough for me and my behaviour made it tough
> for her. When in a conflict, I needed space to withdraw, when
> she needed to address the issue, which led to much frustration
> and anger on her side (and on mine through not feeling free to
> withdraw). Those patterns seem far away now, but they were
> very present and overwhelming at first. In the words of my
> girlfriend, I tend to be either very affectionate and demonstrative –
> overwhelming at times – or quite cold. I come from a fusional type
> of relationship pattern of behaviour and tend to express a lot and
> very clearly what I feel and want – she does too. We thus have very
> open and intense sharing and that has been the case since the
> beginning of our 11-year relationship. 55

Katharina describes how serene her relationship is:

> 66 Eventually, my best friend became my boyfriend and husband
> and we both need harmony and plenty of space, so this has
> been working well for 12 or more years now. He is my favourite
> person to be around. I keep joking that I only married him for the
> fantastic sex, but it is so much more. He is my rock to lean on and I
> know he would do anything for me and our family and has proven
> so many times, not just with words but mostly with actions. He
> doesn't talk a lot or in fact probably not at all about his emotions,
> but he knows when to hug me and hold me and is there for us
> when we need him. He simply gets me and we are a great team.
> We don't fight, we talk things out logically usually. We have the
> same type of humour that makes us laugh about the craziest situa-
> tions in life and he makes me feel safe and loved no matter
> what mess I am in – he sees the true me and loves me for it. 55

Beth's partner is very supportive, making Beth feel safe enough to cry in front of him. She recalls that people used to say, 'What are you crying for now?', making her hide her tears. But with her partner, she doesn't feel embarrassed any more. Neville says that when his wife is upset, he will try to comfort her by being there and being a listener. It's wonderful to see what a difference we can make in someone's life when we show them that we're accessible when they're feeling emotional, that we very much love them and want to be present when they're feeling overwhelmed, even when they don't necessarily like themselves.

Lorraine also shares how difficult it can be to stay present when someone's upset. She says she's good with practical aspects, like offering drinks or food, but is not very good at the nurturing aspect. She says she doesn't really know how to comfort someone.

Fabrizio also wonders about the right approach to provide emotional support to his partner:

> 66 I had three romantic relationships. I married the woman I met in my last relationship. I now realize that my condition deeply influenced all my relationships. My first girlfriend complained that we were always alone and she was right. I read about how to show empathy and how bad is it to say 'other people also ...' or 'at least you have this ...'. I try to say 'Yes, it is very hard' or 'I understand and I am sorry for this', I am not sure if this is helpful. This may sound 'constructed' or 'dishonest', but how can I show that I care otherwise? How can I show that I care if, naturally, I do not know what to say? I can only make an effort to build a mechanism that makes people feel better, and although it may sound 'fake', isn't the effort, the intent, what counts? 99

Melanie explains that she and her husband have a great relationship. She says:

> 66 He looks after me and I look after him. He has a packed lunch for work every day and I try to take care of the small things for him so he doesn't worry. He brings me a coffee each morning which means so much. It's always the best coffee. We rarely argue or fall out and if we do, we can resolve it quite quickly by talking. I feel

safe, secure and understood by him. When I was starting to explore the possibility that I was Autistic, I came downstairs after reading an article about how autism presents in women and I said, 'The more I read, the more I'm starting to wonder if I'm not actually neurotypical after all.' He looked at me, smiled and said, 'Did you really think you were? I've always known you weren't from the moment I met you.' He knows me so well. But never rushed that as he knew it was mine to discover. He's truly amazing. We make a good team. 🙶

Emily says that her partner is incredibly supportive. She describes him as her 'own personal cheerleader'. That's wonderful. Everyone who wants to be in a relationship deserves to be with someone who will appreciate them for who they are and believe encouraging.

Michele shares how she feels about her wife:

🙶 She is the first person I feel like I can openly be myself with (aside from stimming, which I will not do in front of her ever). We have had arguments and most come from communication barriers in certain situations. She knows when I need a break, but occasionally I do feel guilty for not being able to live up to a standard I have epitomized in my mind. I cry. I usually withdraw and isolate, but she knows I need time to get my thoughts together. I process the disagreement on my own, then reconnect once I no longer feel upset. I learned a long time ago that talking about it right away results in too much honesty or an inappropriate tone that is not conducive to resolving the issue. 🙶

She also shares that it wasn't always easy for her to choose someone who'd be good for her:

🙶 Before, I think if anyone paid me any attention, I felt romantically towards them. I don't think I really understood what a relationship was or what healthy love felt like until now. I never had a type and it mostly had to do with personality, status and/or looks, not commonalities. Now I have someone that makes me laugh, has a good personality and good looks, likes to work out with me and eat healthily, and we like most of the same types of things aside from my special interests (same music and extracurricular activities like pool, darts, working out, swimming at a pool or beach, and skateboarding).

Linda has also found it initially difficult to express her emotions. She shares:

> Before I knew I was Autistic I had serious problems with understanding my own feelings and needs and I was very often judged and told I was 'too extreme and exaggerating and your display of emotions/behaving are not normal'. This led to me developing uncertainty and shame about my emotions and I tried my best to suppress *all* feelings the best I could, which of course only led to extreme stress and anxiety building up and in the end resulted in explosive outbursts, frustration, irritation and uncontrolled crying, followed by even more shame and guilt. Total trauma response. I became very defensive and felt attacked and criticized all the time and felt I needed to defend myself and apologize for my whole existence. This way of acting/reacting resulted in the creation of a very unhealthy and unbalanced communication pattern and we were arguing loudly very often over a lot of stuff. In retrospect, after now knowing I am Autistic, I also see how our different ways of expressing ourselves play a *huge* role and I can just imagine how many times we fought because we just missed each other in translation.
>
> Lately, the last year, after working extremely hard on self-healing trauma and meditation-mindful-distancing, I have started to communicate my feelings and needs – to myself and to my partner – in a much clearer and more straightforward way and I ask my partner to try to do the same to me. Today, we meet each other with much more respect and less judgement and we are coming up with a new kind of communication style together that will suit us both through a kind of trial and error – evaluate, modify and try again. Compassion and patience…. Before I knew I was Autistic, I had no idea how to understand or regulate my feelings and reactions, which resulted in explosive anger, yelling, frustration, blaming, defensiveness and the inability to stop arguing until I felt

we had come to some kind of solution. It was always followed by
me crying, uncontrolled anxiety and shame. Nowadays I work very
hard at staying in the now, grounded in the real, conscious me (not
entering the ego or letting the trauma response take over), and
create an overview of the situation (conflict) by rationalizing what
is happening with a neutral state of mind and figuring out if I and/
or my partner have entered the ego – if so, I suggest we continue
the discussion later when we are grounded and capable of listening
to each other and finding a solution or an understanding. A conflict
solution that still is really new for both me and my partner, so
the result is varies a lot. **"**

Sarah shares that she's had a number of relationships and has now been
with her husband (whom she describes as undiagnosed ND) for
26 years. She says:

" We talk all the time and he's very loving and supportive. We
have our moments and do sometimes argue, but it's a healthy
and close relationship. I'm very proud of us. I tend to get
frustrated and angry ... he tends to withdraw and avoid. It's taken
time, but we're getting better at navigating this. I can't handle
having things unresolved ... I hate the sadness it makes me feel.
So, I need to clear the air and make up. My husband comes from a
family who refuse to ever acknowledge when things are wrong, so
he's done really well to improve his emotional communication. My
own family were very poor at dealing with conflict as well, so this is
something we've had to work at a lot. Fortunately, we're good with
honesty and directness, so that's helped.

We both like cuddles. I like kissing more than he does. We both
initiate hugs, but he does more so and I like that. When he gets
upset, I hold him and stroke his back. I'll also make sure he's physically comfortable, making food, drinks, running a bath, getting a
blanket, etc. He doesn't get upset often. I tell him I love him, make
eye contact, hug him. I also tell him all the ways I appreciate him
and how proud I am of him. We both love having occasional times
of reminiscing together about our life with each other. When I feel
aroused, I tell him! I'll also initiate kissing and touch him intimately.

I'm attracted by talent and sense of humour. It's also important that I feel safe with someone. In addition, some of the things that most attracted me to my husband were his strong work ethic and his desire to take care of me. Physically, it's that indefinable spark. He still makes me melt to look at him. I'm very physically attracted to him, even after 26 years. **"**

Toxic relationships

Many participants have shared that they have been in a toxic relationship. Of course, being in a toxic relationship can happen to anyone, but we do observe that many Autistic people can end up trapped in relationships with people who will disrespect or abuse them. This can be for various reasons, of course. Some people stay in abusive relationships because that's all they've known (people who grew up in violent contexts, for instance) and they think the abuse is somehow unavoidable or tolerable. Some people have such low self-esteem that they will be convinced they don't deserve better – of course, the problem with that is that toxic relationships tend to diminish our sense of self-worth, thus making it harder to realize that we do deserve to be treated better! Some people can be naïve or simply not notice the subtle ways in which manipulation and gaslighting can occur, thus making them 'easy prey' to people who will abuse their trust and kindness.

Naomi tells us what makes her vulnerable to manipulative people:

" I think I have a vulnerability to people who are a bit manipulative. What makes me vulnerable to manipulative people is the fact that I like to question myself, I am not at all fixed in my opinions, in my thoughts. I would say that I am quite malleable and flexible because I actually understand, I like the complexity of the world and I like to try to understand them and to delve into complex things. Faced with someone who is a bit manipulative, it's almost a hyper-fertile ground because I open up and the person can go and poke around in the mess and then I'm ok up to a certain point. I open up very easily and there are people who take advantage of that. It's very easy with me. In fact, I've always shifted a bit between two styles of relationships. Between someone quite brilliant and almost fascinating who makes me a little bit addicted and who drives me a little bit crazy, and people who are much more stable, settled, good people in fact, but with whom I get a little bit bored. **"**

Isabella explains how in order to find shelter after having been homeless, she has been in relationships with abusive people (with whom she would live), meaning that for her, finding a place to live meant being mistreated. She said that while you're not economically stable, it's difficult finding a partner who will truly respect you. She says her husband is often very mad at her, insulting her, and that it feels like hell when he's angry. But this relationship is also giving her and her daughter the safety of a roof over their heads, which she cherishes. When Marie-Laure told Isabella that it sounded like she had had to choose between two basic needs – having a roof over your head or being treated with respect – she said: 'Now, I have no choice because I have a child so I don't want to be homeless, absolutely not, this is out of discussion. So now, my only hope is to get some help from the state and to find some job, but it will take time, so for now, it is like this.'

Lucy used to be married to an abusive husband who just wouldn't allow her to be different in any way. She couldn't look after herself or her needs, she just had to be normal. He was Neurodivergent himself and he wanted to act 'normal' and wanted her to act 'normal' too. After that, it was a process of unpicking what was actually going on, of getting to know herself again and responding to her own needs.

S. also recalls that she has been in a toxic relationship:

" I was married for 18 years and we were together for 22. I do feel he was Neurodivergent. We struggled to communicate with each other. There were arguments when I felt able to stand up for myself, but mostly I didn't as the repercussions were worse in that the emotional abuse got worse. I did not confide in him a lot as he used my concerns against me in front of people. There was domestic violence towards the end of the relationship. He was an alcoholic (which eventually killed him). He had suffered a lot of traumas in his life as he grew up in Belfast at the height of the Troubles and he never really dealt with it. He was a very intelligent man and spent a lot of the time seeming surprised if I knew the answer to something. It was a toxic relationship. I woke up one night with his hands round my neck, and then a couple of nights later, while drunk, he swung for my eight-year-old son as he tried to wake him from a drunken stupor. I decided that was enough and had his bags packed for him coming home from work the next evening while my son was visiting my parents. I endured two hours of verbal abuse and then drove him up to his parents' house, giving him money as he had just spent his month's wages in the betting shop and the pub.

I have had a couple of short relationships since then but I have realized in the past year or so that those relationships happened because I settled with two men who weren't really what I liked, I just wanted someone to validate me. I have been on my own now for eight years and while I would like a relationship, I don't think I have the headspace for it. I am concerned that I might revert to the same needy person I was years ago, despite all the work I have done on myself. I am also concerned that I might end up with the same kind of assholes that I ended up with years ago!

Virginia also recalls having been in an abusive relationship:

My first husband was NT, but unfortunately had psychopathic traits and was abusive emotionally and financially. He spent four years having not only a secret affair but more of a double life. When I divorced him, he brought down his full wrath on me to try to ruin my life in every way, but I fought back and eventually did not see him any more. I remarried, a friend I had known for many years, and we know each other really well, so my life is great. He is NT, but he is really supportive and likes my 'weird ways'. If there is ever conflict, I like to resolve it calmly. I think we work because we were friends first and foremost and there is total trust. I had many toxic relationships. To be honest, if I was not with my husband, I wouldn't be worried about being single. I used to confuse sex with love, and feel under pressure to pair up, marry or have children, but I know myself better now. I can't explain attraction at all. I have to like a person and feel connected to want to spend any time with them, or I am happier alone. When I was single, and sometimes now, I get asked on a date. Now I say no, of course, I am not interested, but I found it difficult to say no when younger, so I got into lots of horrible situations. I have no idea how I 'seduce' someone – but I seemed to have been successful in the past, getting too much unwanted attention. I think I put on a 'sexy' persona when I was younger. This probably got me into dangerous situations when I was too naïve to handle it. I never really knew what was appropriate. Thankfully I am older and wiser now. 　　

Kate recalls that she has also been in verbally, emotionally and physically abusive relationships in the past. In those relationships, she masked heavily to be what she thought they wanted of her, and that never turned into anything sustainable. Thankfully, she has since found a new partner, with whom there are very few fights, she feels safe to share how she feels, and who she describes as 'extremely supportive'.

Tanya has commented that being able to feel appreciated by someone when we're not masking is an important criterion in a healthy relationship. She says she knew her husband was the right person for her as she did not mask with him. He gets her, he doesn't judge, he accepts all her quirks and need for routine. Just as her cats give her sensory pleasure, so does her husband. She likes kissing him, though she never liked kissing before him. He knows how to make her feel good about herself and who she is.

Gillian has had a similar experience, noticing a clear difference between a healthy relationship and a toxic one:

> 　　 I was in a relationship with someone previous to the person I am with now and it was very damaging to my self-esteem. Also, going into that relationship, I had been in relationships that weren't healthy because I wasn't. I was very, very vulnerable. I had really absorbed the message that there was something wrong with me. You can't get into a healthy relationship when you're not in a good space. Then, that person I was in that relationship with would make comments such as 'You've made a show of yourself' (when we came home after having been out) or 'You embarrass me', 'You talk too much', so just reiterating all those things that I thought about

myself anyway. I used to be very apologetic, saying 'Sorry I talk too much', 'Sorry I'm doing this', etc. Which I now know is a trauma response that comes back to how I was treated in my childhood. Now I'm in a relationship with someone who is just so accepting of anybody. I used to get so mortified, so embarrassed if I was stimming in front of him. I'd be like, 'Oh my god, I'm so sorry' when I realized I had been stimming. And he was like, 'You don't need to apologize.' **"**

In therapy, Marie-Laure often has to remind her patients that, while it is normal in a couple to be supportive of one another and to remain present through hardships, that does not apply to cruelty. If someone is being disrespectful to you, staying does not make you a 'good partner' but a victim of abuse. You have a right to be surrounded only by people who appreciate you and care about your wellbeing.

Seduction

The art of seduction is a complex one, as it relies a lot on implicit communication and subtle messages. This can make it very difficult for Autistic people to know how to flirt or to notice if someone is hitting on them. S. shares how confusing seducing can be, saying she doesn't think she has ever seduced anyone and wouldn't know how. Christine explains that her interest in others can often be misunderstood. She is fascinated by people, but when she shows an interest in them, especially men, this can be misinterpreted as her having a sexual or romantic interest in them when she really doesn't.

Najib, who is passionate about cards, says he doesn't know how to seduce a woman per se, but since October 2020 he has sometimes sent or showed a playing card to kind women, such as the Queen of Hearts. We love the idea of finding a way of seducing someone based on our special interests, that's so creative!

Kevin shares that he feels lucky to have got to the point where he has several close friends, including several close female friends, but he remains lost about how to get to the next step. He is hoping that this is something that will come soon now that he has his own place to live and independence, but the pandemic has not been an ideal time for dating.

Nia-Eloise doesn't know how to flirt. She says she thinks she doesn't actually have the capacity to flirt and wouldn't be able to tell if someone was flirting with her. So if anyone wanted to ask her out, they would just have to come out and say it. They would have to spell it out. Otherwise, she says she will never pick up on it. Grace also comments on how difficult flirting is. In her 20s she felt very awkward as she would either ignore a guy if she liked him or end up doing things that she later felt mortified about, in an attempt to hint that she liked them in case they liked her.

Karol has experienced how difficult the 'getting to know each other' part of flirting can be:

> 66 I've never been in a romantic relationship but quite recently I had a guy interested in me. It was really overwhelming because that has never happened to me. I still struggle with day-to-day conversation and this is something different and seems to be even more complicated. I asked for advice from my friends and family but they all had different experiences with dating so they all gave different advice. I want to be in a relationship because some of my friends are and they seem happy, but this guy was basically a stranger to me and that made me feel anxious. Then once we were talking about social anxiety and so I mentioned my autism and he said, 'Oh you're Autistic, but you seem so normal!' and it seemed like he meant it as a compliment, as some sort of a chat-up line, but to me it felt very hurtful because he implied that there is something wrong and not normal about Autistic people.
>
> My whole life I thought that there was something wrong with me and I aimed for that idea of 'normal' and that completely wrecked my mental health. It took me a while to process what he said and by that point he was already on a different topic so I didn't mention it then. Later on, he messaged me on Discord and asked for my number. I was still thinking about the 'you seem so normal' comment so I didn't want to give him my number. But I thought that maybe he just doesn't know much about autism and he did mean it as a compliment. He didn't mean to be hurtful.

So, I talked to him about it. I wasn't really expecting an apology or anything but at least some acknowledgement that he understood that what he said hurt me. So, I tried telling him more about my autism and it seemed to be going well, but then I talked about some of the stuff I struggle with and he told me to cheer up, that I'm too serious. That made me angry because he told me how to feel about my autism, about the things I struggle with because of my autism. And it just felt really condescending. Like the reason I struggle with my autism is because I'm purposefully feeling bad about it. And then he kept repeating 'cheer up' when I told him to stop. I just think that maybe this experience will make me scared to share things like that about my autism when someone else is interested in me. But then I don't really want to be in a relationship with someone who won't be respectful about my autism and I won't know that unless I talk to them about my autism. 〞

Paul shares his moving story:

〝 In my young days I attempted to meet people through 'lonely hearts' magazine ads. I had a number of relationships. These never lasted very long: a few months to a year. I often felt awkward because I was still picking up neurotypical social skills and sometimes would be called weird. People would criticize me because of how I acted or dressed or what I talked about. They expected me to socialize in ways I didn't want to. I didn't like crowds or noise. I didn't like being too close to the stage at a play or live music gig – it was too intense. In retrospect, I experienced a lot of rudeness: I would never behave like they behaved to me. Sometimes, I left the relationship because I felt completely misunderstood; sometimes they dumped me.

I married in my 40s and that was as a result of a dating ad, but we clicked when we first met. We had a lot in common but there were times of miscommunication – neither of us knew that we were Autistic. If we had an argument, one of us would withdraw. I would feel unable to cope if she felt hurt because I had said the wrong thing or didn't say what she expected me to. I always had the feeling that I wasn't good enough and that she would tell me to go. I like physical affection, kisses and hugs, but we were both reserved and didn't express our affection all the time. We gave each other lots of presents and she was a good cook. I would do a lot of jobs around the house. We shared some activities, including being involved in cat rescue as we both loved cats. I was her carer when she contracted cancer and she passed away when I was 60. After a few years, I began online dating and made a few platonic friend- ships but no romance has occurred yet. I am beginning to feel that I might be alone for the rest of my life. 🙦🙦

Lynne says she thinks almost everyone she has dated has been Autistic too, without them, or even her, knowing at the time. She believes that we have a 'radar' and are drawn to similar personalities. She had a summer when she slept with someone different every week, saying she was subconsciously conducting her own experiments about relation- ships and emotions, more than sex. She also never understood why her dating life didn't go the same way it does in movies, where she'd just roll into bed laughing, waking up in the morning and still having the relationship. She adds: 'Most of my life has been confusing, to be honest.'

Affection and intimacy

Of course, the difficulties of the art of seduction are far wider than simply trying to get someone to date you. Once we're in a relationship, the art of seduction remains important. For instance, some people struggle with initiating sex. Dan's partner always initiates sex because he has no way of knowing what arousal feels like, in the same way he doesn't know what being hungry or satiated feel like. He thinks there's an expectation around men to be visual, so a sexy woman in lingerie is supposed to be an instant turn-on, but he doesn't work like that and needs to have developed a loving relationship first.

AutieMum also shares that certain displays of affection don't come naturally to her:

🙦🙦 He's a very affectionate person and I'm the opposite, so sometimes he struggles with this. He has had moments where he's felt like I don't love him because I don't show him affection and that I don't find him attractive because I don't initiate physical interaction. But we have a policy in our relationship where we talk about how we feel, even if we are worried the other person won't like what we have to say. This really helps us to understand where the other person is coming from and discuss everything without resorting to arguments. We do argue sometimes though, but they are mainly just me ranting when I'm about to have a shutdown. It's hard sometimes because I feel like he'd be happier with a neuro-typical partner who isn't awkward with physical contact and who knows how to react when he's sad (I tend to hug him and pray that's all it takes to make him feel better). He assures me that he wouldn't, but there have been occasions where he's sought attention from neurotypical females because I wasn't showing him enough affection. This nearly broke us because I cannot possibly change the way I am. I'm Autistic and I'm always going to be Autistic. But for now we are happy and that's all that matters. **"**

Michelle enjoys being held and comforted when she's upset, like a big reassuring hug, and also likes intimacy if she's in a good place within herself. She says she can't be intimate with her husband if there's been a disagreement because it's like a shame overcomes her and she believes she doesn't deserve to feel any pleasure.

Although Lorraine appreciates most displays of affection, she usually has to be asked because she doesn't often think of initiating them.

Danielle has a similar experience:

" I am not very good at initiating affection. I would have to set a schedule or task to do this as I probably wouldn't think to otherwise. I love it when my boyfriend comes to me with affection, yet I often decline or pull away as I am usually in the middle of something else. I will later that night lie in bed reflecting on the day and really regretting that I had not made the most of it when he tried to give me the affection, but the next day I will behave the same again. I don't know how to instigate sex; I would wait for them to. Probably because I am scared of rejection. **"**

Sarah tells her husband that she loves him every day, several times a day and always when he's leaving the house. If she's feeling aroused, she will kiss him. She adds, 'Not just a peck, a proper kiss!'

We all have different preferences when it comes to affection. Some people like to be hugged very tightly, others would find that pure torture. Some people prefer to be touched in a very light way, while others would find that extremely uncomfortable. Also, we all have certain types of touch that we simply don't like, or types of places we do not want to be touched. And all of that can change depending on the moment. That's all completely normal; it is wonderful to have that awareness about yourself. It is important that you let your partner know about your preference. They can't guess, they're not mind-readers. We would encourage you to tell them not only the types of touch that you dislike but also the type that you do like – that way, they won't feel rejected.

If initiating affection or sex doesn't come naturally to you, that's completely fine too. We don't all notice our needs in the same way, it doesn't necessarily feel obvious to us when we'd like to be hugged or to have sex. Our sense of proprioception can vary from one person to the other, meaning that some people will find it easier or harder to notice when they're hungry, thirsty, feeling hot or cold, nervous, excited, aroused, craving tenderness ... If you rely a lot on your partner to initiate intimacy and affection, we recommend you let them know that you appreciate them doing that. It can make a big difference to them to know that you do want them to come to you in that way so they don't feel that they are bothering you when they are initiating contact.

Attraction

Katharina describes having always been more attracted to the 'mind' than the body and finds good humour and a sharp mind way more attractive than some outside features. Nia-Eloise says that for her the biggest romantic attraction is definitely intelligence, but also characteristics like kindness, humour, honesty, patience and calmness. She says she couldn't be in a relationship with someone who is loud and disruptive, that's very triggering for her. She explains that while she would like to be physically attracted to her partner, looks are not high on her list. She adds, 'I enjoy intelligent and deep conversations, so I don't really care how good looking someone is or how big their biceps are, can they challenge me intellectually?'

Amélie wonders if she should consider herself straight or pansexual, saying that she is straight and attracted to men, and feels it has always been like that. However, there has been an exception, where her previous partner (who died of cancer) was a man who liked to 'transform himself into a woman' (clothes, make-up, hair, jewellery, etc.). She says she didn't fall in love with the woman or the man he was but with the person and therefore thinks she might be pansexual.

Melanie says that for years she identified as heterosexual, although she remembers writing on a survey at school when she was 13 that she was bisexual. She now thinks she's best described as pansexual, as gender really doesn't define who she's attracted to. However, she says she has just never had much opportunity to explore that ... and probably wouldn't have because she has always been too fearful of being something very different, which she attributes to her Baptist upbringing.

M. describes what her experience is like as an Autistic asexual person:

> " Since learning what a staggeringly high proportion of Neurodivergent people identify as LGBTQIA+, I've realized that my relationship experiences definitely fit into a very strong pattern among ND folks, and I'm not broken or a failure just because I haven't ever had a 'normal' couple relationship. My strongest desire is for a very deeply attached and committed, intensely loving friendship and companionship with one special person: some people might call this a queerplatonic relationship, and to me this is much stronger than most of the standard couple relationships that I see around me. I've never had a relationship with an Autistic person, just as I've never been half of a couple, but I have had both ND and NT men attempt to form 'romantic'

(creepy possessive) and/or sexual (manipulative and exploitative) relationships with me. Most people just assume I'm straight, and because it took me so long into adulthood to become aware of asexuality, I haven't told many people. Despite finding most physical romantic and sexual touch highly tickly and repugnant, I struggle to say 'no' because it's difficult for me to verbalize words when I'm stressed and overwhelmed. I hate dating and have no desire to seduce anyone, but I have no problem telling someone I like or love them or find them attractive non-sexually. Feeling aroused has usually felt very painful to me because of some traumatic experiences, but it's not easy to explain that in conversation.

I'm very lucky to have a great loving relationship with someone amazing now and he understands that I sometimes need to explain things through writing or body language during my mute episodes. I feel safe to be myself in this relationship, to be open about my neurodivergence, to share my feelings and to know I am supported, even when I'm melting down, crying or going non-verbal. I love to hug and sometimes hold hands or kiss (on the mouth is much less pleasant though), but even in this supportive and caring relationship, many types of touch are a tickly sensory nightmare to me. We are both doing our best to learn and grow together and communicate well. We don't argue very much, but it feels like a lot to me because I'm not used to disagreements with people I'm close to. Every disagreement with my beloved feels heart-breaking and overwhelming and like the end of the world to me, and I struggle to keep a positive frame of mind. We usually put aside our arguments after I melt down and focus on being calm and loving together, but this is still stressful to me in the back of my mind because our differing opinions (e.g. political) never get resolved. This relationship is massively more positive than argumentative though, and I'm so happy to be learning other viewpoints (even if they're wrong to me) and seeing how we change our opinions as we develop and grow. I love to show affection through hugs, shared time together, conversations, sharing books, caresses, cute and happy emojis, compliments, gifts and baking. I feel super lucky to have this relationship in my life, and whether or not it ever develops to become more of a coupleship, I don't want a relationship with anybody else. **"**

Noah has also been wondering if a long-term relationship would work for him or not. He's a trans man who was assigned female at birth. He says:

" While I have dated people, I think my concerns about a long-term relationship is that I have trust issues and I am extremely independent. If I'm ever in a long-term relationship, they're gonna have to be a researcher or a pilot or someone who travels for half the year so I can have my own space and they can have their own space. Being independent is a positive in the sense that I'm alive because of it, and it's a negative because I am really bad at accepting help and really bad at asking for help, and I almost see it as a failure to myself to have to accept help. It's much more relevant in the past few months, which have been very rough. My independence has made me figure things out, forced me to confront my weaknesses and things that I find difficult. Almost from a scientific perspective, rather than 'it happens to me and my personal body'. I'm definitely not very connected to my physical body ... my sexual functions are close to zero. It can be because I'm not very connected to myself. That can be very tricky to a partner. If you're in an intimate relationship and if for instance I don't react physically to their intimacy, to sex, then it can be tricky. In my last relationship, she felt almost like she wasn't doing it right, even though I explained to her that it just doesn't work. I don't masturbate, I don't have curiosity about my own body. Though I do a lot more since my transition, I'm a little more interested or curious about it. I don't really get aroused. Physically, my body just doesn't react, which can be discomforting for people. It definitely has started after the transition. It was at zero per cent before and it's at 5 per cent now. If it's at 5 per cent now, maybe there's the possibility for more. I may be asexual but I really don't want to be because one day I want to have really good sex – even if it's just once – just because I like having specific experiences. I have a list of experiences I'd like to try someday and having really good sex is on that list. **"**

Lucy has made a very interesting point regarding the fact that a lot of Neurodivergent people are bisexual. She says:

> 66 I think Neurodivergent people fall passionately for the person. When you do find a link, it is very, very intense, and it just seems completely superfluous whether they are a man, a woman, older, younger (obviously, over 18!). These gender categories are hideous for Neurodivergent people, it creates an awful lot of confusion for neurodiverse teenagers. 99

We can't deny that we live in a society that puts quite some pressure on being in a couple. It is true that a romantic bond can bring a lot of happiness and support, but one should never force oneself to be in a relationship unless it is one where you find yourself sincerely respected. That is essential for everyone, in particular Autistic people who have learned to mask and to conform to the behaviour that is expected from them. Finding someone with whom you can be fully authentic, who is supportive and generally on your side, with whom you enjoy spending your time, can be truly delightful and help you navigate through the tough times of life.

12

Parenting

Joe James' experience

From an early age I wanted to be a father. I had an extremely complicated relationship with my own dad and the only real father figures
I had were my older brother or TV dads on sitcoms. I used to dream
of having Uncle Phil from *The Fresh Prince of Bel Air* as my dad. A man
who would be tough but fair and you could trust had your best interest
at heart even if at the time you couldn't see it. I desperately needed
structure in my life growing up and because I didn't really have any, I
fell off the rails. I needed guidance, helpful advice, a shoulder to lean
on, someone to be there for me when I was being bullied, someone to
teach me how to ride a bike, swim, go camping with me, how to talk
to girls, how to shave and give me a moral compass I could follow and
pass on to my own children one day. What I got was a dad who ignored
me most of the time, unless I was interested in his hobbies, and didn't
once come to any of my basketball games and cheer me on. He did his
best to avoid me and when he did spend time with me it was on his
terms and we always ended up arguing. He often belittled and insulted
me, and occasionally hit me. His own father had died before I was born,
but from what I heard about him I'm glad I never met him. He made
my dad seem like Dad of the Year. That's the problem with abuse, it
becomes a family trait, passed down from generation to generation,
only getting better because the world becomes slightly less accepting of
it as time goes by. Suffice to say, I was not prepared to be a father, and
especially not at 19 years old.

My older brother did his best to guide me, despite having no
guidance himself. He was a child, really, who never had a dad before my
parents fostered him, and then only had my dad to look up to. He took
me under his wing, but really just taught me how to be independent
and have the confidence to stick up for myself. He had a lot of toxic
masculinity and I learned how to be a man from him. I look back now

and see how ridiculous it all was. Drinking beer, smoking, fighting, chatting up girls and riding motor bikes, like we were in an 80s' movie without the happy ending. I have no idea what my life would be like had he not died in the motor bike accident, but even though I love my life, I still wish he could be here to see it.

So, there I was, 18 years old and Sylvia was telling me she was pregnant. I was terrified, and that's an understatement. I spent the evening celebrating, which was just an excuse for me to get drunk so I could put off facing my fears. But when I woke up, she was still pregnant and I had a choice to make. Sylvia said she would go back to Poland and raise the baby there, or I could step up and be the dad she knew I could be. To me it was never a choice, I would never have even considered not being a good man. Out of everything my brother taught me, that was the main lesson I took to heart, and there was no way I wasn't going to do my best.

I remember the day Simon was born as if I could close my eyes and travel back in time. Sylvia went into labour at 1 am and we made our way to the hospital. We got stopped by the police even though I was sticking to the speed limit and I'll never forget the look on the officer's face when I screamed at her that my wife was giving birth. She did a double take and then asked if we needed an escort. I said no and sped off as fast as I could, leaving her standing in the middle of the road staring blankly at us.

Sylvia was in labour for nearly 13 hours and by the end I'm pretty sure she would have happily killed me to stop the pain. She has always been a saviour to me, and in that moment I saw her as the ultimate warrior, an invincible queen, an angel creating life. I stayed with her the whole time and even helped pull my son into this world. I held him and cried with joy and promised him that I would always be there for him no matter what. In that moment my life had more purpose than ever before, and it is the main reason I have been able to cope with so much trauma all my life. My family give me strength and determination to be a better person every day and that has never changed in 21 years of being a father.

Simon was always a curious boy. He would ask so many questions and want to learn everything he could about his latest interest. He didn't speak until he was almost four, but as we had never had kids before, we didn't realize that was unusual. People mentioned it, but as we didn't really have many friends, we didn't care what they said. We decided to let him grow in his own time, as we believed every child was different, so why compare them all the time? I hated it when the teachers would tell me that he wasn't doing things like the other children. I would think, 'Great, he's not a robot clone then, thanks for letting me know my son is an individual human.' They frustrated me so much and I realized very quickly that if my son was to succeed, I would have to teach him at home. I would do projects with him each week, letting him decide the subject, and he would always make me proud.

The main issue we had was his inability to follow instructions. It was like his brain was programmed to disagree and do the opposite of everything he was asked to do. This made it very difficult for us as we would clash over the smallest of things, from cleaning his teeth to what club he should use when playing golf. He was incapable of sitting still and hated being confined to his buggy when we went out. He would struggle to get out of the straps until we believed he would hurt himself, then I would have to hold him tightly so he didn't run away. It was a constant battle and I wasn't very patient. I didn't understand any of it and no one even once mentioned he might be Autistic or have ADHD. He was just a naughty child, but I knew that wasn't true. I empathized with him and was very protective if others told him off. But because I had my own issues, he would trigger me and I made mistakes. I never once hit him, I never would because I thought it was weak and pathetic to hit a defenceless child. I was taught that you only fight to protect – but I would shout and I would lecture. Sylvia would do her best to calm me down when I got upset, but the main issue was that she never once tried to guide him. We agreed when we got married that we wouldn't have children who had no structure. We agreed we would share the guidance and discipline between us, but when it came to it, it was all down to me. She took a solid back seat and would tell me to sort the kids out when they misbehaved. I don't believe this was her fault, I think she was copying her own upbringing where her father was the dominant disciplinarian and her mother was the hardworking but quiet housewife. This wasn't uncommon in Poland and it was enforced by her father's approval of the way we were doing things.

When Sophie came along, I was more prepared to be a father. It was only two and a half years later, but I had grown so much in those few years. We had planned to have another and I wanted to give Sylvia the daughter she always dreamed of. Sophie's birth was shorter and, for me, not as magical as Simon's had been. I wasn't well and the smells of childbirth made it worse. This pales in comparison to what Sylvia went through, but I just need to explain how it was for me, for context. When we got home, I found it difficult to connect with my new child. The reality of bringing up and being responsible for a girl suddenly overwhelmed me and I shut off emotionally. It wasn't until a few days later that, while I was holding her, she smiled at me. It was probably gas, but it did the job and I was smitten. It was like a light switched on in me and we were inseparable for years to come.

Sophie, like her brother, didn't speak until she was almost four, then we didn't know how to stop her. She was like a tiny gossip queen, always telling us about her friends and their dramas. It was so enter-taining seeing her blossom, and she guided me as much as I tried to guide her. I was always easier on her than her brother. My perception of how to treat women was warped and I overcompensated by being too easy on her and too hard on Simon. I had this warped idea that boys should be tough and girls needed protecting when in truth I should have been firmer with Sophie and gone easier on Simon.

When I look back, I know I did the best I could at the time. I was always present in their lives, spending as much time with them as possible and making sure we did everything as a family. I would make up stories for them when I put them to bed and sung them to sleep every night I was home. I definitely spoilt them, especially with toys and games. Simon got obsessed with video games far too early in his life because I was desperate for someone to play them with me, and Sophie learned how to emotionally manipulate those around her to get what she wanted. I always said that if a child misbehaved, it is the parents' fault, and as far as I am concerned that is my truth. It was our responsi-bility to raise our children and who they are is down mainly to us. I take responsibility for how my children turn out, but I can also take credit, and absolutely do, for their successes.

Over the years our children have shown how individual and very different from each other they are. Simon is very easy going but doesn't have the driving force of his sister. He would prefer to do what he needs to do and enjoy his spare time. Sophie is very intense and always wants to achieve and prove herself. She takes everything to heart and hates not living up to her own high standards. Both of them are very loving in their own way, and both of them are clearly Autistic. We never had a clue when they were young and only discovered it after I found out I am. At first we thought it was learned behaviour, especially with Sophie as she was always following me around and wanting to be like Daddy. But over time I could see clearly that it was always obvious, we just didn't know about it. It upsets me that the school never had a clue. When we tried to get Sophie assessed we were told there were children who were 'more Autistic' than her and she would be on a list for a long time. This was typical of the attitude of the educational professionals and I have heard many such statements, some even less helpful, since becoming an autism advocate. As far as I'm concerned, the current educational system isn't fit for purpose for neurotypical children, let alone any child with additional and specific needs. We ended up getting a private assessment and Sophie was diagnosed at the age of 17, four years after we first suspected she was Autistic. Simon wanted to be assessed for ADHD as he believed the medication would help him study. He was told he didn't suffer enough and therefore he wasn't a priority. That was after a single conversation with an untrained staff member, so we are seeking a private assessment for him now. I know both my children are Autistic and have ADHD because I know them and I am also Autistic and have ADHD – and it's hereditary. Neurodivergence is supposed to exist, and I have passed it on to my children, which is the best thing I've ever done. I have contributed to the creation of the most important humans that have ever existed because it is Neurodivergent people who have shaped this world, and the technology, discovery, science, art, music and uniqueness in it.

I cannot wait to see what my children go on to achieve, and I know that whatever problems they face, my wife and I will always be there for them and I have grown to be the best father I could possibly have dreamed of being. At the time of writing, Simon is a trainee accountant and doing really well in his new job. He's engaged to a wonderful young lady who is like another daughter to me and regularly hugs me for no reason, which I love. Sophie is living in

Cornwall and is studying marine biology and wants to work with turtles. She has had this dream for many years ever since we visited a sea life centre in Brighton and she saw turtles for the first time. She has a great boyfriend and is also an autism advocate who helps mentor Neurodivergent children and teenagers. I could not be more proud if I tried.

My advice to any parent out there who has an Autistic child is, don't wrap them up in cotton wool. Our job is to prepare them for the real world, not shelter them so they can't cope with the reality life throws at them. Protect them from others who don't understand them by advocating, not mollycoddling, and learn as much as you possibly can about being Autistic from Autistic people. There are far too many 'professionals' who think they know better because they've done a course, or some training, or have worked with some Autistic kids. You know your child better than anyone and you are their guide and they are yours. Learn from your child how they learn and what makes them happy, because let's be honest, being happy is the most important thing. But being prepared for what is to come is a close second.

Don't panic and push them into therapies too young, give them a chance to grow. Early intervention can be harmful and often gives false hope and sets the child back. Just being there for them, patiently waiting for them to develop, and not comparing them to their peers is in my opinion the best way to truly help them. Imagine you were a child, would you want to be forced into 20-plus hours of intense therapy when there is nothing wrong with what you are doing, only that society sees it as wrong? We need to adapt our perception of what we should expect, and expect our children to be happy.

Participants' experiences

In this chapter, we're sharing what it's like for our participants to be a parent as an Autistic person. We want to make it clear that while many of them have Autistic children, the questions we asked them were centred around 'What is it like for you as an Autistic person to be a parent?'. These are not the stories of neurotypical parents sharing what it's like to raise an Autistic child.

Parental burnout

Eva shares her experience on being a parent as an Autistic person and how crucial it is to take some time for oneself as a parent:

> It can be really overwhelming and I think that for me that experience is really hard, it is really, really hard because I get really overwhelmed and you can't stop being a mum but I still have to take that time sometimes for myself but when they are all in the middle of a meltdown or shouting or one is talking at me ... And I say 'at' me as it feels like it is at me – it seems sometimes like a machine gun with words being fired at me because I am so drained and I am so tired and I just need quiet while another one is shouting and somebody else is asking what is for dinner, completely oblivious to what the hell is going on around him and then my husband likes having music and having the radio on and he is sitting with a lot of noise and there is like noise all around me and I just want to cry because it is really overwhelming.
>
> As a mum, you can have your little ones just talking at you about something that interests them and you can have your teenagers being oblivious to the world, but as an Autistic mum it seems to be so hard. I love my children so much, sometimes to the point that I can't sleep at night because I love them and I worry about them and I think about what could be better for them, how I could be a better parent, sometimes it is really hard. I think my own need for solitude is so different from their need for having a mum the whole time and it is just really hard. I think that mothers who are Autistic deserve to know that they are not alone. And also, that it is important to take that time for yourself. Don't really leave a child when they need it, if they need you. But if you can and if there is a need, then go and take that time. In terms of boundaries, that is really important. It is absolutely a need and it can be so hard to actually manage to do that and it doesn't – for me – come without guilt, but I still know it is a need and I have to do it because otherwise I actually can't function. It is so important because for me it affects my mental health. Not taking that time has led me to self-harm, to actually want to kill myself, because when I get out of ... my whole self just feels like I just don't want

to be here any more. And I can't think of any other way of coming out of it. I know I need to take that time for myself because otherwise I just can't function as a human being, as a person. **"**

Parental burnout is a real threat that parents should be aware of. Eva's recommendation to check up on yourself as a parent rather than trying to be a superhuman, always available, is essential. As a therapist, Marie-Laure always keeps in mind the message displayed in aeroplanes. It goes something like: 'If cabin pressure were to fail, masks will be deployed from the ceiling. Put your own mask on before helping anyone else.' This makes perfect sense, because if you're suffocating, you won't be able to help anyone else. Therefore, even if your child needs you very much and very often, try to still check up on your own needs. Recharging your batteries can mean a different thing to each person. For some, it is quiet time alone reading, for others it is to go dancing ... While we can't always afford a long week of quiet away from everyone, sometimes self-regulation can be as simple as taking 30 seconds to breathe. You can read more on everyone's experience in Chapter 5 on emotional regulation.

Corrinne finds the sounds of screaming and crying overwhelming sensory-wise. Christina's sensory sensitivity is an issue a lot of the time and she needs a lot of space. She recalls that when her kids were babies, it was hard. She says that parents have Neurodivergent children and Neurodivergent children are often more sensitive to their surroundings. Tapping into their needs and trying to meet her own was impossible. She feels she went into parenthood with her eyes closed and wishes she had had more tools and understanding about what was happening.

Many parents agree with Corrinne and Christina and struggle with the loud noises. Sometimes, wearing earplugs or noise-cancelling headphones can really make a difference as it is essential for a parent to remain within their zone of tolerance before being able to be present for the child. When the child is old enough to understand, it can be helpful to explain to them why the parent is wearing earplugs, so that the child doesn't feel that they're the problem there, simply that we all have a different sensitivity and that it's important to check up on our needs. The child – when old enough – can also try to wear noise-cancelling headphones to see what it feels like, so they can feel included and not left out.

AutieMum shares how difficult yet beautiful being an Autistic parent is:

     66 Parenting a child with complex needs is hard enough, but when you yourself are Autistic, it just makes it harder. Complex needs mean lots of hospital appointments, tests, phone calls, reports, meetings – all things that fill me with anxiety. His meltdowns are loud and violent, and I struggle with loud noises and touch, so they are so hard for me to deal with. But as hard as this journey is, I'm the person who understands him the most. I can understand why he gets so upset over things that others would think are silly, because they'd upset me too. I'm his voice when he can't communicate his feelings, his cheerleader when he's struggling to cope, and I feel so honoured to have that job. 99

Melanie also shares how wonderful yet demanding being a parent is:

     66 I adore my kids and being their mum is the best thing I've ever been or done. It also makes me want to drive off a cliff at times. It makes me want to punch people in the face. It makes me want to scream into the wind. It makes me want to write a book about each one of them as they're so incredible. I'm fiercely proud of them all and for them, I will make phone calls, be assertive and fight their corner. I'm intensely angry that the system has let them down so badly so far. 99

Kanan shares how becoming a parent has negatively impacted her sleep:

     66 I went through that whole hyper-vigilance and, being a very light sleeper, if I heard a noise, then I was like, 'Oh my god, they have fallen out of bed and I need to go and pick them up or check on them.' So I had horrendous sleep when I became a parent. I wouldn't go to bed until two or three in the morning and it was always broken as well because I was constantly in my head and worrying about every little thing. So, it was really exhausting. My mind was so busy anticipating and thinking 'what if this happens, what happens, what I am going to do?'. Also, projecting into the future the worst that might happen. Because that would wake me

up and show that I could not take care of my kids the best I could. So, that intensity meant that I couldn't sleep very well. And then, combined with that I didn't know that my son was also Autistic at that time – or even what autism was about at that time. It was really like a double whammy for me. I was sleep deprived and going through that mental exhaustion. 🙳

Isabella shares that in her experience, to be a parent means to have a reason to be a better person and to live surrounded by love and to be worried about the future of your children. She adds that it is difficult because of the lack of sleep and so it is easier to go into burnout being a parent. But she feels that overall, being a mother has helped her to be healthier and more stable, and she absolutely loves it.

Hannah has learned that if she doesn't look after herself, she is hopeless to her children. She adds: 'I can't be the best mother possible unless I am somewhat happy and fulfilled.'

It is essential to allow yourself to keep up with your own needs, for instance having some alone time (even if it's just a few seconds/ minutes). For that, it is important to have some outside help and it is usually up to us to ask for help – waiting for others to spontaneously offer help leaves us very vulnerable and depending on others. It is a real power move to ask for help when needed! Also, pretty soon, children can understand that a parent might need some alone time to regulate themselves. Explaining to our child/ teenager that we love them very much and will be back in two minutes because we simply need to breathe first can help our children understand that the parent has their own limitations, which is completely normal. Someday, your children might grow up to be a parent too and then they might remember the positive role model you've been in showing them that they matter enough to be allowed to look after their own needs.

As much as possible, try to ritualize the moments where you need to be alone. Let them know beforehand that you'll be taking some time for yourself. Tell them for how long you'll be gone (be specific and don't make it last longer), tell them what the two of you will be doing together when you return, and so on. The more predictable and understandable these moments are, the easier they will be for the child/teenager. Of course, make sure that your child doesn't feel responsible for cheering you up or making you feel happier. To them, it can also be reassuring to know that their parent can take care of themselves and is strong enough and sufficiently self-aware to regulate themselves. Keep in mind that showing your child that even adults need to look after themselves at times is setting up a very human and validating example. This way, they will know that it's ok to not always feel invincible, that even awesome parents get overwhelmed at times.

Charlotte is a parent to multiple children and she says she hopes to have a large family. She states that being a parent is the best thing she has ever done and she only wishes she could have done it sooner. She says that many things about parenting are challenging, particularly the long hours and time commitment, but it's also very easy in that it's extremely fun and rewarding. She adds that nothing has been more fulfilling and that she would pick parenting over anything else that she could do, always!

Katharina explains how she experienced pregnancy and giving birth:

> 66 I have two children, both Autistic and at least one ADHD and dyslexic. I never really found anything wrong with them because after all they were mini versions of us, but they were high-need babies and I was absolutely not equipped for being a mother. Pregnancy was a nightmare. I lost 20 kg in my first pregnancy from hyperemesis gravidarum and spent plenty of time in hospitals, which is a sensory nightmare for me on so many levels. I passed out from fear during the planned C-section, making it an emergency C-section. My first child really had a hard time sleeping and constantly needed to be on my body. The losing control over my body, the hormones, the sensory overload, the helplessness, the anxiety all went into overdrive. It was not easy, but I thought it was like this for everyone.

> What came naturally for other moms, I tried to read from books, and I read a lot about everything and anything in relation to children, but still it was not easy. I was relieved when they started to talk very early because that made things much easier. I still learn with them every day and the biggest challenge is manoeuvring through the demands of the outside world of school systems and kindergarten and all of that. If it was just us being together, we would all be perfectly happy. Covid lockdowns were actually a relief for us, not having to go anywhere. **"**

Tanya has two children who are both Autistic. It was thanks to their diagnosis that she learned she was Autistic. She regrets the lack of parenting books for Autistic parents, as there is no advice on what to do when you and your child are both having a meltdown, or what to do when your child's sensory behaviour triggers you to become overwhelmed. To all aspiring authors out there, there's an idea for a book!

Gillian remembers going to a breastfeeding group and just feeling so different. She said it was like 'being back in school'. No one talked to her. She felt lonelier in that group of people than if she had stayed at home by herself. She says, 'You're meant to go to these places to find support, but you actually end up feeling more isolated.' So, there's a lot of work to be done around Autistic parenting.

Michelle has two sons who are also Autistic and has recently worked out that when her youngest child would melt down, she would too. In therapy, Marie-Laure often meets with some parents who feel they're failing as parents because their child is having a meltdown. They feel that if they were better parents, their child would somehow be always happy and calm. The reality is that all humans experience a variety of emotions; children do not have the cognitive abilities to make sense of the physio-logical feeling associated with the emotion (knot in the stomach, heart beating faster, etc.). They literally feel overwhelmed and they can't make sense of it. The fact that they're showing it means that on some level they feel safe enough to show how they feel. A child who always seems happy and calm and never complains can sometimes feel insecure, in that they're not sure whether or not it is safe for them to express how distressed they feel. If your child shows you how overwhelmed they feel, it can also mean that they trust you and know you're safe enough for them to show you this very vulnerable side of themselves.

Sometimes, we tend to compare ourselves to other parents. Of course, others always seem so happy and cheerful, and we often feel like such a failure because we know how much we are struggling. Keep in mind that there can often be a difference between what others show as blissful parenting and how they actually feel deep down. Lucy has experienced that. She used to be married to an abusive person and one of the reasons she stayed with him was because she thought she could never cope with the children without help, that she's just not built for it. When she was on her own, she recalls it being absolutely terrifying. She went into a sort of strange place in her mind, as though she was high, and she was 'coping, coping, coping!'. She seemed quite cheerful, but inside she remembers struggling so much.

Raising children

Gillian has two Neurodivergent children and she shares her experience of raising them and promoting self-awareness:

> 66 Teaching my eldest how to regulate and honour their sensory profile meant that we adapted our whole life. We have built into our life that if we consider going somewhere, we are going to plan that day off and everything that we do, we do a risk/benefit. Is going to this place going to be worth the fallout? Having a child who is also Autistic helped me be better about doing that. There are days at the weekend where we don't go anywhere. The kids are sitting on a sofa, doing colouring or reading books. There's no expectation, there's very low demand. Because I am quite demand-avoidant myself, I try to honour that in my kids as well. It's a family thing, we all honour each person's sensory profile. My eldest is nine years old and they're amazingly self-aware. They'll say things like, 'I think I need to go bounce on the trampoline; I'm feeling very overwhelmed.' Or 'I need to do some colouring' or 'I need to hide under a blanket', etc.
>
> Most of our friends are understanding. They have children who are Neurodivergent and are Neurodivergent themselves. From very early on, when we'd get somewhere, I'd set up a table for my child

with things that would help them calm down. And I didn't give a shit that the other parents were looking at me like 'What are you doing?' because personally, I think every child needs that. A neuro-typical child is never going to be harmed by the environment being set up for Neurodivergent children, but that isn't true the other way round. So learning to advocate for my child has helped me know that's it's ok to do that for me.

I'll also tell my children that I can't go somewhere or that my misophonia makes the sound of someone eating an apple terrible. Speaking to them about 'I find this difficult', 'I find this very noisy', 'I like this touch', 'I dislike this touch', teaching them about sensory profile, is acknowledging our needs. It's great to see how self-aware my children can be. When they were younger, we used to go to the library and my child would always get books about feelings and emotions. I just thought they liked the pictures, but after a while my oldest child said, 'I don't really understand feelings. I don't understand other people's feelings and my face doesn't do the right thing.' This is how aware they are of their own self.

To be perfectly honest, it is true that their face doesn't show feelings in the way other people do. If someone hurts themselves, my child will be looking at them smiling, which can be surprising, but it's because they're overwhelmed, completely overwhelmed with the emotion. The poor child is very, very empathetic. They will really absorb other people's emotions and the dynamic in the room. Every time I'm premenstrual, they get really sad, they can just sense my emotion even if I haven't been snappy or anything. And I would be the same. It's a really weird feeling where I know that I'm not upset, I know that I'm not feeling down, but because I'm absorbing your feelings, I then get this really horrible feeling of 'this isn't my real emotion, this is somebody else's emotion that I'm taking on'. I can't go to funerals. I remember going to the funeral of a friend's dad and I only met the man once. He was a lovely man but I had only met him once. Everybody was there crying and being really upset and I was there crying, nearly as much as the family, and I remember worrying everybody would think, 'Who does she think she is?' I get very overwhelmed with people's feelings. I have a lot of empathy but I do not have performative empathy. I have effective empathy, I feel,

I know when people are upset, but I don't necessarily get the 'why'. I can sense people's emotions and sometimes I see someone and their words are saying something but their body is giving me a whole other message and I find that very confusing. **"**

Gillian concludes with a comment regarding parents who speak in a demeaning way about their Neurodivergent children:

" I am a parent of two children who are Neurodivergent, I know it's not easy. I know there are difficulties. Our healthcare service is awful, there are such long waiting lists. I understand the problems in the system, I understand how difficult it is. I don't understand talking about your child in a derogatory way while they're there. Yes, parents need support. Yes, parents need to have somewhere to vent. I have a real problem with talking about your child like that. Yes, it can be difficult, but your child isn't challenging. Your child is challenged. They're struggling. You're struggling to cope with their struggling, but it's not about you, it's about them. **"**

Mark shares what his experience of raising children is:

" We did struggle, a lot at times, to cope with their neurodivergence. I related hard to our son's oppositional behaviour and to our daughter's executive dysfunction without knowing what either of those things were. I found looking after them incredibly tiring and during my own low times my wife took on much more than her fair share, and I feel guilty about that and I hope that my behaviour did not affect their development too badly. We've chatted about this at length and they're both adamant that they knew that I was doing my best. Our daughter in particular developed mediation and avoidance skills from a very early age, we now realize, to head off or cope with her brother's tantrums and our parental anger and frustration and my usual withdrawal from the situation. **"**

Beckie fights really hard not to be triggered or melt down with her children. She explains that they're all very different and therefore have very different needs. She feels that she's fighting for all four of them, carrying their burdens and the weight of the world on her shoulders alone. She explains that her son is very aggressive and that she rolls with the punches in more ways than one.

Grace explains that despite feeling sometimes triggered, she really loves being a parent:

> 66 I love a lot of things about being a parent. Number one is that my kids are amazing humans and I'm so lucky to get to be their mom and to have the opportunity to get to know the unique individual that each of them is. I love seeing them grow and learn and accomplish things and overcome struggles. At the same time there are things that are immensely challenging, but I've come to realize a lot of that is my own baggage from my childhood, and how hard it is to break cycles of family dysfunction and abuse (but I'm giving it my best shot!). Also, it's difficult when my kids have a hard time being kind to each other – that's one of the hardest things to deal with as a parent. Well, that and the noise, especially since my ears are hypersensitive. I try not to scold them for just being kids though, and one thing that helps is my earbuds, which cut down on the intensity of the sound. 99

Hélène also shares that her childhood has had an important impact on her hopes as a parent:

> 66 All my life I have longed to have children (an intense preoccupation). I was able to do this at the age of 41. I have only one child, who is also Autistic. Being a mother is the consolation of my life, the happiness that I was waiting for and that almost passed me by. Even though it would have been difficult to manage several children (respecting my qualitative criteria as a parent), I would have liked to have had more. If I had been younger, I think I would have conceived a second one despite the fact that it is quite a challenge as an Autistic person. Having gone through an unhappy childhood, through my child I experience the joys and pleasures that I didn't get to experience when I was young, I relive the missed aspects of my childhood through my child.

I live alone with my son half the time and that suits me fine. The father is present from a distance in case of difficulties. It's not the same as single parenting, but when he's away, the comfort of not having to adapt to my partner as well as my child is a great comfort.

What is difficult: the sensory saturations, especially auditory, induced by my child's activities and emotional states or vocalizations. The management of my executive dysfunctions amplified by all the unpredictable aspects of daily life with a child. 🙸

For Nicky, becoming a parent feels like having found something that really matters to her and she puts a lot of effort into being a good mum. She shares that it's tough though, as with kids come lack of sleep, noise, movement and demands, all of which are stressful to her. Nicky's child is also Autistic, currently going through diagnosis. She feels that this gives them a deep connection as she understands her child like nobody else does. Mickey also experiences that being Autistic themselves, it can be easier to build a connection to other Autistic children. They are presently child-free by choice but spend a lot of time around children in their work life and with friends' children. They communicate extremely well with their friend's non-speaking Autistic three-year-old son.

Michele has neurotypical children and explains what that's like for her:

🙸 I competed on an international level in judo from the ages of 13 to 17. Grown men weighing over 200 pounds would cry during some of the judo training because they were so brutal. Being a parent is harder. My kids are neurotypical and I do not understand the majority of their behaviours, motives and why they do the things that they do (synonymous with my childhood). The only conclusion that I have come to is to stay quiet and only provide guidance and consequences when needed. I feel like they speak a different language. It is hard because I know that I will probably never connect with my kids the way anyone else does, but I always tell them that I am like a mommy bird getting her baby birds ready to fly and be on their own. If I don't teach them how to fly, then they won't have a good life. 🙸

Joanne finds that being Autistic has been helpful for her kids as she understands their needs better than anyone, having been there, done that! It has also meant that getting her voice heard and acknowledged by schools is easier as she speaks from a place of experience.

C.A. also shares how they can relate to Autistic children more easily than others would:

> I don't know what it is to *not* be an Autistic parent and as such I have no idea if it's harder or easier for me being an Autistic parent compared with being a neurotypical parent. I definitely know it's easier for me than many other parents who describe parenting. I often have people complaining that they never get to go places, but I like not going places and staying at home. People complain about needing to drink at the end of the day because it's been so rough with their kids, but I could spend all day every day with my kids and I'd be fine. In a lot of ways, I know that being Autistic makes things harder, but for me, I feel like parenting is quite easy.
>
> When it comes to Autistic kids, such as my students, I find I can connect with them more easily than their parents can. The parents, the teachers, the therapists, who often complain about the inability to get anywhere with certain Autistic students, clients or children. I don't see it, or I can understand what the dynamic is. I can see where the issue is. I can recognize what's going on and so my relatability in connection to that child through a shared experience makes it easier for me to understand what's going on with them, and that inherently makes it easier for me. The kids that others find difficult are often my favourite kids and I often specifically hold them close for that reason, because I am desperate for them to get through their lives knowing that at least one person had their back, at least one person knew what they were truly capable of, and at least one person would never give up on them.

S. shares how she dealt with educating the school about her son's needs, as well as being a single parent:

> I have a 19-year-old son. As much as I love my son, parenting has been difficult due to my son's autism, ADHD and PDA. I had to parent a completely different way to how others

parented and this was challenging when others thought that I was being too soft or not doing it right. At times this was true but I did what I thought was best at that time. The easiest part is spending time with my son. We have some great conversations and he has been very witty from a young age. To love him has been the easiest part of it all. The difficulties were really around school and getting him there, trying to inform teachers who had never heard of PDA what the best strategies were for supporting and teaching my son, and butting heads with those who thought he just needed more discipline. There were many who blamed my poor parenting, not accepting that my methods, while not conventional, suited my son's needs. Working out what type of day we were going to have was also difficult, as that dictated how many demands I could place on him but not make it sound like demands.

While my husband lived with us for the first eight years of our son's life, it was difficult as I would have said no and he said yes. There was no consistency. When we separated, while the parenting became easier in that things in our home were more consistent, doing it alone with no respite was very difficult. He only saw his dad twice a week for one hour at a time and I felt quite hard done by as there were others who got a break when their children's father took them at the weekend. The only person for my child to play with was me and the only person for him to argue with was me. I had to deal with temper tantrums, meltdowns and all the difficult things on my own, including how his dad was full of empty promises and often let him down. I fought my son's battles with the school. It has been very difficult at times since his dad died, as his dad was the one person who could talk him round even when the rest of the world couldn't. It was very lonely at times and no one really understood just how much. 🔳🔳

Neville loves being a parent, despite the fact that he felt very anxious when his daughter was born. He remembers that she was so tiny, he would be worried to even pick her up, or he would worry that something was wrong when she would constantly cry and he couldn't figure out the reason. It felt as if the bond wasn't there from birth and took maybe six months plus to come, but now it's the best feeling he has ever experienced. He says she is easy to communicate with, always happy, and gives him a sense of purpose and the desire to do better.

Richard is the parent of two Autistic boy teenagers. He explains his relationship to each of them:

> 66 One is verbally limited and the other talks a lot. I love to do stuff with them. I love taking them on adventures. But I struggle with my oldest because we are similar and butt heads a lot. He is closer to his mother and likes to argue with me, literally all the time. I also tease him a bit, which winds him up because he does not like it. I'm also a bit immature so act silly. My youngest is not non-speaking, but he lives in his own world a lot. So, getting through to him can be a challenge and frustrates him. But I have a closeness to him, like my other son has with his mother. I love being a dad. I take the responsibility with all my heart and love to interact and spend time with them. Being teenagers, they don't really want to spend time with their parents much. But I love it when I get it. And as my oldest said, 'I love spending time with you when you are not being cringe!' Autism made me a better father. I learned to appreciate the things that NT parents don't even notice because they take it for granted. Every small win feels like a milestone. And I am in awe of them both. 99

Bob has two grown-up children and she shares that her experience of having children is really stressful as you're now responsible and attached to two separate beings whom you want to protect and care for but they go out without you and live separate lives. Now they have moved out, she feels she copes much better with worrying about them. If one comes over to visit, she will still worry about them travelling back home and whether they got there ok, but she won't worry the rest of the time. She recalls that she used to argue a lot with her son as he was growing up, as he is a lot like her. She says he is very black and white in how he sees things and he doesn't do tactful!

Christine saw her daughter as an apprentice person, not an extension of her or a possession but someone to show how to be a good person, to learn responsibility and to be able to function in the world.

Marie-Laure remembers once hearing someone telling her that for years they'd hoped their child would be 'normal'. Until some day they realized that was not what they wished for their child. They wanted their child to be happy, to be themselves, to be unique. Their child deserved to be so much more than 'normal'.

Emily concludes by saying:

> ❝ As a parent to ND children, I'd love to think that they can become adults in a world where they can be accepted as whole people, not just viewed as patients, and to be celebrated for the uniqueness they bring to society. That's my dearest wish, for them and for Autistics around the world. ❞

13

Advice

We've asked our participants to share any advice they might have. We hope these lifehacks and recommendations will be helpful to you too, just like they've been to them. They're all perspectives that have made a difference in their lives and we hope they can be an inspiration to you.

Advice to Autistic people

'Find your voice strong and loud, even if it's not verbally. I also find it helpful to slow down and learn to see the good, to think about things that bring peace rather than just the stress that scares the body. Also, make time to have fun.'

Danielle, 20, USA

'I would definitely recommend integrative counselling to help with coping strategies and finding new tools to help deal with some problems if someone is really struggling with anxiety or depression. Having been in a bad way with both conditions myself I know that this may help. Try to find someone who can offer you more than six sessions at a time. The NHS has a limit on this, sometimes it really isn't long enough and is like putting a sticking plaster on things. Also, you don't have to do CBT or mindfulness if you don't want to. It isn't for everyone. Don't let someone who doesn't know you try to tell you what's best for you.'

S., 52, Northern Ireland

'You're not alone. I hear you. I see you. You're a valid person. Autism is an intrinsic part of you and that's not something to ever be ashamed of.'

Lola, 27, England

'There are a lot of Autistic people in the community, find us so we can help you. Embrace your Autistic identity, it helps to take off the mask and feel empowered.'

Tanya, 44, Australia

'I think the biggest piece of advice I would give is to accept yourself. You are not broken or missing a piece, you are not a disease or a disability, you are just you. Be your own authentic self.'

Lorraine, 50, England and South Africa

'Learning to not be too hard on yourself, that you only have so many spoons to use each day. That being Autistic is ok, it's not a death sentence. I am unique and that is good.'

Michelle, 47, Australia

'My one piece of advice would be to stick with what you are comfortable with until you are ready to move on, and ignore anyone forcing you to move on when you are not ready.'

Thomas, 14, England

'Be proud to be different, don't try to adjust to suit others. Be you and let everyone else adjust their mindset instead.'

Sarah, 50, England

'You just be you. Don't try to change yourself for anyone, and be happy. Find your own way to do something, there is no one box that fits all. Everyone has their own ways of doing something, you will figure it out. We all have strengths, it's figuring out a way to use them, be it doing something a different way instead of a traditional usual way. We always think outside the box, that is what makes us unique.'

Sadie, 40, UK

'It is ok to be you. There is nothing "wrong" with you. You are stronger than you think. Society is still based on NT people, so if you are struggling with how to cope, that is perfectly fine and "normal". Find people/animals/things that make you happy. You matter.'

Milène, 31, The Netherlands

'Embrace your autism. Be your authentic Autistic self as much as possible, every day. Work *with* your autism, not against it.'

Michelle, 48, USA

'I would say breathing exercises for meltdowns can be good, and although I'm not good at it myself, learning the importance of saying no to things that you aren't comfortable with is important. If not already doing it, focusing on an activity, perhaps a physical or creative one, can really help also, the "healthy body, healthy mind" knock-on effect.'

Neville, 44, England

'Surround yourself with people who get you and cut off those who cause you problems. And work on emotional self-regulation. Get help where possible. And be willing to learn and grow, but without compromising your identity. Don't allow yourself to be manipulated to keep others happy.'

Sarah, 51, England

'Don't feel under pressure to act like the others – rejoice in being different and practise a lot of self-care. Learn to speak up for yourself or find a trustworthy advocate when you are not sure. Feel able to say no. Knowing yourself and embracing your difference is the key to a happier life. Accepting your flaws and failures is part of being human, so live the life you want to live, not the one everyone else thinks you should. It gets better as you grow older. If you need support, take it.'

Virginia, 51, UK

'Become an expert on yourself and your needs.'

Linda, 45, Sweden

'There is nothing wrong with the person you are, it just needs understanding on how you operate and honour that. This is really important because we are so often trying to do what everyone else is telling us or make us feel like we should be doing. And when we lose ourselves, then we would become really more anxious, more sad, more suppressed, and that's when all the trouble happens. I feel like I want to give Autistic people permission to be exactly who they are. And that is where there won't be a problem. They need to know who they are and express who they are and have that freedom. That is not easy, though. So, find people who will allow you to do this as well.'

Kanan, 46, UK

'My biggest tip for other Autistics is to please be yourself. Be proud of your interests and never doubt yourself.'

Lauren, 20, England

'I would say most of all to find your niche. Special interests can be a source of great joy and fulfilment to us, and can also be useful in finding a community so that you don't have to be lonely in a world of NTs.'

Charles, 35, UK

'Find your people, even if it's just one or two people. Have some shoulders to lean on where you can be fully, gloriously and unashamedly yourself.'

Emily, 40, UK

'My advice to other Autistic people would be to create a situation
for themselves where they are masking as little as possible. While
it is unfortunately sometimes necessary for short-term situations, it
should *never* be the norm in a person's life.'

Kevin, 33, USA

'I suggest learning more and more to express yourself, unmask, stim
freely, find ways to accommodate yourself to make life and your
sensory needs easier. There is no need to suffer just to please neurotypical people.'

Corrinne, 27, USA

'Seek out other Autistic people. You won't agree with all of them. You
won't suddenly be best friends just because they're Autistic. But you
will get information that's more accurate. Seek out those voices on
social media that will help you with the voices of internalized ableism.'

Gillian, 45, Ireland

'Stim as much as you need and find ways to unmask because at
some point, you'll burn out. I'm speaking from personal experience.
Find safe spaces to unmask. Don't just unmask for the heck of it
because the world isn't that welcoming. Something that has helped
me is going back to my special interests or stims from when I was
much younger. Go back to things that brought you happiness when
you were younger or made you feel a bit calmer.

'Observe when you're very distressed or very happy. Your
reactions tend to be more innate, authentic, and allow yourself to
be that version of happy, be it flapping or jumping, and that version
of sad. Allow yourself to be that around people who you love or who
love you or both. And even those little expressions, if you know
that it's been seen and accepted as it is, it makes it a little easier
to tune into your emotions. But in terms of unmasking in real-life
situations – oh, I wish someone would tell me how to do that!
I wouldn't know how to do that. It's almost like I have a switch in my
brain. I can be on my own planet and I can switch in a millisecond
and be completely professional, back straight, speak clearly, as if …
It's harder to go back to relaxing after masking, but it's really a must.

'A lot of talk now is self-care and a lot of it is retrospective and
reactionary rather than proactive. If you know you're gonna have a
really rough day, do something in the morning to give you a head
start, a little bit of calm, to give yourself a little bit of space just to
be you and in your unmasked state before you start. For everybody,
it's always reactionary, like 'Oh, I feel so stressed, I'm gonna go for a
run'. Go for a run first so you don't feel stressed!'

Noah, 30, Switzerland

'Weighted blankets put pressure on your skin, it helps with anxiety and sleep.'

Isabella, 40, Italy

'I'm not sure what advice I can give others as we are all so different, depending on our socialization, upbringing, culture, race, circumstances, strengths and complex difficulties we all seem to share in this neurotypical world. But there's one thing I have learned: this world is not catered for us. So, we suffer. But we too are amazing human beings and we deserve to shine in this world too. If you're thinking about diagnosis, go to your GP for a referral. I'm not sure if you can access through any other service at this point. If they are not understanding, look for a second opinion. I was lucky to have an understanding (and possibly Autistic) GP and I'm grateful for that. However, I realize that not everyone will have the same experience and of course, we are also privileged because of the NHS despite 2–3 years' waiting and more for some. If you're in therapy, maybe ask your therapist, if they are understanding, to write a supporting letter to your GP.'

Sarah, 49, England

'Talking to peers, going out to meet other Autistic people and finding those with whom you can develop affinities. It is among Autistic people that we know the subtleties of Autistic difficulties, that we feel understood and that we can share the best tips.'

Hélène, 45, Switzerland

'Develop your strengths. They will make you happiest and can be turned into a career. Reach out when you struggle. Find ways to communicate when you feel anxiety, stress or physical discomfort. Communication is key to helping you get the best support. Never be afraid to ask for help. Surround yourself with people who care about you. Toxic people will only drain you. Lastly and most importantly, love yourself. Big yourself up. Fill yourself with confidence. Be your biggest fan. Tell yourself you are amazing. And back that up by trying every day to improve yourself. Sometimes it can feel like the world is against you. Especially those hard days. Don't join them. Don't be against yourself too. You're the one who is going to keep picking yourself up, overcoming the obstacles in life.'

Richard, 51, UK

Advice to relatives and friends of Autistic people

Let's start with Maisie, who is 52 years old and comes from the USA. She would like to summarize how her parents made a difference for her. Maisie says:

> **"** They believed in me before I could believe in myself. They changed their dreams for me when they realized that I would be much happier with my own. Special interests were always valued in our family. Everyone had unique ways to occupy our down time, from collecting cars, stamps, containers or watching sports events. **"**

Maisie created the list below to reframe autism for parents and any other adults in a position to guide an Autistic person:

- Find neurodiversity-affirmed professionals to help support co-morbidity or co-occurring conditions, such as apraxia, dyspraxia, depression, dyslexia, or extreme sensory regulation difficulties. It is important to find therapeutic professionals who take the time to get to know us as a family instead of giving us a to-do checklist.
- Every day is an opportunity to learn something new about a person less experienced than us and it is up to us to turn it into a two-way discovery.
- Books, training, strategies, online tips or professional advice can do very little unless the person we are trying to help wants to work on the same goals.
- Autistic people have excellent skills, what they need is an opportunity to demonstrate those skills, not just 'talk' about them.
- Every time we meet someone Autistic, we need to put away our checklist, prior training or what we think we know about 'a type of Autistic person' and start over by connecting with the person as an individual.
- Sometimes we don't know 'why' someone is the way they are and the best thing we can provide is a radical acceptance and a compassionate presence.

- A diagnosis without self-acceptance is a very difficult path to walk at any age, unconditionally accepting our Autistic child at home is a game-changer.
- Progress does not have an expiration date!

Maisie adds:

> " There is no shame in admitting that we came from a less informed place. Keep an open mind to learn from Autistic voices of all ages. Even an Autistic non-speaking child can show us a new way of thinking.
> I want to remind everyone that Autistic children will become Autistic adults. If you are a parent of an Autistic child, help your child to understand what it means to be an Autistic person. Empower your Autistic family member to problem solve for sensory and communication needs as much as possible, and when they do ask for help, honour it even when you don't understand the reasons. Surround your family with positive influences and 'insource' instead of outsourcing. You, your Autistic family member and the rest of the family are the best support for one another. Your journey as a family is yours to write, in your own time and words. Don't let anyone outside of your family make you feel incompetent as a parent, partner or sibling. You've got this! "

'To the relatives and friends of Autistic people, thank you for all your love. Don't be afraid to connect. We (or at least I) always want to be included even if that looks different and I'm not appearing engaged. I take everything in. See us as regular people that want to be included and respected.'

Danielle, 20, USA

'For parents and relatives, please remember they are amazing as they are, they don't need changing or making normal. Be proud of them and advocate *with* them. They have their own voice, whether it is verbal or not, and they deserve to be heard.'

Lauren, 20, England

'Parents need to learn to accept their children the way they are instead of obsessively trying to change us – that is not going to get anyone anywhere or make anyone happy. Yes, a lot of the things "wrong" with us are annoying to others and a challenge. If only everyone would stop seeing them as symptoms and defects and simply start accepting them as part of who we are (because these things as challenging as they are will never go away, they might get less intense but it's part of us). If we stop seeing things as problems and stop trying to remove them, we can learn to accept and maybe someday love them as parts and flaws of that person. How is a child or a grown-up supposed to live and grow up if we are treated as a mistake and as a symptom? How are we supposed to believe we are worth being loved if we learn that we are a mistake that needs to be fixed and changed? We will simply live a lifetime of trying to be what we can never become, feeling like a useless mistake.'

S., 19, Switzerland and Morocco

'The Autistic people I have seen who are successful and happy in life, they have had unconditional love and acceptance from their partners and parents. So, it is not easy but it is simple and to do that you might need be more of a detective, like telling someone what to do, rather be a director, be a detective kind of thing. It is like seeking understanding of what is going on inside them because there is a lot going on in them and people just see the outside and in fact, we also cover it really well, so if you can allow that person to open up, be curious and non-judgemental, this is what we get in mindfulness, this Buddha talk, being non-judgemental, being curious. Have a beginner's mind, that is how you learn stuff.'

Kanan, 46, UK

'We need to be listened to. I keep reading things on social media about how Autistic people are being gaslighted by things like "that doesn't smell bad", "why are you tired?" and that sort of stuff just kills you eventually, you sort of stop sharing your needs.'

Lucy, 46, UK

'If you're going to an Autistic adult for advice regarding your child, be aware that it's a big ask. So, be appreciative of us doing it. Don't attack us because you don't like the message. Realize that people are doing this for your child. Our focus is on your child so they don't go through what we have. I am getting a little bit burnt out from the expectation of being a free resource without acknowledging that this is triggering. It's very triggering for me to hear you talk about your child and to know that these are things that people would have said about me. It's bringing me back to difficult situations. I'm doing it because I want your child to have a different experience. But then you get that thrown back into your face with parents saying, "You're not like my child, you're too high-functioning." Or they're not even saying "thank you". I know you're struggling and want help, but do you have any idea what you're asking me to do? I'm doing it but I am more like your child than you realize. This does take a toll.'

Gillian, 45, Ireland

'Don't give me surprises. If my friends surprise me, they're gonna be amputated. I had a few friends who tried to surprise me and I left. I hate surprises. I don't mind presents. But surprises in terms of trips, it's like "nope, never!". They gave me a surprise birthday party and I just walked out. But every person is different, some Autistic people might love surprises. So, know your friend!'

Noah, 30, Switzerland

'Don't be dismissive, don't condescend, and listen to us. We are different from you. Being different isn't a bad thing. It's one thing to post on social media how disgusting bullying of the disabled and others is and how you support people being themselves, but we also see your condescension and dismissiveness at family gatherings. It's not good enough to just say these things any more. Live it too.'

Charles, 35, England

'For relatives of Autistic people, I wish you patience to listen to them and let them lead you. Watch closely what makes them happy and what stresses them and learn from it. A well-regulated Autistic will be a happy person. Throw out the window what other people might be thinking of you and only care about what works for you as a family. Best advice I got from one of our doctors was – there will be many therapies suggested to you but be aware not all will be working for you or your family, so try out many things and see what actually works. Be proud to be different.'

Katharina, 42, Austria

'Abandon the box. Children aren't meant to be moulded into cubes. Allow your child space and they'll grow the wings to fly.'

Kate, 34, USA

'Stop making your child mask, stop taking away their stim. They need it to express themselves and to comfort or regulate themselves. Stop wrapping them in cotton wool, saying my child can't do that. Teach them living skills, self-care, give them the opportunity to be able to live a life and meet their full potential.'

Beckie, 40, England

'Listen. Put aside what you think you know about autism and listen. Be prepared to make adjustments. And love them how they need to be loved. Don't try to mend them, they're not broken. If you are an Autistic parent, understand that your autism might not be the same as your kid's. And teach your Autistic child to have agency, let them know it's ok to ask for what they need and build with them a tool kit which allows them to do so.'

Emily, 40, UK

271

'Don't try to get them to act NT. Learn how to communicate with them. A happy Autistic person is not someone acting NT, it's someone comfortable being themselves.'

Ben, 41, USA

'My advice to family, friends, colleagues of Neurodivergent people. Give them time to process the question. Be mindful of what they don't like or what triggers them. Also learn the signs when they are not comfortable. Early intervention can de-escalate and avoid meltdowns. They don't need to look you in the eyes when talking. Eyes are not designed for hearing. That's a scientific fact. Love them, help and support them to reach their full potential.

'This one is especially for parents. When you see your Autistic child playing on their own, don't force them into playing with others. It's very possible that they are not even aware of the other kids and happily playing in a world of their own. It might feel like they are sad and alone. But that's on you, that's your projection because that's your perception. So always ask first.

'Be very vigilant and mindful of bullying. Because if your Autistic child does not experience this, they are one of the very lucky few. Bullying can set back all the hard work you have helped nurture in your child by years.

'On the subject of a very common issue I see in me and many Autistic adults I meet, demand avoidance: its real, it's a pain in the ass and it's not easy to overcome. Be patient here. It's borderline quite literally painful to do things you don't want to do.'

Richard, 51, UK

'That they learn about the "Autistic culture", that is to say the whole dimension outside the "problematic aspects", which is very important to know in order to respect the Autistic functioning and avoid discomfort, ill-being. To get rid of the exclusively pathologizing (and very condescending) perception of their child, brother or sister.'

Hélène, 45, Switzerland

'I would strongly advise seeking an advocate. If an educational or health professional says they will do something, don't take it at face value. You have to badger them, bulldoze your way in and make sure they know you cannot be fobbed off. Educate yourself as much as possible, join parent forums and talk about your issues. And just love your kids. Don't touch ABA with a barge pole – there's nothing wrong with your children. They just don't fit into the boxes that society finds easiest. You can help them make their own box ... or even better, forget about boxes altogether. Let them fly. Let them soar.

'Autistic people and Neurodivergent people are the ones who have led humanity to progress. Without that mutated gene, early man wouldn't have explored, invented, travelled, experimented. Your kids are amazing!'

Melanie, 41, UK

'While it is common for parents and relatives to talk about their children and young people to other parents who also have an Autistic loved one, it is human nature for them to focus on the negative aspects, e.g. things your child or young person cannot do. I get it that you need to offload your worries or just share news with someone who gets it, but *please, please* do not have these conversations in earshot of your child or young person. All they hear is that they cannot do something and the more often they hear you say it, the more you reinforce it. As their parent/relative, they will believe what you say. In years to come it may be something they are more than capable of doing, but your words are still in their heads, convincing them otherwise to the point where they may not even try.

'Talk to Autistic adults – your children will one day be adults too. Try not to get upset when you hear something you don't like and please do not go for the jugular – remember, we have feelings too! I see it in support groups on social media. Adults may advise that what you are doing could be upsetting to your loved one, maybe as a child it upset them. They aren't saying you are a bad parent, if anything in asking for advice or sharing your struggles, you are showing your vulnerability and that takes courage. It shows that you are looking for other suggestions as to how to help you and your child. Autistic individuals can be blunt and to the point. More often than not, sugar coating does not come naturally to us, so sometimes our response will sound harsh. We don't mean to be, we are just trying to help.

'Our children and young people all have different abilities and there are many areas where parents struggle and when talking about these troubles sometimes disagreements happen. That is also obvious in the various support groups. While there is stress involved in parenting, it is not about whose struggles or child is worse. They may simply be different from yours. It isn't a competition, you do not need to win.'

S., 52, Northern Ireland

'Listen to Autistic adults. Follow advocates. Listen more than you speak. Be willing to learn. Be positive. Don't make assumptions, or talk over us. And most of all, don't make it about you!'

Sarah, 51, England

273

'Be patient, give space when needed, make them feel safe to be themselves and not hide who they are as this will give them confidence to grow at their pace. Also really, really listen – their feelings are valid and important even if you think it is silly. It is not silly or stupid to them.

'Be very open-minded. Do not treat them like they may not succeed in life, they will succeed, just in a different way. Make accommodations – yes, it may take longer to do something or get somewhere. Allow extra time to get somewhere.

'Allow extra time for them to process information and give small pieces of information at a time, don't overwhelm them by giving too much in one go so that the person is unable to process it all – this can cause anxiety and make them feel pressured. And don't compare them to another Autistic person you may know, this is never a good thing. We are all different.'

Sadie, 40, UK

'Your Autistic relative is not broken or crazy or a burden. You are not a victim. If you struggle with an Autistic person having a meltdown, stop and think about how much they must be struggling. Communicate with them, find out how to help them, show them that you care about *them* and not about making them easier for you to handle.'

Nia-Eloise, 19, England

'I would encourage parents of Autistic children to have patience, and encourage them to pursue what makes them happy, not just to conform to societal norms and work on getting a job they may later hate.'

Neville, 44, England

'Normalize communication that is other than verbal communication. Don't poke fun at things that are "weird" about Autistic family members. It's easy for anyone to internalize that stuff but even harder when you end up fixating on it.'

Mickey, 28, USA

'Listen to the actually Autistics– their true experiences, explanations and needs – in an open, non-judgemental way. Be ready, open and positive to learn. Increase your knowledge, through correct sources (not outdated, incorrect, harmful sources).'

Linda, 45, Sweden

'Please, don't see us as a problem to be fixed, we are thinking and feeling human beings who are being asked to fit into a world that doesn't cater for us and we are doing a great job. All we ask is that you support us, love us and choose to spend time getting to know us.'

Lorraine, 50, England and South Africa

'Families should be around Autistics too. The more allistics know, the better they will understand the Autistics in their lives and the results will be life-changing. There are so many barriers to be broken down by understanding each other. Get therapy, for everyone. Find a Neurodivergent-affirming therapist and get into family therapy. Game-changing.'

C.A., 30, Australia

'When someone is diagnosed later in life, allow them to feel special for being diagnosed and finally understand why they have done certain things all their lives. Don't tell them that everyone has a bit of autism in them and we all do these things. Don't play it down too much as if it's a bad thing.'

Danielle, 40, England

'Be patient, be understanding. Autistic people burst more often than others, some of us like to clarify stuff during the wrong moment. Do not despair – in the right environment, with the right support, we can achieve great things.'

Fabrizio, 39, Italy

'Being from a mutated species means we will always be different, like Spock in *Star Trek*. These films and series show us that we are all different and we have a knowing of something way beyond what people are able to receive in this reality. Always encourage this gift to be turned up, not dimmed down.'

Geraldine, 50, UK

Advice to medical professionals

'For neurotypicals, please listen to us. If we ask you to use identity-first language, please respect it and use it.'

Tanya, 44, Australia

'Having the possibility of making an appointment through the internet or having an assistant call us back to make an appointment. To know in advance the time slots/days of available consultations. Having access to a medical secretary who is aware of our difficulties in describing symptoms, or a single secretary who knows us over time (sometimes there are several secretaries, turnover, it is very impersonal and increases the difficulty). For the doctor to be punctual. Having the possibility of waiting elsewhere than in the waiting room.'

Hélène, 45, Switzerland

'In my role as a therapist, I've worked with people who are diagnosed or identify as Autistic and some who don't even know. I estimate at least 25 per cent (if not more people) who refer to our services are Neurodivergent, yet there is little understanding. I want to see services funded to support Autistic adults more. I know there are some, but usually not for those who "appear" to be coping. I want us to be recognized for our strengths and abilities as well as an understanding of what we find difficult in this world that hasn't been built for us.'

Sarah, 49, England

'Please look more into neurodivergence in women as well. Even if that only means Googling Hannah Gadsby, simply learn about us. Ask us for information if you're not sure you know enough yet. The current system is still so outdated and changes are happening slowly. We are not all Rain Man or Dr Murphy or Sheldon.

'When it comes to the medical office and places like that, keep the colour scheme in mind. Bright colours can be 'fun', but they can also be very overwhelming and a hurdle that prevents ND people from even wanting to step inside.'

Milène, 31, The Netherlands

'Largely, the medical community needs to overhaul its understanding of autism. Many of the perceptions of Autistic people are actually observations of our trauma responses. There needs to be more research and understanding of Autistic women and non-binary people. There needs to be more understanding of the PDA profile and the intersection with ADHD. We'd also like a lot of our physical problems addressed, such as IBS, EDS, etc.'

Sunny, 25, USA

'While I appreciate that you are coming from a medical perspective and are looking at symptoms, diagnosis and potentially treatment, the attitudes of some staff shock me to the core. Please look at the human being underneath.'

S., 52, Northern Ireland

'The medical community needs to be more aware of sensory issues and should always consult each person about their individual needs.'

Lauren, 20, England

'I think it would be great if medical professionals could have some more education about autism and that we are not children. Just because we are Autistic doesn't mean that we are children and that you have to talk to me like I'm a fool. I am a mother of four and I manage my things in daily life as ok as anybody, really. But I am not a child and it is offensive if people talk to you like this.

'And I see that with my children as well. I took my 16 year old to the dentist and it was marked in the medical notes and you could see she read the medical notes and she said, 'How are you, champ?' and then she was talking to me and I said, 'Why don't you ask him?' She was like 'Mummy has to make sure he brushes his teeth' and I was like 'Why don't you tell him? He brushes his own teeth'. It is just rude.'

Eva, 41, Denmark

'When choosing a professional, I am very aware about materials used (as I feel better in a room with all natural objects versus plastic and synthetic) and the amount of stimuli (lots of space versus lots of stuff).'

Thomas, 45, Switzerland

'People like myself can't even afford the consultation to start with, so maybe making it free, or at least affordable in a lot of countries, is important.

'I would really appreciate it if you could look more into the relationship between PTSD symptoms and autism. I was subjected to severe trauma (crime related) as a kid and my symptoms are not getting better. My fears are irrational and my fears are 'too extreme' and I 'should be over it'. I am convinced that the strength of our reactions to trauma has to do with our sensitiveness, but hardly anyone looks into trauma (not autism-related trauma, trauma that is in no way related to our already existing issues).'

S., 19, Switzerland and Morocco

'Listen to actual Autistic people and their experiences rather than make assumptions. Provide helpful supports rather than trying to fix us or get rid of our Autistic traits. Help us get support and accommodation for our needs.'

Corrinne, 27, USA

'It would be great if the medical community could know from my records that I have autism and instead of trying to do general small talk to take my mind off things when I attend appointments they could talk me through specifically what they are doing.'

Danielle, 40, England

'Listen. And really listen, try to understand, empathize. So many people I know have developed serious mental health issues from not being believed. Even if there isn't much you can do to help, you can at least listen. The Hippocratic Oath is to do no harm, but far too many of you do by not listening.'

Emily, 40, UK

'Ask questions in a different way: What are you perceiving (rather than what are you "feeling"?)? What are you aware of?

Stop treating their differences as labels to define people. That then limits their capabilities, based on what they are not able to do and keeps kids and adults in a state of not functioning. This reality loves to label and limit people and put them in boxes. Learning to perceive their abilities is a way to empower them rather than disempower them with what they struggle with.'

Geraldine, 50, UK

'I don't have suggestions for the medical community. Maybe one, lower the ***ing light?'

Fabrizio, 39, Italy

'They need more information on girls with autism and how they present.'

Faith, 17, USA

'Communicate with Autistics in whatever way is comfortable for them and stop looking for body language and facial expressions. Also, recognize that some of us experience pain differently.'

Ben, 41, USA

'Listen when Autistic people speak. Listen if someone comes to you and says, "I think I might be Autistic, but you've diagnosed me with anxiety/OCD/personality disorder. And here's why I think that..." There are already so many barriers to care and support for Autistic people, so listening to what they have to say is important. I now have trauma from my dealings with medical professionals who didn't believe me when I presented them with evidence of misdiagnosis. If you can, provide a second opinion or review instead of pretending the problem isn't there and putting a medication plaster over it when it's not needed.'

Beth, 34, UK

'Get educated about autism and get an autism evaluation for the whole family and ADHD too. Always investigate why a child has problems, always try to help. There is always a reason why.'

Isabella, 40, Italy

'Be kind! Listen to what autists tell you and don't dismiss us. Ask us what we need to feel comfortable, and give us time to process our answers. Recognize that we don't always know what we're feeling and need... especially under stress, so keep checking in and make appropriate suggestions (Would you like the overhead lights off? A glass of water? Somewhere quieter? etc.). But also, try not to overwhelm us. Speak gently, but directly, and check we've understood. Give us time.'

Sarah, 51, England

'If you are assessing a child – listen to the parents! Nobody knows their child better than a parent. If they believe their child is Autistic, trust their judgement. Don't make a lifelong decision based on a two-hour interview. Masking isn't always noticeable to the experts. What you see is not who they are at home.'

Sarah, 50, England

'I'd love if more medical and other appointments could be made without phone calls.'

M., 44, New Zealand

'The more that medical providers can create calm environments, the better it is for all patients. For example, I had a pelvic ultrasound recently and the room had low lighting, an image on the ceiling panel right above of some hot air balloons, and it just made it really relaxing. Versus a colposcopy appointment I had a few weeks later in which the fluorescent lights were on bright and the environment was very sterile versus welcoming/relaxing.'

Mickey, 28, USA

'*Listen* to your patients. *Recognize* that every single thing you were taught as doctors about the human body were about a neurotypical human body and that much of that information is not the same for Autistics. We do not feel pain the same. We do not respond to medications the same. We do not present the same, for anything. We do not have the same symptoms. We have issues with interoception, so we may not even know all of our symptoms. Work *with* us and listen to us – and believe us.

'Please change your lighting choices. Those long tube lights are quite hurtful to us. Literally painful, on several levels. Yet these lights are in schools, doctors' offices, grocery stores, post offices, libraries, making those buildings inaccessible for us unless we are prepared to be tortured for the time we are forced to be in them. Please adapt.

'Autism has been around since the dawn of time. We are not an "epidemic", we are not the result of vaccines or dietary choices. We are not broken, we do not need to be fixed. We are not diseased, we do not need to be diagnosed for a disorder. We do not need treatment, we do not have "special" needs. We are human, with human needs. Our needs may be different than yours, that is all. If you want to know what those needs are, talk to us, but more importantly, *listen* to us.'

Michelle, 48, USA

'Update your knowledge about autism and meet us in the way *we* need, which is only possible if you have a mindful and flexible mindset and actually ask us what we are comfortable with and need to feel calm and safe. Though keep in mind that it might be the case that some Autistic persons don't even know the answers to that or are scared to actually ask for accommodation even when being encouraged to do so.

'Keep in mind that just being in a stressful environment like medical offices for many of us has a *huge* impact on how we are able to focus, express ourselves and take in and process information.'

Linda, 45, Sweden

'Send us a photo of the doctor, the hospital and the consultation room ahead of time.'

Nicky, 45, UK and France

'You need to study autism in females. You need to be balanced and not just focus on males.'

Nia-Eloise, 19, England

'Offer Autistic people priority passages to avoid long waits, and show them kindness.'

Najib, 32, France

'I feel there is a lack of understanding of the Autistic experience in most and I would love it if they would just educate and listen to the Autistic people who are now speaking quite loudly I think, just to broaden the perspective.

'I am judging them but I know a lot of people speaking today, they don't feel understood and it is frustrating and you feel like down and you shouldn't because you have gone to someone for help. And a lot of the time we end up helping ourselves instead. So if they want to help us, they need to understand us.'

Kanan, 46, UK

'Listening to Autistic people – what makes you feel comfortable or uncomfortable? When I'm in a very uncomfortable situation, I can't speak, but I can answer questions. I will tell people, "I can't talk, but I can answer questions." As a professional, don't be, "Oh, but I don't want to be asking you questions." If you're looking to help, ask the questions. Always ask precise questions. I don't want to infantilize it, but it's very much "Have you eaten today?" – No. "Do you have a preference between lasagna or a salad? Can I get you one?" Don't just say, "Hey, how are you feeling today?" Also because you're gonna get the real answer and most people don't want the real answer.

'Therapy's a tricky one, friends is easier. When I feel very vulnerable, I need a lot of deep-pressure contact. The strongest hug that you feel like is gonna bruise me, that is gonna make me feel extremely safe. Which a legal therapist can't do. Something like "Could we do breathing exercises?", for example, or "Can we brainstorm things that would make you feel a little bit more grounded?" would help. That's what I feel is very tricky, it's that what I need is not what people can give because of professional boundaries. I'd love for the therapist to hug me in that moment. I feel extremely vulnerable so it's almost like if you feel this strong pressure, it's almost like someone is gluing you together again. I'm also very aware that my emotional needs can be quite child-like in the sense that I will sit on the edge of the couch in a fetal position. I will completely curl up and hide as much as I can.'

Noah, 30, Switzerland

'Certainly, from what I've observed both in primary and secondary care there needs to be more understanding and recognition of what it means to be Autistic from an Autistic person's perspective. There needs to be more recognition of the so-called "female" traits of autism or rather the lesser-known traits that can appear no matter what gender you identify as. Professionals in the services need to understand that our experiences throughout life can impact our mental health, our physical self and our energy levels. That's why we can be treatment resistant. There is no cure for autism, we are Autistic, and with adaptations and accommodations for our neurotype, we too can thrive. Stop medicalizing us. Once we understand this, then we can look at appropriate support in a multi-disciplinary way, whatever our needs are.

'To remember for those of us who are non-verbal and have high support needs that this doesn't necessarily equate to low intelligence and those of us who "seemingly" have low support needs struggle too in different ways. Change needs to happen in the mental health services and services for Autistic adults in general. Governments are very short sighted if they think investing in Autistic services would be a loss. On the contrary, I think investment in us would help us bring our brilliance into the world, adding colour and diversity. At present I don't think there are any services or support for late-diagnosed adults.

'Our difficulties can only be understood by Autistics themselves, who have gone through lived experiences of how non-affirming and unaccepting this harsh world can be. Even then we all have something to learn from each other. We're at a turning point now and we need to, somehow, come together and change this for future generations, no matter our neurotype. I know I have, and some even more have been badly treated by this world, and we are angry. But that will only get us so far. We need to educate others about ourselves, so we are no longer feeling put down or not enough. Maybe that sounds grandiose, but it's our time. I hope this suffering can end and we can have understanding and a world where we can all co-exist and feel supported and accepted despite our differences.'

Sarah, 49, UK

Advice to people working in the school system

'They should look beyond the textbooks and see what actually works to help each person. That answer isn't in one book or one "study". Please, listen, listen, listen to each individual in whatever way they best communicate. Listen to their parents or those closest to the individual if the student has difficulty communicating directly to you.'

Danielle, 20, USA

'Avoid implicit phrasings or phrases that lack contextual precision.'

Hélène, 45, Switzerland

'Incorporate coursework that matters in relation to special interests. Use their special interests to translate the world around them.'

Michele, 39, USA

'Destigmatize autism being talked about in general, disrupt the idea that it's a problem or something that needs to be fixed, and don't speak about it in pathologizing ways. Ask Autistic students (and all students!) what they need to feel safe and comfortable in their environments. Allow Autistic students various means of communication and options for participation.'

Mickey, 28, USA

'No more shaming, forcing/motivating them to fit the neurotypical mould. Adapt the sensory (sound, light).'

Linda, 45, Sweden

'I am genuinely angry about the lack of recognition of neurodivergence in society. An example: my daughter presented with typical symptoms of "female neurodivergence" in school: perfectionist behaviour, limited friend group, withdrawal, going from gifted and talented at her first school to underachieving at high school, hidden self-harm, acute anxiety and so on. Her teachers were uniformly wonderfully kind and supportive and could not have helped more – but not one of them had received enough training to recognize autism. That needs to change. I appreciate that we as parents have a responsibility here, and that we failed her too, and that neurodivergence is a very broad spectrum of conditions and can be difficult to identify because it presents so differently from person to person. But for all this to happen, for all these indicative factors to be displayed for years, and for it to never even be mentioned, seems like a failure in the system.'

Mark, 55, England

'Recognize that a child who is gifted in one area may not be gifted in others and accommodate. Also, recognize that when a child is picked on, it is the bullies who are the problem. A bullied child defending themselves is a failure of the school, not the child.'

Ben, 41, USA

'We are people too and we deserve to learn like everyone else can, we just need support and alternative methods to do so. Listen to us, do not dismiss us. Speak to Autistic adults who have been through the school system, ask children what they need in order to learn. Tailor the experience to people's needs.'

Lauren, 20, England

'Admit your limitations. As long as the school system pretends it has everything under control, these children will continue to suffer from entirely inadequate supports.'

Kate, 34, USA

'These kids do not speak like kids. They go directly to adulthood. They have a totally adult concept of reality from the start. They have a total awareness of their past lives and they are going to bring that into this life. They get super bored very quickly too. You are trying to teach them at a first-grade level of things and they are already at the 12th stage. It's very important to recognize that these are not disabilities, they are actually abilities, and start to talk to them as though they are adults.

'Ask kids what they perceive and know, not what they think or feel. Change the language you use with them. Ask them questions and talk to them as adults, not their chronological age.

'Invite them to show you what they have learned and would like to share without looking at their eyes too much. Soften your energy and tone of voice. If you have had a bad day and you are showing some anger in you, kids pick this up and will become overwhelmed by the energy that you are radiating.'

Geraldine, 50, UK

'I strongly recommend using (paid) Autistic delegates to come into the field, review the course materials, and provide their insight and comments, which I think is essential. I think it's very unfortunate that non-Autistic people, no matter how trained, consider themselves sufficient. It's not very ethical that on the rare occasions when they ask Autistic people to bring a contribution, it's done on a voluntary and unpaid basis. It is also a form of exclusion, especially as Autistic people have less access to employment.'

Hélène, 45, Switzerland

'Educational professionals including health visitors, PFSAs, even SENcos (special educational needs co-ordinators), do not know the correct information about autism. In my own experience, they go by outdated criteria my mum learned in the early 90s and it's wrong. My own health visitor came out with the classic 'everyone is on the Autistic spectrum'. No, Autistic people are on the Autistic spectrum! It's like saying, 'Well, we're all a little bit Black, aren't we?' It's devaluing and belittling to our experience as Neurodivergent people. Because my daughter is hyperlexic, they have told me she can't be Autistic. This is incorrect. Hyperlexia is a trait of autism. Because she is three, I have been told she is too young to know how to mask. This too is incorrect.

   'The problem with this is that misinformation and ignorance are a huge barrier to children getting the diagnosis and support they need and the longer the parent has to fight, the more chance the child will incur adverse mental health. Every person that works with children should know the very basics about autism and other common neurominorities.'

Melanie, 41, UK

'Having quiet spaces is a gift to mankind. It doesn't have to be a fancy sensory room. Of course, if it's a fancy sensory room, I'll come to that school. But if there's even just a quiet room, it means there's a place where you can go without the bright lights, the noise, the running, the drilling. It's difficult because teachers have 20–30 kids in the class, so it's hard to pay attention to the six kids who have dyslexia, the four kids who have mental health issues, the three Autistic people, etc, it's tricky. So, it's not "do this!", but have a communication feature in the classroom that allows students who need your attention in a given moment to communicate that. A lot of teachers will put a board outside the classroom with a high five, a hug or a bow and welcome the kids in and each kid will tap the one they want and I think having that for all the kids in an adapted way would be helpful. Something like "I need time out" or "I'm having a quiet moment". It can be discreet but it can communicate the needs in an effective way where you don't have to draw attention to yourself. You don't have to make a big deal and you can still get your message across effectively, that can be so helpful.

'But being a teacher is very, very tricky and they're only human. The teachers have 20–30 children in a classroom so they have no time to interact with each kid individually. I always got on better with the teachers than the kids. I'm still very good friends with a lot of them. One of them said, "You're so smart, I don't understand why you don't see it." And she just left it at that, left me hanging. I couldn't access the work because the way she taught didn't make sense to me. I often feel very, very dumb. I'll rank extremely high on the IQ tests ... It might be true on paper but it does not relate to my ability to work. So, stop telling me I'm smart because firstly I don't feel smart, but ok, if I'm smart, then maybe have some magic ideas on how I can study here better. Help me out! Help me find more effective learning strategies and give me the space to figure it out. My education was not in any way mainstream. The school I went to didn't have an awareness of dyslexia, autism, etc. You just had the good versus naughty kids, kids from good or not good families. Education is very much trying to individualize a uniform system. Everyone has to take the same exam, but ultimately, you're all taking the same exam.'

Noah, 30, Switzerland

Conclusion

This book shows that the trauma the participants have been through has shaped the person they have become. We need to stop perpetuating the idea that we are suffering because we are Autistic and understand that we are instead experiencing trauma and anxiety from not feeling valid as our authentic selves.

Hopefully, in the future, we as a society can be more accepting of neurodivergence. The future can be brighter for our people if society changes the way it thinks about autism. The current representation of stereotypical autism is generally incorrect. Autistic people have created many changes throughout history, so hopefully, as a collective, we and the other Autistic participants can contribute to achieve the most important change – to change society's negative views on autism.

We imagine a world where being Autistic is seen as an ability to learn and understand things in great detail. That being Autistic is thought of as a strength that needs individualized support in order for the Autistic person to reach their full potential, just like any other human. And in this world, we are not judged by our deficits but celebrated for our achievements. Autism is not a problem, the treatment and the environment are.

One of the key messages we find in this book is the importance of neurotypicals needing to work with Autistic people in order to make a better future for everyone. Only by working side by side and each side trying to bridge the gap in communication can this be achieved. A lot of books have been written by neurotypical people about autism and we are constantly spoken about, for and over, but never truly allowed our own voices. This book is written by Autistic people. These are the silenced voices finally heard.

Glossary

ABA therapy	Applied Behaviour Analysis, a therapeutic approach which has sparked a lot of controversy; it is widely rejected by the majority of the Autistic community.
ADHD	attention deficit hyperactivity disorder
AFAB/AMAB	assigned female/male at birth
ASD	autism spectrum disorder
DSM	*Diagnostic and Statistical Manual of Mental Disorders*
GP	General Practitioner (Doctor)
NHS	National Health Service (England)
OCD	obsessive compulsive disorder
OT	occupational therapy
PTSD	post-traumatic stress disorder
SEN	special educational needs
Ableism	discrimination or prejudice against people who have disabilities.
Actually Autistic	a term used by Autistic people to describe that they are Autistic and speaking about autism, and not neurotypical and speaking about autism.
Alexithymia	a trait characterized by the inability to identify and describe emotions experienced by oneself.
Allistic	a person who is not Autistic.
Dyscalculia	a specific and persistent difficulty in understanding numbers which can lead to a diverse range of difficulties with mathematics.

Dyslexia	a learning difference that primarily affects the skills involved in accurate and fluent word reading and spelling.
Dyspraxia	a common disorder that affects movement, co-ordination and planning.
Interoception	the awareness of our feelings, our emotions and our internal sensations.
Neurodivergent (ND)	a person whose brain has evolved and developed differently to bring diversity within the human species.
Neurotypical (NT)	a person whose brain has developed in a typical way.
Pathological demand avoidance (PDA)	a profile of autism that affects the way demands and expectations are met to an extreme degree.
Rejection sensitivity dysphoria	the experience of severe emotional pain due to a failure or rejection.